Russian Hajj

Russian Hajj

◆◆◆◆◆◆◆◆◆◆◆◆◆◆◆◆◆◆◆◆◆◆◆◆◆◆◆◆◆

EMPIRE AND THE
PILGRIMAGE TO MECCA

Eileen Kane

Cornell University Press *Ithaca and London*

Cornell University Press gratefully acknowledges receipt of a subvention from the Research Matters program of Connecticut College which assisted in the publication of this book.

First published 2015 by Cornell University Press
First paperback printing 2020

Library of Congress Cataloging-in-Publication Data

Kane, Eileen M., 1972– author.
  Russian hajj : empire and the pilgrimage to Mecca / Eileen Kane.
    pages cm
  Includes bibliographical references and index.
  ISBN 978-0-8014-5423-3 (cloth)
  ISBN 978-1-5017-4850-9 (pbk.)
  1. Muslim pilgrims and pilgrimages—Russia—History. 2. Islam and state—Russia—History. 3. Muslim pilgrims and pilgrimages—Saudi Arabia—Mecca—History. I. Title.
  BP187.3.K266 2015
  297.3'52—dc23   2015010887

For my mother and father
and in memory of my brother Matthew (1978–1998)

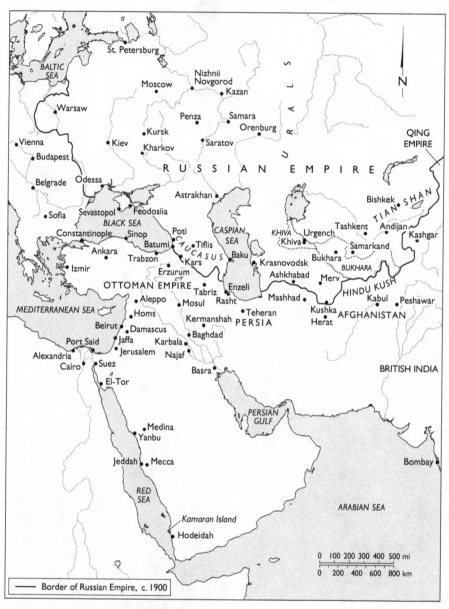

Map 1. The Russian Empire and neighboring lands, ca. 1900

CONTENTS

MAPS

PREFACE: SOURCES AND MAPS

THIS study was made possible by an accidental discovery in the Russian imperial foreign policy archives in Moscow (AVPRI). Looking for material on Russian Orthodox pilgrimage to Jerusalem, I found folders of correspondence about Muslims making the pilgrimage to Mecca, most of them with blank tags, indicating that they had never been read by researchers. AVPRI, I later discovered through a more deliberate search, is a trove of documents on the nineteenth- and early twentieth-century hajj, as understood by Russian consular officials posted along routes to Mecca in Ottoman, Persian, and Indian lands. Reading through these sources, I was struck by the confounding image of the Russian Empire they conjured—seemingly disparate regions of the empire were revealed to be closely connected; imperial populations appeared out of place; and Russian officials operated in parts of the world and in ways not captured by standard narratives. Gradually, these sources revealed to me a system: a cross-border hajj infrastructure that the tsarist state built to support the movement of Muslims between Russian-ruled lands and Arabia. This infrastructure had administrative and political coherence of its own, and it seemed ideally suited to study, given the abundance and accessibility of material.

I wrote this book to document a fascinating and virtually unknown chapter of Russian history, and in the hope that a history of Russia told through a focus on human mobility might illuminate how rapid changes sweeping the globe in the late nineteenth and early twentieth centuries shaped Russia's history in ways that conventional domestic frameworks have so far obscured. One of the challenges of writing a history of human mobility is that sources tend to be fragmented and scattered across great distances. In the case of the hajj, the story is not inscribed in the Russian archival record. The tsarist state's ambivalence and secrecy about its involvement in the Meccan pilgrimage, together with Soviet cataloguing conventions, conspire to bury the subject. And so, the story must be uncovered by seeing beyond categories in archival registers and against narratives that Soviet-era archivists sought to create, and by piecing together documents from disparate places.

Having picked up the thread of the story in Moscow, I next investigated archives and manuscript collections in Tbilisi, Odessa, St. Petersburg, and Istanbul. A network of Russian consulates in Ottoman lands anchored the tsarist state's hajj infrastructure, and I use the records of these institutions—mainly those from Beirut, Damascus, and Constantinople (Istanbul)—to anchor my study as well. The archives of tsarist Russia's Jeddah consulate, arguably the most important of the network, are missing. To fill the gap, I have pieced together records of this consulate from other collections, including the Russian Interior Ministry archives and especially the Ottoman Interior and Foreign Ministries archives.

To access and represent Muslim experiences of the hajj and Russian involvement in it, as well as to balance state and nonstate perspectives, I draw also on sources produced by and for Muslims in Russia. These include articles, letters, and advertisements from Turkic-language newspapers, as well as firsthand accounts of the hajj written in Old Tatar. I found hajj memoirs from the late imperial period (1880s–1910s) to be particularly valuable as geographical sources. Often dry and boring reads, these were intended not to entertain with tales of exotic places, but as practical guidebooks for would-be pilgrims. As such, they contain rich and precise data on pilgrims' routes and itineraries between Russia and Mecca. Few scholars have studied these sources; they are poorly catalogued in collections across the former Soviet Union, where they await discovery and study by scholars of history, religion, and migration in Russia's vast imperial expanses.

The maps of hajj routes I include in this book are original. I made them using GIS (geographic information system) software, by plotting textual geographic data, gathered from both hajj memoirs and state sources, onto a visual map. Each of these sources has its flaws. Hajj memoirs tend to reflect the routes and experiences of elites, rather than the more numerous poor. And state reports on the hajj can be of questionable accuracy. Written by Russian officials who often could not communicate with Muslim pilgrims—and to whom, as non-Muslims, the holy site of Mecca was closed—these reports tend to be detailed yet unforthcoming about their sources. They all start to sound the same by the early twentieth century, suggesting that some Russian consular officials simply read and repeated data from other reports, rather than doing local, ground-level investigations into hajj patterns. By comparing and combining data from these two sources, I have tried to reconstruct as accurately as possible the geography of Russian hajj itineraries and routes in the tsarist and early Soviet eras.

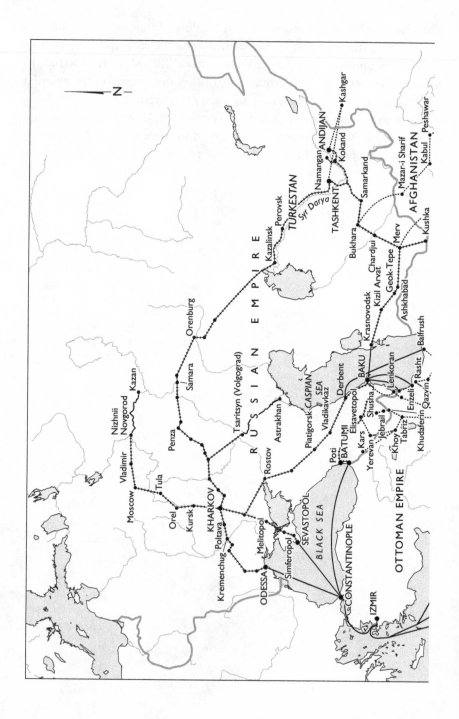

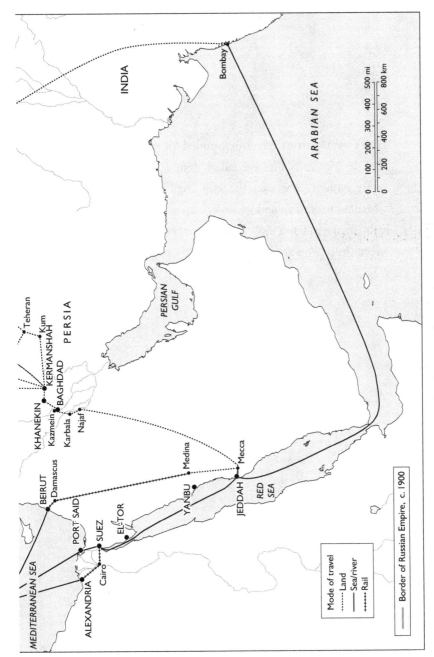

Map 2. Main Russian hajj routes, late nineteenth and early twentieth centuries

Mode of travel
..... Land
—— Sea/river
++++ Rail

—— Border of Russian Empire, c. 1900

INDIA

Bombay

ARABIAN SEA

500 mi
800 km

PERSIAN
GULF

Teheran
Kum
KERMANSHAH
PERSIA
KHANEKIN
BAGHDAD
Kazmein
Karbala
Najaf

Medina
Mecca

BEIRUT
Damascus

PORT SAID
SUEZ
EL TOR

YANBU

JEDDAH
RED
SEA

MEDITERRANEAN SEA
ALEXANDRIA
Cairo

The First House of Worship founded for mankind was in Bakka [Makkah]. Blessed and guidance to mankind. In it are evident signs, even the Standing Place of Abraham [Maqam Ibrahim]; and whoever enters it is safe. And the pilgrimage to the temple [Hajj] is an obligation due to God from those who are able to journey there.

QUR'AN 3: 90–91

Introduction

Russia as a Crossroads of the Global Hajj

In the late nineteenth century Russia took on a new role in the world: patron of the hajj, the Muslim pilgrimage to Mecca. Citing its policy of religious toleration, the tsarist government subsidized transportation for Muslim pilgrims on Russia's railroads and specially outfitted "Hejaz steamships," and built a cross-border network of facilities along their routes between Russia and Arabia. It created special passports for hajj pilgrims and passed new laws to protect them during their long-distance travel. By the early 1900s the tsarist government had built a sprawling, transimperial hajj infrastructure that spanned Russian, Ottoman, Persian, and Indian lands. One of the architects of this infrastructure, foreign ministry official N. V. Charykov, described it as a system of "cut-rate steamship service through Constantinople," organized with the "active participation" of Russian consuls abroad to ensure safety, comfort, and low costs for Muslim pilgrims.[1]

An Orthodox Christian state, Russia would at first glance seem an unlikely supporter of the hajj, one of the five pillars of Islam, and a sacred Muslim ritual. In imperial Russia the ruling Romanov dynasty embraced Eastern Orthodoxy as its official faith. Orthodox tsars claimed divine right to rule, and the Russian Orthodox Church enjoyed prestige and legal privileges as the empire's "preeminent" church. From the late eighteenth century, Russian tsars claimed to be the "protectors" of global Orthodoxy—the mid-nineteenth-century Crimean War was fought largely on these grounds—as part of Russia's self-fashioning as heir to the Byzantine imperial tradition, and its competition with Britain and

1

France for influence over Christian populations in the disintegrating and increasingly weak Ottoman Empire.

But the tsar's Orthodox imperial rhetoric concealed an important truth: nineteenth-century Russia was not uniformly Orthodox, but a multiethnic and multireligious empire. This was the result of centuries of aggressive Russian imperial expansion that began in the fifteenth century, much of it into former Mongol lands, and at Ottoman and Persian expense. The greatest land empire in world history, the Russian Empire circa 1900 held within its borders large and internally diverse Christian, Buddhist, and Jewish communities, and especially large Muslim populations. Much has been written about imperial Russia's five-million-strong Jewish population (a result of the strong émigré presence in the field), but far less attention has been paid to its more numerous Muslims. An 1897 census revealed that Muslims were the empire's second largest confessional group overall, after Orthodox Christians. No monolithic community, imperial Russia's Muslims were internally divided by religious beliefs and culture, language and geography. They included Sunnis and Shi'is, sedentary and nomadic peoples, and dozens of ethnicities that spoke various Indo-European, Semitic, and Turkic languages. They lived in eighty-nine provinces and territories of the empire (in addition to the semi-autonomous protectorates of Bukhara and Khiva), above all in the Volga-Ural region and Siberia, Crimea and the Caucasus, the Kazakh steppe and Central Asia. By the turn of the twentieth century, at its greatest territorial extent as an empire, "Orthodox" Russia ruled far more Muslims than the neighboring "Muslim" Ottoman Empire—twenty million, compared to fourteen million.[2]

Through its dramatic conquests of Muslim lands and peoples, Russia became integrated into global hajj networks. By the nineteenth century, long stretches of ancient Eurasian caravan routes that had been forged in earlier centuries under Muslim rulers, and had long served as hajj routes to Mecca, now lay within the Russian Empire's borders. This made the hajj a diplomatic issue in Russia's dealings with its Muslim neighbors to the south. In the early nineteenth century, Persian and Bukharan rulers routinely petitioned Russia's tsars, as a matter of their own legitimacy and authority, to allow their subjects access to these routes in making the Meccan pilgrimage. Russia's tsars, for their part, often honored these requests, and assumed ad hoc a role historically performed by Muslim rulers—that of patron and "protector" of the hajj—securing routes for hajj pilgrims through their realm, and subsidizing their travel to Mecca. Tsars did this with an eye toward developing economic and diplomatic ties with their Muslim neighbors. It is impossible to know how many Muslims made the hajj through Russian-ruled lands before the nineteenth century; most would have gone undetected by tsarist authorities, whose presence was light in Russia's vast expanses. But surely the hajj happened on a small scale. Long distances, high costs, and the dangers and uncertainties of travel limited Muslims' access to Mecca before the modern era.[3]

This situation changed with Russia's construction of a modern transport network inside its empire. Russia built this network very quickly over the second half of the nineteenth century, following its humiliating defeat in the Crimean War (1853–1856), and as part of a rapid "modernization" campaign that aimed, among other things, to develop Russia's domestic economy and foreign trade. It comprised a dense web of railroads that linked disparate regions of the empire (and drastically shrank distances between them), and connected to brand-new steamship lines that operated out of Black Sea ports. In Russia, as elsewhere, the introduction of railroads and steamships reorganized and accelerated existing patterns of human movement.[4] Nowhere was this more apparent than in the case of the hajj. If previously the Meccan pilgrimage had occurred on a small scale within Russia, it was suddenly a mass phenomenon in the late nineteenth century. Tens of thousands of Muslims made the hajj through Russian lands every year—tsarist subjects as well as those from Persia, Afghanistan, and China—most by way of the Black Sea. Russia's conquests of Muslim lands and peoples, and its mobility revolution, had, in effect, transformed the empire into a crossroads of the global hajj. To manage the mass hajj traffic moving through its empire and across its borders, Russia began to systematically support the pilgrimage to Mecca.

This book tells the story of how Russia assumed the role of hajj patron in the late nineteenth century, as part of its broader efforts to manage Islam and integrate Muslims into the empire. It explores Russian involvement in the Meccan pilgrimage in cross-border perspective, and reveals how, in the era of mass mobility, the imperial project of governing and integrating Muslims took on global dimensions. Challenging stereotypes about entrenched Islamophobia in the tsarist regime, and Russian officials' attempts to block Muslim movement abroad for fear of Pan-Islamism, it demonstrates that Russia, in fact, facilitated and even increased Muslim mobility abroad in the late imperial period by sponsoring the hajj. I argue that it did this not only, or even primarily, to control its Muslims or keep them under surveillance while abroad, but ultimately in an attempt to co-opt the mass migratory phenomenon of the hajj, and exploit it as a mechanism of imperial integration and expansion.

The focus of my story is the hajj infrastructure that Russia built between the 1840s and the 1910s, and that the Soviets revived in the late 1920s. By using the term *infrastructure* I do not mean to suggest a static structure, but instead a flexible, evolving system that changed dramatically over time, in line with the tsarist regime's growing understanding of the geography of hajj routes connecting Russia to Arabia, and hajj pilgrims' ever-shifting itineraries and preferences for routes. Anchored by a constellation of Russian consulates located in hubs of hajj traffic, and along popular Russian routes to Mecca, at its greatest extent in the early 1900s it included outposts in Odessa and Jeddah, Bombay and Baghdad, Constantinople and Karbala.

It might be tempting to think that the idea for Russia's hajj infrastructure came from high-level meetings of tsarist officials sitting around map-strewn tables in St. Petersburg, and was decreed by the tsar. But this was not the case. Instead, it grew out of improvised encounters between Russian officials and Muslim pilgrims, both inside the empire and in spots abroad, and from Muslim pilgrims requesting and in some cases demanding help from Russian officials in making the hajj. Hajj pilgrims ultimately determined the geographic shape the infrastructure took. As more than one Russian official conceded, pilgrims themselves decided which routes to take, and whether or not to avail themselves of Russian services along these routes. And so this infrastructure was very much in flux throughout this period, as railroad construction in Russian and Ottoman lands reorganized the traffic and lured pilgrims to new routes, and Russian officials studied the traffic to build new services around it.[5]

Until recently, scholars tended to gloss over Russia's 500-year history of ruling Islam, and Muslims were often left out of standard accounts of Russian and Soviet history.[6] This neglect stems in part from practical and ideological constraints on Cold War–era scholars, which made it nearly impossible to study the history of Islam in the Soviet Union or its predecessor, the Russian Empire, during the second half of the twentieth century. The Soviet government discouraged work on the subject, and blocked foreign researchers' access to archives as well as travel to Muslim regions. Many Western historians, for their part, accepted Soviet rhetoric about having eliminated religion, and pursued other topics.[7] Neglected by scholars, Russia's Muslims dropped out of sight: they went missing from narratives of Russian imperial history, and featured little in histories of Islam and European colonialism. Only since the 1990s, when the USSR unexpectedly broke apart into fifteen separate nation-states—six with Muslim majorities—have Russia's Muslims "reemerged" as a subject of scholarly study.[8]

Taking advantage of newly opened archives and manuscript collections, scholars in recent years have written works that offer important insights into

Figure I.1. Central Asian hajj pilgrims on board the Hejaz railway in Ottoman Arabia. Note the samovar at the man's feet, with tea brewing. 1909. (Library of Congress, Prints and Photographs Division, LC-M32-A-357)

how Russia governed its Muslim populations, as well as Muslim experiences of tsarist rule. These new studies go some way toward integrating Muslims into broader narratives of Russian, Soviet, and global Islamic history.[9] Recent works have also sparked debates among scholars about how best to characterize relations between Muslims and the state in imperial Russia. Challenging standard "conflict-driven" approaches, the historian Robert Crews has argued that Russia ruled Muslims with relative success in the modern era not by "ignoring" or repressing Islam, but by sponsoring it. In the late eighteenth century, inspired by Enlightenment thinking about religion as a useful tool of governance, Russian tsarina Catherine the Great (r. 1762–1796) announced official toleration of Islam and created for the empire a domestic Islamic hierarchy (the Orenburg Muhammadan Ecclesiastical Assembly) headed by state-sanctioned clerics.[10] Through this hierarchy, Crews argues, the state effectively instrumentalized and institutionalized Islam, facilitating the state's direct involvement in Muslim religious affairs, and integration of Muslims into the empire. By institutionalizing Islam, Crews argues, Russia ultimately sought to "seal off the borders of the empire," and isolate the empire's Muslims from foreign Muslims and spiritual leaders.[11] Scholars may disagree over the results of the Islamic hierarchy that the Russian state built—whether it functioned, as Russian rulers hoped it would, as a means of state control over Islam, and the extent to which Muslims actively participated in it.[12] But there is little debate about the goals behind it, of domesticating Islam in Russia, and isolating Russia's Muslims from global Islamic networks.

A central goal of this book is to challenge this stark view. I argue that alongside efforts to cultivate domestic sources of Islamic authority and encourage Russian Muslims to adhere to state-created Islamic institutions, Russia also sponsored, indeed reinvigorated, the Islamic institution of the hajj. Far from constantly trying to cut Muslims' ties to the wider world, in this example Russia worked to facilitate and even expand them. These efforts were reflected in the hajj infrastructure that the Russian state built over the late nineteenth and early twentieth century, at great expense and effort. Russia built this infrastructure in an effort to harness and exploit perceived benefits of the hajj for the state and the empire. This would prove to be difficult: like other pilgrimages, the hajj was a largely spontaneous phenomenon that was in many ways difficult to predict, let alone control and co-opt. Russian officials were often disappointed by Muslim pilgrims' unwillingness to follow state-sanctioned routes, or avail themselves of services offered by state officials along their routes. Nevertheless, Russia's construction of this infrastructure is testimony to tsarist officials' complex understanding of the hajj and its implications for Russia. If some saw it as a liability, many others saw it as an asset. Islam's global dimensions were not merely a problem that the tsarist state (and later the Soviet state) struggled to manage, let alone dismantle, but were instead a phenomenon that also created new, positive opportunities for Russia, and that Russia tried to exploit for economic and strategic purposes.

THE story of how Russia inherited and grappled with a hajj tradition is part of the broader history of global European imperialism. By the end of the nineteenth century Europeans had brought most of the world's Muslims under colonial rule (of the world's Muslim states, only Persia, Afghanistan, and the Ottoman Empire escaped colonization). Each of the leading imperial powers of the day—the British, Dutch, French, and Russians—ruled more Muslims than did any single independent Muslim state.[13] And most hajj pilgrims who showed up in Mecca by the late nineteenth century were colonial subjects. They arrived in unprecedented numbers, as many as 300,000 a year by the early 1900s, the result of the global mobility revolution that went hand-in-hand with European imperialism.[14] Across colonial contexts, the introduction of railroads and steamships had transformed the pilgrimage from a small-scale ritual performed mainly by elites into a mass annual event dominated by the rural poor, who packed onto the decks of Arabia-bound steamers on third- and fourth-class tickets. Their wretchedness at the hands of greedy ship captains made headlines in Europe, and provided the scandal at the heart of Joseph Conrad's 1900 novel *Lord Jim*.[15]

A growing body of work explores how Europe's imperial powers all began to sponsor the hajj in the nineteenth century, as part of broader efforts to accommodate Islam in their empires. As an obligatory ritual and a cross-border migratory phenomenon, the hajj posed unique challenges to these efforts. Unlike other Islamic institutions, such as mosques or law courts, which had a local, fixed character and an obvious hierarchy, the hajj was loosely organized, had no official leadership, and involved long-distance travel along ever-shifting

Figure I.2. Hajj pilgrim praying on the deck of a steamship. Early 1900s. (Library of Congress, Prints and Photographs Division, LC-M34-A-355)

routes that were largely beyond the view or comprehension of colonial officials in any given setting. Also, colonial officials worried about the hajj as a source of infectious disease and subversive political ideas. Many would have liked to abolish it. They feared Mecca, which was (and is today) closed to non-Muslims, as a center of anticolonial political agitation, where Muslims from around the world converged to plot the overthrow of European empires. However, because the hajj was a duty for Muslims (the Qur'an stipulates that all adult Muslims who can afford it must perform the pilgrimage once in their lifetime), it was not possible to ban it. At the same time, colonialism, with its railroads and steamships, opened up access to Mecca and intensified Muslims' attachment to the Holy City and desire to make the pilgrimage. In the colonial era, Islam worldwide became more Mecca-centric than ever before in history.

Figure I.3. *Shamail* print produced in Kazan, reflecting growing interest in Mecca and the hajj among Russia's Muslims. It depicts Mt. Arafat, outside of Mecca. Notes in Old Tatar in the Arabic script describe the religious significance of the site. Early 1900s. (*Tatarskii shamail: slovo i obraz* [Moscow: Mardzhani, 2009])

Following the historian William Roff's influential "twin threat" thesis, scholars working across colonial contexts have argued that the European powers sponsored the hajj essentially for defensive reasons: to contain the spread of cholera and Pan-Islamic ideas. In Russia, Daniel Brower has argued, tsarist officials were essentially forced into permitting and even supporting the hajj by the late nineteenth century, because of Russia's policy of religious toleration, and out of concern for the negative political and sanitary effects on the empire of the unregulated hajj.[16]

But historians have been too quick to assume similarities across empires. A close look at the Russian case reveals a more complex set of motivations for involvement in the hajj than standard histories allow, and unique aspects related to the peculiarities of imperial Russia's geography. A land-based empire with large Muslim populations living within its borders, rather than in remote overseas colonies, and hajj routes that cut through its central Slavic-speaking lands and busy Black Sea ports, Russia had both internal and external interests in the hajj. For Russia, the hajj was not a matter limited to far-away regions and populations—invisible at home and separate from domestic issues—but instead a highly visible, annual event that took place largely within Russia's borders and was deeply entangled with domestic issues.

Russia's goals in sponsoring the hajj were different from those of other European powers, and they were more ambitious. What is striking overall about Russia's decision to sponsor the hajj is not that it was undertaken to guard against perceived sanitary and political threats, but that it was ultimately an attempt to instrumentalize the pilgrimage to advance secular state and imperial agendas. At a time when Russia was simultaneously trying to cultivate a broader, collective sense of imperial belonging and "Russianness" among the empire's diverse peoples, and to develop the empire's economy to fund empire-wide reforms, the tsarist government embraced hajj patronage both to integrate newly conquered Muslim populations and to channel lucrative profits into state coffers. To this end, Russia organized seasonal service for hajj pilgrims on state-owned railroads and steamships, hoping to streamline the traffic onto Russian transport and capture millions of rubles for the state. In this sense, the Russian case more closely resembled that of the Ottoman state, in which the sultan undertook elaborate and expensive patronage of the hajj not only because it was expected of him as ruler of the Muslim holy places, and caliph of all Muslims, but also for non-religious and strategic reasons—namely, to integrate Arabic-speaking Muslims into the empire, and to justify posting Ottoman troops in the empire's far-flung Arab provinces.[17]

Figure I.4. *Shamail* print depicting the newly built Hejaz railway, which connected Damascus and Medina. The Ottoman government built the railroad with money gathered from Muslims worldwide. Russia's Muslims were among the donors, and the Russian consul general in Constantinople helped to deliver donations to the Ottomans. Kazan, 1909. (*Tatarskii shamail: slovo i obraz* [Moscow: Mardzhani, 2009])

Unlike France and especially Britain, Russia had no entrenched trade interests or extensive consular presence in the Ottoman Arab provinces, which had become a focus of European imperial rivalries by the mid-nineteenth century. This region encompassed the Muslim holy cities of Mecca and Medina, together with other important Islamic shrines and sites in Jerusalem and Damascus, which many Muslims visited as part of multi-site hajj itineraries in the nineteenth century. Not surprisingly, then, Russia embraced hajj patronage also for strategic reasons, as a means to extend influence into Ottoman Syria, Arabia, and other areas of imperial interest and rivalries abroad, where it had few or no interests to claim besides the hajj. In strategic terms, then, Russia's embrace of hajj patronage was less about protecting established interests forged over centuries of overseas colonialism, and more about extending Russia's imperial reach into new parts of the world.

◆◆◆

THE story I tell in this book reveals Russia's involvement in one of the great global migratory movements of the modern era. The hajj was the largest pilgrimage in the world in the nineteenth century, as well as Russia's single largest pilgrimage.[18] And yet for all the attention scholars have paid in recent years to Russia's diverse migrations, the hajj is missing from this historiography, which tends to focus on internal peasant migrations, and, to a lesser extent, mass emigration from the empire in the late imperial period (mainly by Poles and Jews).[19] The puzzling absence of the hajj from the historiography of Russia's migrations reflects broader neglect of Muslims in narratives of Russian history. To be sure, scholars in other fields—mainly Islamicists and anthropologists working in Europe, Russia, and Japan—have produced a robust literature on Muslim mobility and networks of exchange and contacts in modern Eurasia. As this work demonstrates, Muslims were among the most mobile of Russia's imperial populations; connected to coreligionists by networks of trade, pilgrimage, and scholarship, they moved frequently across imperial regions and borders. However, this body of scholarship is largely overlooked by historians of Russia, and has yet to be integrated into the history of Russia's migrations.[20]

By including the hajj in this history, we can begin to rethink some of our assumptions about patterns of Russia's migrations, and their effects on the empire. As it turns out, migrations were not simply an internal issue for Russia; nor were migrations abroad necessarily permanent. The mobility revolution in nineteenth-century Russia had transformative effects not only on Russian peasants and Jews, but also on the lives of the empire's Muslims populations. With railroads reaching the Caucasus and Central Asia in the 1880s, Muslims living in these places gained sudden access not only to Mecca, but to other parts of the Russian Empire and the world as well. Some moved out of their home regions, and many more began to ride the rails and explore the empire. These internal Muslim migrations raised questions within the regime about what Muslims "saw"—what impressions they gained of the empire—and prompted Russian officials to forge new ties with their counterparts in other parts of the empire and the world, to assist them in their efforts to integrate Muslims. Not all Russian officials saw Muslim migrations as a problem—some, in fact, saw them in a positive light. Many Russian officials saw the hajj not as a destructive but as a creative migratory phenomenon, one that generated economic activity and opportunities within Russia, offered ready-made connections to other parts of the world, and opened up possibilities for the expansion of Russian influence and power in the world.

A study of the hajj also pushes the boundaries of conventional spatial framings of Russian imperial history. Historians of the Russian Empire often take space for granted. They tend to approach their subject as a discrete territory circumscribed by formal borders, the same Russia represented on a Cartesian map, as though Russian history unfolded neatly, if improbably, within these borders.[21] Such an approach is convenient, but it can make it difficult, if not impossible, to see complex processes, phenomena, and cultures of contact and exchange that transcended Russia's formal borders. It also does not capture the geographical complexities of Russia's connections to and involvement in other parts of the world in the era of globalization and mass mobility. It can even, I would argue, reinforce a Cold War–era worldview that ahistorically separates "Russia" and the "Middle East," effectively concealing entire chapters of tsarist-era history and contributing to powerful and false binaries of West and East, Christian and Muslim, and so on.[22]

Late imperial Russia's borders, like those of other empires and states of the time, were porous, largely unmanned, and thousands of miles long. Migrants moved with ease across them, often undetected by imperial authorities, in patterns and processes that connected Russia to other parts of the world in ways that we are only now beginning to explore. Migrants were diverse, and they are all deserving of our attention. Hajj pilgrims serve as particularly useful guides across Russia's formal borders, because their migrations were circular and periodic (they happened at a set time of year, according to the Islamic lunar calendar), and can thus be followed with relative ease.

By tracing hajj pilgrims' routes and movements, we can begin to see empire in a new way, spatially. *Empire* is a flexible term, and here I use it to encompass a geographic space differently shaped and broader than the bounded territory of the Russian Empire that we can point to on a map. It is useful here to borrow analytical concepts and terms from the geographer David Harvey, who distinguished between "absolute" and "relative" space. Applying this theory to the Russian Empire, we might say that the absolute space of the empire is that contained within territorial borders, while its relative space is that produced through migration and exchange, between Russian subjects and places and peoples elsewhere.[23]

The hajj is a point of entry into this relative space, and a chance to explore little-known dimensions of how the Russian Empire was made over the nineteenth century. Tracing the history of the hajj reminds us that Russia's late imperial borders looked different to contemporaries than they do to us today: they were often insignificant to those who crossed them (often unknowingly), and fuzzy in the minds of imperial officials, many of whom saw them as impermanent. And so the geographic shape that the Russian Empire took in the nineteenth century was not foreordained, nor can empire simply be reduced in spatial terms to its familiar rendering on a map, as a clearly defined and self-contained unit.

MUSLIM responses to Russian involvement in the hajj were mixed. Glancing through the pages of hajj memoirs, one can find both praise and harsh criticisms. Not surprisingly, praise often came from Muslim elites, whose privileged status derived from their service to the Russian state, and who thus had good reason to voice approval for Russian involvement. Such elites included people such as Mufti Sultanov, the head of the Orenburg Assembly, who made the hajj in 1893 and stayed at the Russian consulate in Jeddah for three days on his way back from Mecca. Sultanov gushed in his account about the Russian consul, A. D. Levitskii, who was "so friendly and hospitable" to welcome him into his home, in spite of a raging cholera outbreak in Jeddah and the risk of infection.[24] But others complained about invasive policies and rough treatment, and being gouged by predatory agents who worked on behalf of the state. In one account from 1909 by a Muslim Tatar from Astrakhan, the author warned readers to avoid the "dishonest" mullah in Odessa, Sabirzhan Safarov, who worked as an agent for Russian steamship companies, and made a killing preying on poor hajj pilgrims.[25]

And yet it would be wrong to conclude that Muslims simply resented Russian efforts to sponsor the hajj, or avidly sought to avoid the hajj infrastructure that Russia built. By and large, most Muslims from Russia relied to some extent on tsarist support in making the pilgrimage to Mecca. The Russian consular archives are stuffed with correspondence between hajj pilgrims and consular officials that reveals that Muslims regularly turned to consular officials for help making the hajj: asking for money, directions, a place to stay, to mail a letter back home to relatives, medical care, and so on. The list of requests and demands is long, reflecting pilgrims' great needs during the long and arduous travel between Russia and Arabia. And many pilgrims wrote to Russian consuls to thank them for their help, promising to pray for them and the tsar, and expressing their gratitude to be subjects of the tsar and to receive diplomatic protection abroad.

Russian consular officials often took these letters at face value, as evidence that support for the hajj was working to instill in Russia's Muslims pride in their status as Russian subjects, and loyalty to the tsar. However, we should be more circumspect. Many Muslims were surely grateful to receive Russian protection while making the hajj, but there is little reason to think that the experience transformed their attitudes toward the tsar or the empire. More likely, their willingness to make use of Russian services, and the gratitude they expressed in writing, are evidence of their resourcefulness in mobilizing their status as Russian subjects when it suited them, and when they needed protection or help.

Whatever their true feelings about Russia's involvement in the hajj, pilgrims effectively assisted Russia in constructing its hajj infrastructure by appearing at its consulates, availing themselves of Russian services, and taking Russian railroads and steamships to make the pilgrimage. By the eve of World War I, Russia and other European powers were involved in virtually all aspects of the hajj, even in Ottoman Arabia. In Jeddah, the Dutch had set up a multi-service "Hajj Bureau," the British ran a medical dispensary out of their consulate (run by the vice-consul, a Muslim doctor and British subject from India), and European doctors and nurses staffed quarantine facilities set up to screen hajj pilgrims in El Tor (at the bottom of the Sinai peninsula) and on Kamaran Island (in the Red Sea).[26] Most Muslims would have found it impossible to make the Meccan pilgrimage in this era without interacting with European officials. This state of affairs shocked and dismayed many Muslim observers, who did not expect to be greeted in Ottoman Arabia by Europeans. Abdürreşid Ibrahim, the Pan-Islamic intellectual and activist from Russia, was surprised when he showed up at the quarantine station on Kamaran Island in 1908, and was greeted at the door of the disinfection building by a Christian woman. "Are we not in Ottoman territory?" his equally stunned companion asked him, to which he replied, "I don't know."[27]

For Ibrahim, Russian and European involvement in the hajj was inconsistent and unwelcome: he, like other Muslim intellectuals, saw it as a contravention of Muslim religion, tradition, and history, and as a thinly veiled attempt to colonize Ottoman Arabia. Interestingly, some Russian officials would have agreed. At a time of growing uneasiness about Pan-Islamic threats to the empire, as well as fears of the erosion of Orthodoxy's privileged place in the empire, some pushed for the tsarist regime to disengage from the hajj and withdraw its support. But this was a minority opinion. A greater contingent within the regime saw benefit for Russia in sponsoring the hajj.

The Soviet regime, too, would embrace a similar position, when it came to power in Russia in the 1920s. Like other revolutionary regimes, the Soviets built their new state in part upon a past that they officially rejected. To this end, the Soviets would begin to build their global presence by reopening hajj routes through Russian lands, and reviving the tsarist-era hajj infrastructure.

The history of Russian involvement in the hajj that this book tells has been overlooked up to this point, in part because it is hard to see, both in the material life of the region and the archival record. Much of what we know about Ottoman patronage of the hajj comes from the physical landscape. Working across the modern Middle East, archeologists have reconstructed Ottoman imperial hajj routes, and studied traces of the old infrastructures the imperial government built along them. They have studied stone cisterns, ruined caravanserais, fountains, and cemeteries to recover aspects of the material history of the Ottoman-era hajj.[28] By contrast, few physical traces exist of the Russian hajj. Unlike the stone-structure-lined hajj routes that the Ottomans created, Russia's hajj infrastructure was essentially a loose network of people and institutions, posted along railroad routes and aboard steamships; there were no stone buildings erected; dead pilgrims' bodies were thrown overboard at sea, disappearing without a trace; and what few physical structures did exist (a Muslim cemetery, in Odessa, for instance, where many dead pilgrims were buried) were demolished in the 1930s as part of Stalinist modernization of the USSR.[29]

The subject of the hajj is also obscured in the Russian imperial archives. Modern state archives tend to be both rich and deeply unforthcoming sources on human mobility, and Russia's archives are no exception. Because nineteenth-century Russian state officials often shared an assumption of immobility and firm borders as desired norms, the hajj, like other forms of mobility, attracted their attention as a potential disruption to local order (as well as a source of opportunities), and they produced mountains of documents about it.[30] And yet while copiously documented, the hajj is effectively "buried" in the Russian archives, by categories of cataloguing that reflect tsarist officials' preoccupation with borders, local concerns, and sedentary populations, and, later, Soviet archivists' Marxist worldview.[31] Because the hajj involved people moving through space, state sources also necessarily exist in fragments.

To recover this history, I have pieced together sources gathered from archives and collections across former Russian and Ottoman imperial lands. Through these sources and fragments, gathered together, this book broadens our understanding of Russian imperial geography in the tsarist era, and integrates Russia into histories of globalization from which it has long and unnecessarily been missing.

I

Imperialism through Islamic Networks

In 1848 a Russian subject named Kasym Mamad died in Arabia while performing the hajj, the annual Muslim pilgrimage to Mecca. Mamad was a native of the South Caucasus, a region Russia had recently conquered through wars with the Ottoman Empire and Persia. Like most Muslims traveling overland to Mecca at this time, Mamad made the long trip as part of a caravan, a procession of people and animals. He took a route that Muslims from the Caucasus, Sunnis and Shi'is, had followed for centuries. It wound through eastern Anatolia and northern Syria down to Damascus, the departure point for one of the enormous imperial caravans to Mecca that the Ottoman sultan sponsored every year.[1] Unlike his ancestors, however, Mamad made the hajj through Ottoman lands not as a Persian subject, governed by Ottoman taxes and laws, but as a newly minted Russian subject, entitled to extraterritorial privileges and the protection of Russian diplomatic officials in Ottoman lands.[2]

When Mamad died, his heirs in the Caucasus appealed to Russian officials to investigate the whereabouts of 300 rubles, a large sum, which Mamad had entrusted to a camel driver in Damascus for safekeeping. Mamad's heirs wanted it back. In earlier times, they would have appealed to Ottoman judicial authorities in Damascus, who for centuries had been in charge of auctioning off estates of the many pilgrims who died on the hajj and disbursing the proceeds to the proper heirs.[3] The local Russian governor referred the case to the viceroy in Tiflis (Tbilisi), who forwarded it to the Russian ambassador in Constantinople. Over the next two years, Russia's consul general in Syria investigated Mamad's estate. With the help of local Ottoman officials, the consul general managed to track down the camel driver in question—a rich Damascene and Ottoman subject named Hajji al-Esmer—and had him brought to the local Islamic court in Damascus. There, under oath before an Ottoman judge, al-Esmer acknowledged Mamad's deposit and testified that he had returned it to his travel companions, two men described in court documents as Russian subjects and Muslim military officers from the Caucasus. At this point, the consul general transferred the case back to Tiflis for the Russian viceroy to investigate further.[4]

Mamad's story and his heirs' quest to recover his estate illustrate a much broader historical change, whose effects would prove wide ranging: by the mid-nineteenth century, as a consequence of global imperialism, the hajj was increasingly coming under European influence and control. This was unprecedented. Since its eighth-century beginnings after the birth of Islam, the Meccan pilgrimage had been performed under the patronage of Muslim rulers, through Muslim-ruled lands, and with the help of Muslim officials along the way. Hajj pilgrims' ultimate destination—the Holy Cities of Mecca and Medina—were (and still are) closed to non-Muslims. This situation slowly began to change in the sixteenth century, as Europeans explored the Indian Ocean and other parts of Asia, conquering Muslim-majority lands and bringing long stretches of traditional hajj routes under their influence and direct control.[5] As European colonization grew, so did Europeans' interest in and influence over the hajj.

Russia was unique among European empires in ruling Muslims as far back as the fifteenth century, and had one of the longest histories of involvement in the hajj. In the sixteenth century Muscovite Russia conquered the former Mongol khanate (principality) of Astrakhan and established itself along a major caravan route used by Central Asians to get to Mecca.[6] Further imperial conquests to the south and the east—of the northern shores of the Black Sea, Crimea, the Caucasus, and Central Asia—added millions of new Muslim subjects to the empire's already large and internally diverse population, and brought a web of ancient caravan routes within Russia's borders.

For centuries Muslims across Eurasia had been traveling these lands and routes to reach Mecca. Many took sailing vessels across the Black Sea to Istanbul (Constantinople) to witness the sultan's investiture ceremonies that marked the departure of the imperial hajj caravan from the Ottoman capital. Others, Kasym Mamad among them, cut south through the Caucasus to join imperial hajj caravans leaving from Damascus and Baghdad. Still others followed land routes through Afghan and Indian lands, to board ships bound across the Indian Ocean to Arabia.[7] This traffic continued and in fact increased after the Russian conquests, with the introduction of railroads and steamships in the mid-nineteenth century that made the Russian Empire a center of global hajj routes and traffic.

Having inherited a hajj tradition through imperial conquests, Russia had to decide what to do with it. As one of the five pillars of Islam, and an obligation for Muslims, the hajj could not easily be banned or stopped—and, it offered Russia opportunities for managing and governing Muslims, as well as for advancing state and imperial agendas. To bring the hajj under state influence and control, Russia began to sponsor it in the nineteenth century. This sponsorship was at first improvised and episodic, as part of Russian efforts to consolidate rule in newly conquered Muslim regions. However, as the hajj grew into a mass annual phenomenon over the nineteenth century, Russia's interests in it multiplied, and state support became systematic. While the tsar periodically announced bans on the hajj in the empire, particularly during wars and epidemics, and tsarist officials often expressed political and economic concerns about the hajj, Russia embraced a general policy of hajj patronage from the mid-nineteenth century onward.[8]

By sponsoring the hajj, Russia was not simply trying to control the pilgrimage, or contain the problems it engendered as a mass migratory movement. Rather, it was seizing a new opportunity created by imperial conquests to tap into and co-opt the hajj, a global Islamic network, as a mechanism of imperial integration and expansion. This was part of a larger process that had been under way in Russia since the late eighteenth century—and, more broadly, across European empires over the nineteenth century—whereby European colonial governments institutionalized Islam and Islamic practices to advance imperial agendas.[9]

Co-opting the hajj would not be easy. Contestation and ambivalence were inherent to the project from the start. Unlike the situation with Russian Orthodox pilgrimage to Jerusalem, which the tsarist government also began to sponsor in the nineteenth century, government support for the hajj was not organized through a centralized process, nor did the tsar ever publicly endorse it.[10] This semisecrecy reflected concerns, widely shared among tsarist officials, that state support for the hajj could upset the empire's Russian Orthodox faithful and the leadership of the Russian Orthodox Church, which enjoyed prominence and a privileged position as the "preeminent" church of the empire and the ruling dynasty. The decision to sponsor the hajj grew from a gradually developing consensus within the government that Russia stood to gain more from sponsoring the hajj than ignoring or banning it. But as a non-Muslim empire, Russia faced unique challenges in persuading Muslims to recognize it as protector of the hajj, and to follow state-mandated routes and regulations.

Notwithstanding these challenges and complexities, Russia over the nineteenth and early twentieth centuries would build a transimperial hajj infrastructure that spanned thousands of miles and supported the tens of thousands of Muslims pilgrims who moved between the empire and Arabia every year. Many of Russia's Muslims were critical of the tsarist government's involvement in the hajj, but most relied on this infrastructure, to some extent, in making the pilgrimage to Mecca. Built upon Russia's expanded consular networks in Ottoman and Persian lands—the result of extraterritorial privileges Russia had gained through peace treaties starting in the late eighteenth century—this hajj infrastructure was testimony to the dramatic changes in Russia's internal demographics and relations with neighboring Muslim states, as well as its changing position in the world after its conquests of Muslim-majority lands.

THE story of how Russia became patron of the hajj begins in the Caucasus. The Caucasus, a Muslim-majority region, was annexed by Russia over the first half of the nineteenth century through a drawn-out process of piecemeal conquest and war. There, against the backdrop of Russia's ongoing war against Muslim anticolonial resistance in the north and its efforts to consolidate imperial rule in the region, tsarist officials in the 1840s first began to organize coordinated, cross-border support for Russian subjects taking the popular Syrian route to Mecca, via Ottoman Damascus. Collaborating with Russian consular officials newly posted in Syria, tsarist officials in the Caucasus organized logistical, financial, and judicial support to assist small numbers of pilgrims, perhaps a few hundred a year, in making the hajj through Ottoman lands. Kasym Mamad was a typical beneficiary of this early patronage, as a Muslim elite with close ties to the nascent tsarist administration in the Caucasus.

This first instance of Russian organization of cross-border hajj patronage reveals how much tsarist officials saw strategic opportunities in the hajj. Russia wanted to establish stable rule in the Caucasus and expand its diplomatic presence and political influence in Ottoman Syria, a site of European imperial rivalries in the first half of the nineteenth century. Russian officials in both the Caucasus and Syria embraced hajj patronage to consolidate Russian power in their region, and in the process forged a new policy of Russian imperialism through Islamic networks.

Russia's conquest of the Caucasus was a turning point in the empire's history. Much has been written about the wide-ranging transformative effects of this conquest on the empire—how it gave Russia an "Orient" to civilize, allowed it to see itself as a colonial empire like its European rivals, and created a new imperial borderland, far removed from the center, to which the Russian state exiled undesirables.[11] This conquest also integrated Russia into the world in new ways, through the web of human mobility networks that connected the lands and populations of the Caucasus to other parts of the world. The nineteenth-century Caucasus was a bridge between Russian lands in the north and Persian and Ottoman lands to the south, and a hub of ancient caravan routes along which people had been moving for centuries as merchants, travelers, and pilgrims.

Throughout the first half of the nineteenth century, the Caucasus remained a center of Eurasian hajj traffic. We see this by piecing together documents from Russia's foreign policy archives. These archives contain numerous petitions from Muslim rulers from Central Asia and Persia, asking the tsarist government to allow their subjects passage to Mecca along their traditional routes, across the Russian steppe and through the Caucasus. These cases reveal the extent to which Russia's southward expansion had made the hajj a diplomatic issue with neighboring Muslim states, whose rulers sought to keep the old routes to Mecca open for their subjects as a matter of their own prestige and political legitimacy.

In the early 1800s, Russia allowed foreign Muslims open access to these routes through a series of treaties with the Persians and Ottomans. In some cases the Foreign Ministry even arranged and subsidized travel for elite Muslims from Central Asia. This was a small-scale but nevertheless significant practice. It shows that rather than try to close these routes and prohibit hajj traffic through the empire, Russia instead embraced an informal role as "protector" of hajj pilgrims and routes in its diplomatic relations with its Muslim neighbors. In so doing, Russian tsars were acting in an ad hoc fashion much as Muslim emperors had since eighth century: they laid claim to the tradition and networks of the hajj for imperialist aims. At a time when Russia sought to develop commercial relations with Persia and Central Asia, its practice of supporting foreign hajj pilgrims was surely motivated by economic and strategic interests.[12]

Domestic Muslims, newly minted subjects of the tsar living in the Caucasus, were another matter. Russian policy toward these internal Muslim populations went through three stages. As the new ruler of the Caucasus, Russia first tried to prohibit the hajj. In 1822 Tsar Alexander I officially banned the hajj for Muslims in the Caucasus, at the urging of his trusted commander in chief of the region, A. P. Ermolov. This was above all a security measure. Like colonial officials operating in Muslim regions elsewhere, Ermolov was suspicious of the hajj as a "clandestine" activity that fed Muslim "fanaticism." Faced with Muslim rebellions across the North Caucasus in the early 1820s, he worried that the hajj was feeding this resistance, and that disguised pilgrims were in fact arms smugglers and Ottoman agents. Writing to Russian foreign minister Karl Nesselrode in January 1822, Ermolov noted that many Muslims in the Caucasus made the hajj every year along routes through Ottoman lands, and he warned that the experience was surely strengthening their loyalties to the sultan and their resolve to resist Russian rule.[13]

Tsar Alexander I was reluctant about the hajj ban. He worried that Muslims would resent it, given Russia's promise of religious toleration, but he agreed to it as a temporary security measure. Ermolov's officials announced the ban throughout the Caucasus in early 1822, and threatened violators with state confiscation of their property, and deportation into Russia's central regions.[14] The tsar's hesitation illustrates how Russia's official policy of religious toleration, introduced in the late eighteenth century by Tsarina Catherine the Great to foster social control and imperial stability, was sometimes difficult for officials to reconcile with broader security concerns about the empire, particularly when it came to pilgrimage to holy sites abroad.

Russia's hajj ban in the Caucasus was short lived because it did not work. Muslims continued to leave the Caucasus for Mecca in spite of it, some with the help of Russian officials, who were often easy to bribe. In 1823, Ermolov complained to his commander in Dagestan, in the North Caucasus, that "many Muslims" from his province were showing up in the South Caucasus carrying travel documents from their local Russian authorities that permitted them to make the hajj, in violation of the ban.[15] The ban also created problems for foreign Muslims. Soon after it was announced, the Foreign Ministry received numerous complaints from Persians and Bukharans who suddenly found their routes through the Caucasus blocked. More than once Nesselrode wrote to Ermolov, reminding him "under no circumstances" to apply the ban to foreign Muslims, who "passed through Russian lands to make their journey easier."[16]

The hajj ban also interfered with tsarist officials' efforts to cultivate Muslim allegiances, and co-opt elites into the emerging Russian administration in the Caucasus. When Muslim elites complained about the ban, Russian officials tried to defend it as a benevolent measure, intended to protect Russia's Muslim subjects from violent attacks along Ottoman hajj routes, and as a "warning about the dangers of traveling through Ottoman lands during wartime."[17] But Russian officials quickly discovered that Muslims recognized, and resented, the ban for what it was: an attempt by their colonial conquerors to restrict their religious practice, and, thus, a violation of Russia's stated policy of toleration of Islam.

In one awkward exchange in 1824, an Islamic judge (*kadi*) representing the Dargin community (one of the largest ethnic groups in the North Caucasus) complained about the hajj ban, and Ermolov conceded that he had no right to "prohibit the performance of religious duties," and thus no authority to forbid Muslims from making the hajj. He urged the *kadi* to see the ban as a measure intended to protect Russian subjects from Ottoman abuses along their routes, "of which there are many sad examples," and he assured him that the routes would "soon be reopened."[18]

Faced with growing Muslim demand for access to Mecca, Ermolov declared the hajj ban "inconvenient," and abandoned it. Following a pattern set by colonial officials managing the hajj in other parts of the world—and surely influenced by knowledge of these colonial practices, about which Russia was gathering information through its foreign consulates—Ermolov went from restricting to regulating the hajj.[19] In January 1826 he introduced new rules and procedures for granting Muslims passports to Mecca. He instructed tsarist officials throughout the Caucasus to monitor applicants for travel documents, and give permission only to "well-intentioned Muslims." Ermolov acknowledged that intentions were easier to determine among elites, whose allegiances were generally known to the Russian authorities. The "simple folk," with more mysterious loyalties, would need a letter of recommendation from their local district in order to get a transit pass for Tiflis. Once in Tiflis, Muslims were supposed to report directly to Ermolov, who would record their names in a logbook and issue them a foreign passport.[20]

By getting Muslims to apply to Russian authorities for passports to Mecca, Ermolov reasoned, officials would be able to determine "how many are going on the hajj . . . and how much money they are taking with them, as this journey typically costs a lot."[21] The ethos and intentions of Ermolov's new rules for the hajj fit the larger project he is credited with as commander in chief of the Caucasus: the creation of a centralized, rational Russian government administration, by understanding local social hierarchies, categorizing populations, and identifying important locals to co-opt into the administration. His decision should also be seen as an urgent security measure. Introduced against the backdrop of Muslim rebellions across the North Caucasus, and renewed war with Persia, when Muslim khanates in the South Caucasus were also revolting against Russian rule, Ermolov's abandonment of the hajj ban was surely an attempt to quell dissent and reassure Muslims of Russia's toleration of Islam.[22]

The 1840s would bring another change in Russian policy toward the hajj. In that decade Russian officials in the Caucasus would begin to sponsor it.

This shift was again a result of Russia's changing geopolitics in the wider region—namely, its growing interest and involvement in neighboring Ottoman Syria. This story of imperial meddling in Ottoman lands is often told as a chapter of Russian foreign policy history, and as part of the narrative of the "Eastern Question"—the phrase that nineteenth-century European powers used to refer to the problems posed by the disintegration of the Ottoman Empire, and the resulting European contest for control over former Ottoman territories. But it was also closely connected to the history of Russian governance of Islam and the integration of Muslim populations in the Caucasus.

◆◆◆

SYRIA became a focus of Great Power rivalries in the Ottoman Empire in the 1830s. It was one of the largest of the Ottoman Empire's Arab provinces, encompassing all of what we know today as Syria, Lebanon, Israel/Palestine, and Jordan, as well as small parts of Turkey. Political instability in Syria, resulting in the Ottomans' temporary loss of control of the region, stoked European fears of the collapse of Ottoman rule in the region, and with it the post-Napoleonic "balance of power" in Europe.

Syria had been in turmoil since 1831, when troops loyal to Muhammad Ali, the renegade Ottoman governor of Egypt, invaded and occupied the region. Taking advantage of Ottoman weakness—the empire had just lost a large swath of territory in the Balkans to the Greeks, who revolted and created their own state—Muhammad Ali invaded Syria as part of his attempt to carve out his own empire from the Ottoman Arab provinces.

Lasting through the 1830s, the Egyptian occupation of Syria opened the region to unprecedented European penetration. Trying to court European support for his imperial project, Muhammad Ali encouraged European merchants to expand their commercial activities in the region, and invited in Christian missionaries. To protect their growing interests in Syria, European powers got permission from Muhammad Ali to open a constellation of new consulates, and moved into places that the Ottomans had long kept closed to them for religious reasons. During the Egyptian occupation, Europeans opened their first consulates in Jerusalem and Damascus, both cities sacred to Muslims, and in Jeddah, which lay within the Arabian Peninsula and close to the Holy Cities of Mecca and Medina. Russia opened a new consulate in 1839 in Beirut, a busy trade port and the emerging hub of European diplomatic activity in Syria.[23]

The Ottomans ended the Egyptian occupation in 1840, through a protracted war they fought with the help of British troops. But the European presence continued to grow after the Ottomans reasserted control of the region. Having gained a foothold in Syria, the European powers expanded upon it. Their presence in Syria and surrounding regions was connected to broader imperial networks and interests, as well as domestic interests. Britain had significant trade networks centered in Baghdad that it wanted to protect, together with its overland communication routes to India, which cut through Syria and Mesopotamia. France, in the midst of an industrial revolution in the 1840s, relied on Syria for wool and silk for its new factories. Russia, for its part, had mainly security concerns, given Syria's proximity to Russia's southwestern borders (the distance between Tiflis and Aleppo is about 600 miles). Each of the powers—Britain, France, and Russia—feared that if Ottoman power collapsed, one of its rivals would move in to fill the vacuum, and colonize Ottoman lands.[24]

With these broader imperial concerns in mind, European powers increased their involvement in Ottoman Syria over the 1840s and competed with one another for influence over local populations. Their interests may have been primarily strategic, but they expressed them largely in religious terms. Standard scholarly narratives describe a process whereby European "Christian" empires sought to undermine Ottoman "Muslim" control over its Christian subject populations by invoking (and abusing) treaty rights, known as Capitulations, secured from the Ottomans. Though Syria had a majority Muslim population (about ninety percent were Sunni Muslims), it was also home to one of the empire's largest concentrated populations of Christians, who numbered in the hundreds of thousands and practiced a dizzying array of rites and traditions. On the grounds of "protecting" Christian "coreligionists" in Syria from persecution by Muslim neighbors, European consuls interfered in local Christian religious affairs, and the powers created infrastructures in and around Jerusalem to support their Christian subjects who visited Jerusalem and nearby holy sites as pilgrims.[25]

Russia presumably had a particular advantage in this imperial competition, since it shared the Eastern Orthodox rite with the largest Christian community in Syria (Eastern Orthodox were about a third of all Christians in the region).[26] To serve as Russian consul in Beirut, the center of European diplomatic activity in Syria, the Russian Foreign Ministry carefully chose a Greek-speaking Orthodox Christian: an Ottoman-born Russian subject named Konstantin Bazili. The ministry hoped that Bazili would gain the trust of the Greek-speaking clergy in charge of the Orthodox churches in Syria. As Beirut consul, Bazili was also officially responsible for helping Russian Orthodox pilgrims, who typically arrived in Beirut or Jaffa by ship, and then proceeded by land to Jerusalem. However, this was more a justification for opening this new Russian consulate than a response to acute need. Only a small number of Russian Orthodox Christians made the Jerusalem pilgrimage; reports from the Russian embassy in Constantinople estimated just a few hundred a year.[27] Surely some eluded the embassy's record, but it is unlikely that they were numerous. The trip from Russia to Syria was long, costly, and dangerous, and Orthodox pilgrimage, unlike the hajj, was not obligatory. But the tsarist government was keen to see the Orthodox pilgrimage increase, to bolster Russia's presence in and claims to interests in Syria. The tsarist government began encouraging its Orthodox subjects to make pilgrimages to Jerusalem by subsidizing their transportation and constructing support facilities along their routes, and in and around Jerusalem.

Over the 1840s, the tsarist government established a Russian Orthodox ecclesiastical mission in Jerusalem, on the premise of supporting its Orthodox pilgrims as well as local Eastern Orthodox churches. By the late nineteenth century, the government had helped fund the establishment of the Russian Imperial Orthodox Palestine Society, which built a network of facilities for Orthodox pilgrims along their routes between Russia and the Holy Land. Traces of this history are visible in the physical landscape of Jerusalem now, in onion-domed Russian Orthodox churches on the Mount of Olives, and the so-called Russian Compound outside Jerusalem's old city walls, a multibuilding complex the tsarist state helped build to support Russian Orthodox pilgrims. (Today parts of the compound house Israeli government offices.)[28]

Russia's support for Orthodox pilgrimage to Jerusalem was part of an emerging strategy to extend influence into Ottoman Syria through religious networks. As tsarist officials would soon come to see, Russia had connections to Syria not only through its Orthodox Christians, but through other subject populations as well. The complexity of Russia's relationship to Syria becomes clear when we start sifting through the archives of the Beirut consulate, looking closely at the kinds of cases Bazili handled in his first years as Russian consul. We find many cases involving Armenian and Jewish subjects from Russia, who had come to Jerusalem and other parts of Ottoman Syria for pilgrimage and trade, and also—in the case of Jews—as permanent settlers. The archives also reveal attempts by tsarist officials to expand Russia's landholding and presence in Jerusalem by laying claim to buildings that the Georgian Orthodox Church had owned in the holy city for centuries.[29] Most strikingly, the Beirut archives contain scores of cases and correspondence involving Russia's Muslim subjects and their connections to the region. By and large these cases involve new Russian subjects from the Caucasus, passing through Syria on their way to and from Mecca.

Syria in the nineteenth century was central to global hajj routes because of the Damascus caravan. It was one of two imperial hajj caravans sponsored by the Ottoman sultan in his empire—the other left from Cairo—and both were ancient institutions. First organized by the Mamluks in the thirteenth century, the two caravans had been taken over by the Ottomans with their sixteenth-century conquests of Arab lands, and as part of the Ottoman sultan's assumption of the role of "protector" of the hajj and the Holy Cities of Mecca and Medina.[30] The Ottomans sponsored the two imperial hajj caravans at enormous cost and effort because it was expected of them as Muslim rulers who now controlled the Muslim holy cities. At the same time, they had strategic motivations. In her study of the hajj under the Ottomans, Suraiya Faroqhi argues that the Ottomans embraced hajj patronage also as a mechanism for integrating the empire's dispersed and internally diverse Muslim populations, and maintaining a military presence in their far-flung Arab provinces.[31]

Figure 1.1. The hajj caravan commander with the *mahmal* (the ceremonial palanquin, representing the authority of the Ottoman sultan) and Ottoman officials. Damascus, ca. 1908. (Courtesy of the Kunstkamera Museum, St. Petersburg, Russia)

For security, pilgrims taking land routes to Mecca tried to join one of these hajj caravans. The Damascus caravan was arguably the more prestigious of the two. It began in Istanbul, where the Ottoman sultan performed public investiture ceremonies to send it off. It carried a ceremonial palanquin (*mahmal*)—an empty wooden chair mounted on a camel's back, cloaked in silk brocaded with Koranic verse, a symbol of the sultan's authority—as well as the "imperial purses" (*surre*). The *surre* contained generous subsidies and gifts from the sultan for the people and officials of Damascus, Jerusalem, Mecca, and Medina, and Bedouin tribes along the desert route.[32]

To make the hajj caravan into an imperial institution and a "centerpiece of Ottoman rule" in Damascus, the Ottomans built an extensive infrastructure to support it beginning in the sixteenth century. This included the construction of a majestic pilgrimage complex in the center of Damascus, the Tekkiya, with a mosque and soup kitchen; shops stocked with supplies for the road, such as riding gear, blankets, and grain; and an enclosed campground reserved for pilgrims in the courtyard of the complex.[33]

To fortify the caravan's desert route between Damascus and Mecca, the Ottomans built a string of fortresses, wells, and cisterns that reached deep into the Hejaz region. To secure the route, they stationed troops along it, and paid off nomadic Bedouin tribes with generous grain subsidies to prevent them from attacking the caravan. They named the governor of Damascus the caravan commander (*amir al-hajj*), and put him in charge of annual preparations for the caravan, and for leading it to Mecca and back. They also organized new ceremonies in Damascus to mark the caravan's departure. This involved a solemn procession through the city with Ottoman troops and musicians, and the delivery of the *mahmal* and *surre* to the caravan by an official from Istanbul.[34]

The result of these efforts was an enormous caravan of people and animals, described by one eyewitness as a "walking administration."[35] In addition to many thousands of pilgrims speaking different languages, with the caravan commander at its head, the caravan consisted of a military escort, its own court and treasury, merchants, Ottoman officials responsible for running the complex logistics of the caravan, and a fleet of service people, including the "torchbearers" who took shifts walking ahead of the caravan at night with a hand-held lantern.[36]

In the late eighteenth and early nineteenth centuries, the Damascus caravan included as many as 50,000 pilgrims a year, hailing from surrounding Arab lands, Anatolia, Persia, Central Asia, and the Caucasus.[37] In good years, it provided pilgrims with safe passage across the desert to Mecca and back. But in times of war or famine, the route was unsecured, Bedouin attacks were frequent, and some years the caravan got stuck in Damascus. During the decade-long Egyptian occupation of Syria, the Ottomans lost control of the Damascus hajj caravan. In 1832 and 1833 the caravan did not leave Damascus because of local revolts and the Egyptians' inability to secure the caravan route. Thereafter, between 1834 and 1839, the Egyptians controlled and ran the caravan between Damascus and Mecca, introducing new procedures and ceremonies and putting their own officials in charge of it.[38] Only in the early 1840s, with the withdrawal of Egyptian troops from Syria, did the Ottomans begin to reassert their authority over the Damascus hajj caravan, and restore their traditional ceremonies.

Even so, by the 1840s the Damascus hajj caravan was an institution in decline. Every year the numbers of pilgrims declined, to as few as 2,000 a year by 1850, compared to tens of thousands at the start of the century. There were two reasons for this. With the rise of steamship travel worldwide, hajj pilgrims were beginning to shift away from traditional land routes to take sea routes to Arabia instead.

Figure 1.2. Procession of the Ottoman hajj caravan through Damascus. Early 1900s. (Courtesy of the Kunstkamera Museum, St. Petersburg, Russia)

Second, following the withdrawal of Egyptian troops from Syria the Ottomans struggled for years to restore order to the region, and to raise taxes from the local population adequate to fund a functioning hajj caravan. As attacks on pilgrims persisted, and word spread about dangers pilgrims faced along the route, many Muslims sought alternate routes to Mecca. In December 1840 the hajj caravan did not leave Damascus as scheduled because the Ottomans were unable to secure the desert route. This left thousands of pilgrims stranded in Damascus, faced with the choice of either making the long journey back home or waiting in the city for a year until the next year's hajj season.[39]

Historians have written about the devastating effects of the hajj caravan's decline on Damascus, whose economy had been based for centuries on the pilgrim traffic.[40] Another consequence, however, was that opportunities opened up for Russia and other European powers to increase their involvement in the hajj through their new consulates in Syria. Opportunities were especially rich for Russia and France, which were connected to Syria and the Damascus caravan through their Muslim populations from the Caucasus and Algeria. In the 1840s both began to organize support for their subjects making the hajj along the Syrian route through their consulates, and to intervene in Ottoman organization of the Damascus caravan.[41]

As the leading Russian diplomat in Syria, Bazili became involved in the hajj in Damascus in December 1840. He knew that many Russian subjects were among the thousands of pilgrims stranded in the city, along with a number of "distinguished" Persian pilgrims who carried documents from the Russian consulate in Tabriz that entitled them to Russian diplomatic protection. When the head of the Persian contingent wrote to the Beirut consulate from Damascus to ask for help, Bazili contacted the newly arrived Ottoman governor in Damascus, Nejib Pasha, asking him to protect these pilgrims, and warning him that among them were notables whose safety was important to the Persian government. At the same time, Bazili wrote back to the Persian leader, inviting him to file any "grievance" he might have with the consulate through an agent Bazili had sent to Damascus who was "authorized" to approach the Ottoman governor on their behalf.[42] Meanwhile, Bazili got to work to reroute Russian and Persian subjects in Damascus through Cairo, asking local Ottoman officials to guarantee their "safe passage" from Damascus to Beirut, and writing to the caravan commander in Damascus directly, asking him to announce the new plan to these pilgrims under his authority.

On their own initiative, some Muslims began to reach out to Bazili from Damascus, sending petitions to ask for his help getting to Mecca. These petitions reveal some of the dangers faced by hajj pilgrims taking the Syrian route in this period, because of Ottoman failures to provide security. They also show that some Muslims from the Caucasus had begun to mobilize their newfound status as Russian subjects in response to these failures, and turn to Russian consulates for help making the hajj.[43]

Among those seeking Bazili's help that winter was a group of Muslims from Kazikumukh, a Muslim khanate in the North Caucasus region of Dagestan, ruled at this time by a Russian-appointed khan (prince).[44] They had traveled overland on foot and horseback, as part of a small caravan of twenty men. Their case, preserved in a thick file in the archives of the Beirut consulate, offers vivid details on the pilgrims' identities, and the conditions under which they made the pilgrimage. Like many pilgrims traveling to Mecca in this period—just before the era of modern transport, and the opening up of the pilgrimage to Muslims of all backgrounds—they were elites with the means and connections necessary to make the long journey. At the center of the group were three mullahs (Islamic jurisconsults), who had been summoned from their different villages by the wife of their local khan, and asked to perform the pilgrimage on behalf of herself, the khan, and their son. She had given them gifts from her treasury to deliver to officials in the Muslim holy cities, and seventeen of her personal servants to assist them in the journey. She had also arranged for them to receive passports from the Russian commander in chief in Tiflis, I. G. Golovin. Golovin had "warmly" received them at his office in Tiflis, giving them more gifts along with foreign passports, before sending them on their way.

This twenty-man caravan had left Tiflis for Damascus in October 1840, taking a land route through Erzurum and reaching Aleppo within a month. Halfway between Aleppo and Damascus they were robbed in a surprise attack by Bedouins who "came out of nowhere," on foot and horseback, wielding spears, clubs, and rifles. The Bedouins stole everything—their money, clothes, passports, dried food stores, and horses—killed eight of them, and seriously wounded the rest. Taking refuge in Damascus, the twelve survivors heard that there was a Russian consulate nearby, and three of them immediately went to Beirut to seek Bazili's help. In their first letter to Bazili, delivered in person to the door of the consulate, they reminded him that it was his "duty" to protect them as "subjects of the tsar," and begged him to do one of three things: come to Damascus to intervene on their behalf with the Ottoman governor, send them to Constantinople to be cared for by the Russian ambassador, or send them back to Tiflis to get help from the Russian commander in chief. They had no money or travel documents and told Bazili, "We are hungry and have no clothes and we will all die if you ignore us."[45]

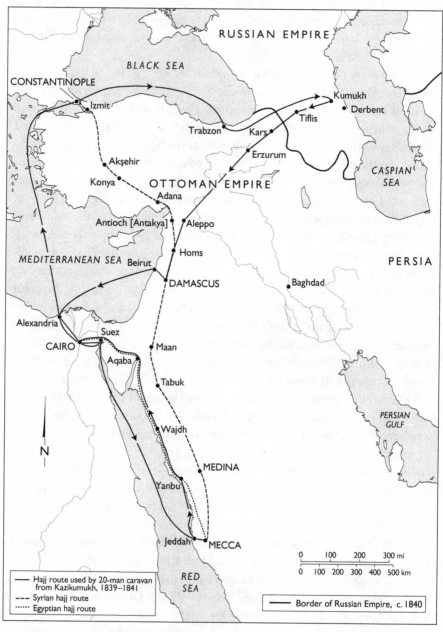

Map 3. Hajj route followed by caravan from Kazikumukh in the North Caucasus, 1839–1841

The following labels appear on the map:

RUSSIAN EMPIRE

BLACK SEA

CONSTANTINOPLE
Izmit
Kumukh
Derbent
Tiflis
Trabzon
Kars
Erzurum
Akşehir
Konya
OTTOMAN EMPIRE
Adana
CASPIAN SEA
Antioch [Antakya]
Aleppo
Homs
MEDITERRANEAN SEA
Beirut
DAMASCUS
Baghdad
PERSIA
Alexandria
Suez
CAIRO
Maan
Aqaba
Tabuk
Wajdh
N
MEDINA
Yanbu
PERSIAN GULF
Jeddah
MECCA

0   100   200   300 mi
0   100   200   300   400   500 km

—— Hajj route used by 20-man caravan from Kazikumukh, 1839–1841
--- Syrian hajj route
····· Egyptian hajj route

RED SEA

—— Border of Russian Empire, c. 1840

32

Bazili immediately took up their case. He took the three pilgrims who had shown up at his door into the consulate, and housed and fed them for several days. He sent money through a consular agent to the surviving pilgrims in Damascus, and a letter assuring them that their case would be "specially handled" by Nejib Pasha. Bazili reported the crime to the Damascus city-governor (*müsselim*), and asked him to provide security for the survivors in his city. In the meantime, he contacted the Russian ambassador in Constantinople, V. P. Titov, who extracted from the Ottoman government an imperial order for Nejib Pasha, instructing him to investigate the case of the "Dagestani pilgrims" and punish the Bedouin attackers. Finally, he wrote directly to Nejib Pasha, reminding him of his "double title" as governor of Damascus and caravan commander, and asking him to "uphold his duties" by "rendering justice" to the Dagestani pilgrims named in the imperial order.[46]

Within nine months the case of the Dagestani hajj pilgrims was resolved. In a final report to Ambassador Titov, Bazili recounted how Nejib Pasha had sent troops out into the desert, found the Bedouin culprits, and seized 425 camels from them as indemnity. With the next hajj season fast approaching, Bazili went to Damascus to supervise the process of selling the camels at public auction, and disbursing the proceeds to the Dagestani pilgrims through the local Islamic court (*mahkeme*). Bazili assured Titov that he had kept the pilgrims out of the Islamic court—given their legal immunities as Russian subjects—and had also "scrupulously" avoided intervening in the division of the money, which the pilgrims had carried out themselves, equitably, "according to their religious law."[47]

With rumors circulating that the Damascus hajj caravan might not leave again that year, Bazili arranged for the Dagestani pilgrims to join the Cairo caravan instead. At consulate expense, he brought all twelve pilgrims from Damascus to Beirut, and housed and fed them for several days before sending them off to Egypt by steamship. As a final gesture, he sent word through diplomatic channels back to their relatives in the Caucasus, assuring them that they were safe and were finally headed to Mecca.[48] A year later, while in transit in Egypt, waiting to catch a steamship back to Russia, they wrote Bazili a final note: they thanked him for his help, told him they had prayed for him and the tsar in Mecca, and reported that they had all made the journey safely but for one, who was buried in Jeddah.[49]

By intervening in the case of the Dagestani pilgrims, Bazili was fulfilling his duty as Russian consul to provide diplomatic protection to tsarist subjects in

Ottoman lands. According to eighteenth-century treaty agreements with the Ottomans (the Capitulations), Russia, like other European powers, was allowed to open consulates "wherever it had interests" in Ottoman lands, and its subjects were entitled to extraterritorial privileges.[50] These included immunities from Ottoman taxes and laws. Scholars tend to think of the Capitulations most often with regard to Russia's Orthodox Christian subjects, but in fact they applied to all Russian subjects in Ottoman lands, regardless of religious faith. Ottoman sources reveal that some of Russia's Muslims began to take advantage of these privileges as soon as they were introduced at the end of the eighteenth century. Ottoman archives hold petitions from the Russian ambassador in Constantinople on behalf of Russian Muslims who complained of mistreatment by Ottoman officials while making the hajj.[51] As Beirut consul, Bazili routinely provided legal assistance to Russian subjects of all faiths, intervening on their behalf with the Ottoman authorities when they were the victims of crime, and acting as arbiter in their financial negotiations with Ottoman subjects.

And yet, it is also clear that Bazili went to extraordinary lengths for these pilgrims from the North Caucasus. He helped them even though they had no documents to prove they were Russian subjects, and in spite of their disregard for warnings from tsarist officials against making the hajj that year, "through a country at war." And his insistence on tracking down and punishing the Bedouin attackers, while ultimately successful, was costly to the Ottoman authorities in Damascus. Toward the end of the case, an exasperated Nejib Pasha complained to Bazili that he had gone "above and beyond his duty" in this case, and that his investigation had already cost his government far more than the pilgrims lost in the attack.[52]

Correspondence surrounding this case reveals that Bazili saw strategic value in supporting the Dagestani pilgrims. He told Titov he had "lavished" care on them in part because they belonged to the "house of the famous Aslan Khan, prince of the Kazikumukhs in Dagestan."[53] Bazili had intimate knowledge of the Caucasus. Before being posted to Syria, he had served in the Caucasus on a Foreign Ministry committee tasked to develop a plan for governance of the region. He knew firsthand about Russia's ongoing efforts to put down rebellions and establish control over the predominantly Muslim North Caucasus, by identifying and recruiting Muslim elites into the Russian administration.[54] His attention to this particular case, and comments to Titov, suggest that he had broader imperial agendas in mind in helping this group, and that his decision was shaped by Russia's ongoing efforts to establish a stable government in the Caucasus.

In the case of the Dagestani hajj pilgrims we can begin to see the outlines of an emerging policy of Russian hajj patronage, based on complex new geopolitical circumstances, and mutual interests among Russian officials in the Caucasus and Syria, as well as Muslims from the Caucasus. At a time when Russia was trying to consolidate its empire in the newly conquered Caucasus and also expand its influence in Ottoman Syria, tsarist officials in both places began to see the hajj traffic that linked the two regions as strategically useful, and well worth cultivating.

In the Caucasus, Russian commander in chief I. G. Golovin and his successors in the early 1840s had started to sponsor the hajj selectively, offering passports and special support—subsidies, gifts, travel assistance, in some cases all-paid hajj trips—to Muslim elites who had chosen to serve the Russian administration or pledge their allegiance to Russian forces.[55] The case of the pilgrims from Kazikumukh fits this pattern of hajj patronage as a colonial strategy to consolidate Muslim loyalties. Meanwhile, across the border in Syria, Bazili quietly began to expand support for the hajj. He hired an unofficial consular agent in Damascus, a local Greek-speaking merchant named Leonidas Telatinidis, to advertise the services of the nearby Beirut consulate to hajj pilgrims from the Caucasus moving through the city, and to help "settle their accounts."[56]

If some Muslims from the Caucasus were happy to invoke their new status as Russian subjects and take advantage of services offered through Russia's consular network in Syria, their reasons were surely pragmatic. At a time of political flux in Syria, and repeated failures by the Ottomans to secure traditional routes and keep pilgrims safe, Bazili and his agent in Damascus offered them the support they needed to perform this sacred religious ritual. The relationship was mutually beneficial: by offering Russia's hajj pilgrims support, and getting them to turn to the Russian consulate instead of Ottoman officials and institutions, Russia was able to gain some understanding of, if not control over, the hajj traffic between the Caucasus and Ottoman lands, and justify the expansion of its diplomatic presence deeper into Syria.

OVER the 1840s Russia expanded support for its hajj pilgrims in Syria. In 1845 it opened a new vice-consulate in Aleppo, and, most significantly, in 1846 it opened one in Damascus. Both cities were nodes along the main routes used by Muslims to get from the Caucasus to Mecca, and the new consulates operated under Bazili's supervision. By opening these consulates, the Foreign Ministry was essentially formalizing activities that had been going on for years, making support for hajj pilgrims central to Russia's mission and policy in Syria. These consulates and the services they offered were something new for Russia: they were the start of systematic efforts to coordinate cross-border hajj patronage, the use of passports to map and regulate hajj traffic between the Caucasus and Mecca, and a new policy of co-opting the hajj to integrate Muslims into the empire and extend Russian influence abroad. They also marked a turning point in the history of the hajj in Damascus. For the first time, a non-Muslim power was asserting itself as patron and protector of hajj pilgrims in Syria, involving itself directly in the hajj caravan and in the estate cases of deceased pilgrims.

Damascus was a city sacred to and visited by both Orthodox Christians and Muslims, but Russia opened its vice-consulate there with its hajj pilgrims in mind. This is clear from Bazili's orders to Telatinidis upon his formal appointment as vice-consul. In an 1846 document, "Instructions," Bazili told Telatinidis that his "main job" was to protect Russian subjects who passed through Damascus to perform pilgrimages to holy places, the majority of whom were "Muslims from the Sunni and Shi'i rites" from the Caucasus. As Russian vice-consul, Telatinidis was supposed to greet and receive these Muslims pilgrims when they arrived in the city, register their passports, and take a list of their names to the Damascus caravan commander so they could receive his "effective protection" during their "punishing journey."[57]

The decision to open a Russian vice-consulate in Damascus was not the result of a sudden surge of hajj pilgrims from the Caucasus into Syria. It is impossible to know exactly how many Russian-subject hajj pilgrims were moving between these two regions in this period. Some show up in the records of the Beirut consulate, and yet many others surely evaded the consulate and traveled, undetected by Russian authorities, their old routes and with the support of long-standing Muslim networks. Scholars often argue that in the era before railroads and steamships, mainly elite Muslims made the hajj. But this is debatable. The development of a modern government administrative network in Russia by the mid-nineteenth century, and increased data on population movements, revealed, among other things, more complex and apparently long-standing patterns of Muslim pilgrimage to Mecca. In the North Caucasus, for instance, officials noted that many from the Dagestan region who made the hajj were poor, traveled by foot along well-known land routes, and supported themselves along the long and arduous journey by hiring themselves out as servants to wealthier pilgrims.[58] Still, if anything, the numbers of pilgrims from the Caucasus taking the Syrian route to Mecca were probably in decline, as word spread about dangerous conditions along the route, and pilgrims began to opt for sea routes between the Black and Red seas, or chose to postpone their pilgrimage.

Nor was the decision to open Russia's Damascus vice-consulate prompted by problems hajj pilgrims were causing in Damascus, or concern about their activities in the city. In instructing Telatinidis to "maintain order" among Russian hajj pilgrims, Bazili noted that he found them to be "generally peaceful and well-behaved."[59]

Rather, the opening of Russia's Damascus vice-consulate illustrated a shift in policy in the Caucasus. By the early 1840s, faced with Muslim rebellions across the North Caucasus that they could not suppress, Russian officials in the Caucasus were increasingly concerned about the hajj. They had little sense of how many Muslims in the Caucasus were making the pilgrimage, by which routes, or who they were. Like European officials in other colonial contexts, many viewed the hajj as a clandestine activity that fed Muslim "fanaticism," and Mecca as a center of anti-Christian proselytizing. Many believed that the hajj was fueling Muslim anticolonial resistance in the Caucasus. Russian officials were especially concerned about how returning hajj pilgrims might influence their communities. They understood that many elites made the pilgrimage, and that those bearing the honorific title *hajji* (meaning, one who has completed the pilgrimage) were accorded great respect in their communities and tended to be among those chosen by Muslims to serve as their local political leaders. If these pilgrims were getting radicalized on the hajj, then they might have an inordinate, radicalizing influence over Muslim communities back home.[60]

One proposed solution was to stop the flow of pilgrims abroad by making passports prohibitively expensive. In 1842 Russia's minister of war, A. I. Chernyshev, wanted to impose a steep fifty-ruble fee on all passports to Mecca, to reduce the number of pilgrims. When this proved unpopular and unenforceable—Muslims complained that their religious freedom was being restricted, and the fee violated existing passport law—then commander in chief A. I. Neidgardt suggested spying on Russia's hajj pilgrims instead. In 1843, he proposed to Nesselrode, the foreign minister, that Russia send one of its "trusted" Muslim officers in the Caucasus into Mecca as a "special agent," who could keep the Russian administration in the Caucasus informed about what pilgrims were doing in Mecca, and whether foreign Muslims were trying to "instill" in them ideas that were "harmful" to the tsarist government. Nesselrode agreed that it was "desirable" to post a Russian agent in Mecca, but doubted that the Ottomans would allow Russia to establish a presence in "a holy place for Muslims."[61]

Under the new leadership of M. S. Vorontsov, named Russian viceroy of the Caucasus in 1844, Russia tried a different approach. It began to actively sponsor the hajj from the Caucasus as a way of bringing it under state control. Two decrees issued by the tsar, in 1844 and 1845, authorized free passports for Muslims traveling to Mecca (they were required only to pay a fifty-kopeck fee for the paper document). At the same time, with an eye toward "strengthening" the network of Russian consulates and agents abroad providing "protection" to Muslims traveling to holy places, Russian officials in the Caucasus began to interview local Muslim clergy about pilgrims' routes to Mecca. These interviews revealed that some Muslims, both Sunnis and Shiʻis, continued to favor the Syrian route through Damascus over an alternate sea route by way of Trabzon, Istanbul, and Cairo.[62] In the spirit of intelligence gathering, the Damascus vice-consulate gave Russian officials in the Caucasus an institution to consult about the hajj traffic abroad, along the main route that connected the region to Mecca.

By sponsoring the hajj between the Caucasus and Syria, Russian officials were not trying to encourage it. On the contrary, Vorontsov instructed local officials in the Caucasus to "limit" the number of passports to Mecca, issuing them only to those whose local district chief could vouch for their trustworthiness and the absence of "harmful intentions" toward the Russian government.[63] Instead, the main goal was to get more Muslims to apply for Russian passports to Mecca, and in this way provide Russian officials in the Caucasus with more information about who made the hajj, and by which routes. Russian officials envisioned passports serving at least two important functions. First, they were a mechanism for identifying powerful elites to recruit into the Russian administration. In a report urging the tsar to decree free passports to Mecca, Nesselrode argued that this measure would allow Russian officials in the Caucasus to identify and "lure" to the government "influential people from among those returning from Mecca."[64] Russian officials also used passports for surveillance. In them they recorded details of the routes pilgrims planned to take, and then contacted Russian consulates posted along these routes abroad to ask them to keep track of pilgrims and report back to officials in the Caucasus on their activities.[65]

This pragmatic plan meshed with Vorontsov's broader efforts to cooperate with local Muslim elites in the Caucasus, and co-opt them into the Russian army and administration. At the same time, it reflected his growing concern about the hajj as a security threat. In 1846 Vorontsov had received credible information that Imam Shamil, the leader of the Muslim rebellion in the North Caucasus, was communicating with and receiving support from Muslim clergy in the Ottoman Empire through Sunni hajj pilgrims who left Dagestan every year for Mecca. Worried that "secret and harmful relations" were being conducted through hajj networks between the Caucasus and Ottoman lands, but believing that it was "impossible" for the Russian government to forbid or even discourage this "important ritual" of the Muslim faith, officials in the Caucasus embraced a new passport system for the hajj in order to map and understand patterns of the hajj traffic, and bring the pilgrimage under the authority and supervision of Russian institutions.[66]

Within months of the opening of the Damascus vice-consulate, Bazili told Titov that hajj pilgrims from the Caucasus were already "drawing heavily" on Telatinidis's services. This was surely due to continued Ottoman failure to secure the Syrian route. The year 1846 was disastrous for the Damascus hajj caravan. Famine had driven the Bedouins to plunder the caravan's food and water stores along the desert route, and when the Damascus authorities sent an official out into the desert with provisions to replenish the caravan, he too was attacked. The attack had driven up the cost of fodder for animals at markets along the caravan route, and camel drivers were forced to demand more money from pilgrims for their camel hires. Hundreds of pilgrims perished in the attack and its aftermath, many from starvation, along with hundreds of horses and camels. Upon the caravan's return to Damascus, many Russian subjects went to Telatinidis to complain about being "extorted" on the way home by their camel drivers, and asked him to take their complaints to the Ottoman governor.[67]

For Bazili, Muslims' reliance on the new Damascus vice-consulate signaled a major shift. Just several years earlier, he noted, most Muslim pilgrims from the Caucasus "did not dare" identify as Russian subjects while passing through Syria, for fear of how "fanatical" locals might react. While acknowledging the dangerous and unstable conditions that had pushed this year's pilgrims to seek Telatinidis's help, Bazili also claimed credit, saying that his persistent efforts to support hajj pilgrims—"especially the amazing punishment of the Bedouins" who had attacked the twenty-man Kazikumukh hajj caravan—had "transformed" Muslim attitudes about Russia. Today, he told Titov, Muslim pilgrims coming through Syria "proudly bear the title of Russian subject," and "glorify" the name of the tsar and the "concern of the imperial government in their favor." Some had even been "overheard in inns and coffeehouses in Damascus and Beirut" openly discussing with local Muslims the "advantages" they enjoyed as Russian subjects, and drawing comparisons between their good life under Russian rule and the "anarchy" and disorder of Ottoman provinces.[68]

By offering his services to Russia's Muslim pilgrims, and registering their passports with the vice-consulate, vice-consul Telatinidis was able to compile data on the hajj traffic from the Caucasus, in a sense functioning as a spy. He kept detailed records on pilgrims who came to seek his help—recording their names, ages, passport numbers (if they had them), and places of residence—and wrote quarterly reports on the hajj traffic that were forwarded on to Vorontsov by way of the Russian embassy in Constantinople. These reports provided Vorontsov and officials in the Caucasus with valuable information on Muslim subjects under their rule: the geography of their hajj routes abroad; Muslim elites they met with during their stay in Damascus; their reception by Ottoman dignitaries; attacks, robberies, and deaths during the journey; and the status of their estates.[69]

Bazili worked closely with Telatinidis to provide services to Russia's hajj pilgrims in Damascus, competing with and to some extent displacing Ottoman officials, institutions, and networks organized around the hajj, as well as the local hajj service industry. He offered the Damascus vice-consulate as a place for pilgrims to store money and valuables. He also advertised the vice-consul's services to settle estate cases for the many pilgrims who died while making the hajj. Bazili noted with satisfaction the "first example" in 1846 of pilgrims choosing the legal intervention of the Russian vice-consul instead of the Islamic court, in an estate case of a Russian-subject pilgrim who died while making the hajj. This pilgrim, from the North Caucasus, had died in Damascus before the departure of the hajj caravan, and Telatinidis processed his case. He took the deceased's property into the consulate, and conferred with notables traveling with the deceased to distribute it to the proper heirs, in accordance with Islamic law. Bazili reported that the pilgrims had "spontaneously" sought Telatinidis's intervention, and he saw this as a sign that they had "more confidence in him than in the Ottoman authorities in Damascus." He noted that the Ottoman authorities were frustrated to be deprived of this "traditionally lucrative" role, but were forced to recognize the legal right of the Russian agent to settle this case.[70]

For centuries estate cases had been an important source of revenue for the Ottoman state. They quickly became one of the main hajj issues for Russia's consular officials, as well as part of the extraterritorial legal protection they offered to Russian subjects.[71] To recall, the Russian subject Kasym Mamad died in Mecca in 1848, leaving behind questions about the fate of a large sum of money he had left with a Damascus camel driver, and setting off a two-year investigation into his estate, led by Bazili and Telatinidis. The archival record in the Mamad estate case ends abruptly, giving us no sense of how it was finally resolved, or if his heirs managed to recover the 300 rubles he left behind. Nevertheless, the case offers valuable insights into how Muslims were responding to Russia's growing involvement in the hajj in this period. Mamad's example suggests that by the late 1840s, Muslim pilgrims were regularly turning to Russian consular officials in Syria for help resolving estate cases. Bazili noted in correspondence with other officials that he had handled "many" estate cases like Kasym Mamad's in the past, and resolved them quickly.[72]

And yet it was also clear that many Muslims continued to rely on Ottoman networks and avoid the Russian consulate, or to use it only when they ran into serious trouble. It took Bazili a long time—almost two years—to investigate the Mamad case, because neither he nor Telatinidis had any record of him. Mamad had not registered with the vice-consulate upon arriving in Damascus, and had chosen to leave his money with the Ottoman camel driver instead of with the vice-consul. Bazili complained to Ambassador Titov that he and the Damascus vice-consul had a hard time protecting the rights of Russia's Muslims if they did not come to the consulate to certify their transactions and deals. Bazili was frustrated that many Muslims were still not registering with Russia's consulates in Aleppo and Damascus, which had been established "to protect the interests of Russian subjects," and many did not apprise the consuls of their business and trade deals. This situation made it difficult for Bazili to deal with cases like Mamad's, and the lengthy investigations they required were costly for Russia's consulates.[73]

Russian officials in the Caucasus who wanted to encourage Muslims to make the hajj through official Russian channels, by getting passports and registering with consulates abroad, took Bazili's complaints seriously. Reasoning that many Muslims did not register their business transactions with Russian consuls out of ignorance of this "necessary formality," Russian officials worked to better inform departing hajj pilgrims about the consular services available, and of the importance of informing the Russian consul or agent of their whereabouts and other transactions with Ottoman subjects. In 1851 the viceroy's office ordered its officials in the Caucasus to "urge Muslims going to Persia and the Ottoman Empire to involve Russian consular agents in their deals," and this order was sent also to Russian diplomatic officials in Persia and the Russian ambassador in Constantinople.[74]

By the early 1850s, officials involved in the hajj in the Caucasus and Syria disagreed over whether to expand support for Muslim pilgrims further into Ottoman lands. This is clear from disagreements between Vorontsov and Titov over a proposal to establish a Russian consulate in Mecca. The idea grew out of the awful suffering of Russia's hajj pilgrims in 1850, and was first proposed by one of Russia's Muslim subjects. In what Bazili described as the "worst hajj in years," 20,000 to 30,000 pilgrims had died in and around Mecca and Medina from a cholera outbreak. As a result of bad decisions by the "inept" commander of the Damascus hajj caravan, who insisted that the caravan go out in torrential rains, several Russian subjects had died along the route through the desert. "It's been many years since the hajj caravan returned in such a state of misery and suffering," Bazili told Titov in his annual report.[75]

Bazili was unsure how many Russian subjects died in the 1850 Damascus hajj caravan. Some had gotten to Mecca by way of Cairo and never registered with him or Telatinidis. They included a group of pilgrims from Dagestan, who came to Telatinidis for help as soon as the caravan reached Damascus. They complained that their camel drivers had double-charged them for the arduous trek through the desert. Telatinidis took their complaints to the Ottoman authorities in Damascus, and got them "justice." Impressed by the assistance they had received, one of the pilgrims, named Ibrahim Bek Mahmudoglu, stopped to see Bazili in Beirut on his way home. Mahmudoglu described the troubles they had suffered, and all that Telatinidis had done to help them, and proposed to Bazili that Russia establish a consulate in Mecca.[76]

Eager to expand Russia's presence in the Ottoman Arab provinces, Titov embraced the plan for a Russian agent to Mecca. He presented it to the Ottoman grand vizier in Istanbul as a way for Russia to "protect the interests of its subjects in Arabia." His correspondence with other Russian officials suggests that he had begun to see the hajj as central to Russia's rivalries with France in Ottoman Arab lands. He pointed out that the French in Algeria were supporting their Muslim pilgrims, by providing them with a free-of-charge steamship to Jeddah every year.[77] And just the year before, in 1850, Titov had praised Bazili for his "ingenious" plan to take over a property adjacent to the Church of the Holy Sepulchre in Jerusalem, on the premise of housing Russia's visiting Muslim pilgrims. Titov warned Nesselrode in an 1850 memorandum that Russia should quickly take over the building before the French could claim it for their own Muslim pilgrims from Algeria, to house them on their way to Mecca.[78]

Elsewhere, from Baghdad to Jeddah to Bombay, Russian military officials began to invoke Russia's duty to "protect" its Muslim pilgrims to justify opening new Russian consulates in areas of strategic interest and imperial competition abroad. In Baghdad, for example, where British communication routes to

India intersected with hajj routes from the Caucasus, the idea of a Russian consulate was first suggested by a Russian military officer named E. I. Chirikov, who arrived in the Ottoman city in 1849 as part of an international team to set postwar borders between Persia and the Ottoman Empire. During his stay in the city, Chirikov noticed large crowds of Muslim pilgrims from the South Caucasus—he estimated at least 6,000 a year—in transit to Mecca and various Shi'i shrines. Many of them approached his Russian colleagues for "help in dealing with the Ottoman authorities."[79] In two separate reports sent to the army's general staff in the 1850s, Chirikov proposed that Russia could use the hajj traffic as an "excuse" to open a consulate there that could "keep the British away from Russian territories around the Caspian Sea and Central Asia" and function as a spy apparatus to "keep officials in far-away St. Petersburg informed."[80]

As for Titov's proposal to have a Russian agent installed in Mecca, the Ottoman grand vizier implied that while his government would not allow Russia to post a formal consular agent in Mecca, it might permit a *kehaya*, chosen from among Muslims in the Caucasus, preferably a Sunni. His job would be to "represent his coreligionists before the authorities in Mecca," supervise the processing of the estates of deceased pilgrims, and "defend" pilgrims from exploitation by locals. Titov next forwarded his proposal to Vorontsov, presenting it as a response to the disasters pilgrims had suffered the year before, and acknowledging the concern that Vorontsov had for the subjects under his authority. He elicited Vorontsov's response to the plan.[81]

Vorontsov received Titov's proposal at a time when he was trying various strategies to discourage Muslims from making the hajj and other cross-border pilgrimages to Shi'i shrines in Persian and Ottoman lands, mainly Mashhad, Najaf, and Karbala. One strategy was to dissuade Muslims who applied for passports by expressing concern for the welfare of the families they left behind during their long absences. Vorontsov was concerned in part about the daunting volume of hajj traffic, and its potential future growth. He acknowledged that because of the difficulties and expenses of the journey, relatively few Muslims made the pilgrimage every year. However, he noted that the overall Muslim population in the Caucasus was enormous, and Russia's policy of religious toleration precluded him from turning down requests to go to Mecca, so he wanted at least to keep the numbers low.[82]

Vorontsov's motivations were also economic. His investigations into the routes and costs of Muslim pilgrimages abroad had revealed huge costs: at least 200 rubles to get to Mecca, one hundred to get to Karbala, and forty to fifty for the trip to Mashhad. Many pilgrims spent "their last kopecks" on the journey, which left their families who stayed behind destitute and created problems for the tsarist administration. With steamships now providing easy, fast transport from Baku and Lenkoran across the Caspian Sea, "huge crowds" of Shi'is had started making the pilgrimage to Mashhad, where, Vorontsov's officials reported, they "fill up on hatred for Christians." As more Muslims were making these pilgrimages, Vorontsov worried, the government was being deprived of taxes in their absence.[83]

Voronstov rejected Titov's proposal out of concern for stability in the Caucasus. "I recognize that the majority of Russian subjects making the hajj are from the South Caucasus," he told L. G. Seniavin, head of the Asiatic Department at the Foreign Ministry, "and I have often thought of the idea of posting a Russian agent in Mecca." And yet he did not see any reason to offer special protection to a religious practice that had "inconvenient" political consequences, and instilled in Muslims "hatred for Christians." Like European colonial officials elsewhere, Vorontsov's fears about the hajj had much to do with Mecca's status as a city closed to non-Muslims, and the anxieties this generated about the hajj as a cover for clandestine political organization and the radicalization of Muslims. It does not seem that Vorontsov had any evidence of connections between the hajj and Muslim anticolonial resistance in the Caucasus. In fact, in other correspondence around this time, he conceded that he had "not seen any bad behavior from returning pilgrims."[84]

While acknowledging Voronstov's local concerns, Titov defended his plan for a Russian agent in Mecca by making a broader strategic argument. In a letter to Nesselrode in June 1851, Titov argued that extending Russian hajj patronage into Mecca would help Russia better integrate its Muslims into the empire, and could even reduce their "fanaticism." Central to his argument was the punishing physical experience of the journey, and Ottoman failures to secure routes for pilgrims, something he knew much about from the reports of his consular officials in Syria. He described the hajj under current conditions in the Ottoman Empire as one of the most "inconvenient" and "ruinous" religious practices for "the majority of Muslims who performed it." Allowing Russia's Muslims to make the hajj through Ottoman lands under these conditions, he argued, would help "neutralize" the great desire of Muslims to make it, and deter "fanaticism" and "the spirit of contradiction," especially when Muslims saw the "facilities" offered to them as hajj pilgrims in Ottoman lands by a "Christian government." He pointed to Damascus as a model: Muslim pilgrims from the Caucasus had a more positive impression of Russia after receiving support from Russia's Damascus vice-consul.[85] Titov essentially argued that Russia could and should embrace a new role as patron of the hajj because it was good for the empire. It would help Russia integrate newly conquered Muslim populations that were proving resistant to Russian rule, allow Russia to expand deeper into Ottoman lands, and undermine the sultan's prestige and influence, such as it was, over Russia's Muslims.

OVER the nineteenth century, human mobility influenced imperial policies and the geographic shape of empires around the world. This observation is central to several recent studies, which show the extent to which empires were built upon the migratory patterns and moving bodies of merchants, missionaries, labor migrants, and others, and, thus, were shaped by pressures from below. These histories offer an alternate perspective to standard accounts of empire building that highlight military conquests and describe a centralized, top-down process.[86]

In Russia, state patronage of the hajj was one way that the government built new imperial agendas upon inherited mobility networks. This patronage began on a small scale in the Caucasus and Syria, where Russian officials discovered the hajj as an important network connecting the two regions, and tapped into it for their own imperialist goals. Russia's conquest of the Caucasus, then, was more than the acquisition of new lands and peoples for the empire. Russia emerged from this conquest a changed empire, connected to the Ottoman Empire and other parts of the world in new and strategically important ways.

Russia would not, in the end, conquer Syria or other Arab lands under Ottoman rule. But from the 1840s onward, it steadily expanded its ground-level presence and influence into these lands, building new imperial pathways along hajj routes. Russian support for the hajj began in response to Muslim needs and demands, stemming from unrest and political instability in Ottoman Syria and the Ottoman government's failures to secure the Syrian hajj route. This impetus came very much from below, from the movement of individual Muslims from the Caucasus along established routes to Mecca, through Ottoman lands and back home to Russia. This movement of bodies in turn generated among tsarist officials who observed and encountered the traffic new ways of thinking about Russia's connections to the neighboring Ottoman Empire, and a new imperial policy centered on the hajj.

New strategic realities thus stimulated a new direction in Russian imperialism. In seizing the Caucasus from the Ottomans and Persians over the first half of the nineteenth century, Russia assumed control over a region closely tied to Mecca by way of Syria. In this same period, Russia was in the process of expanding its consular presence in Syria, as part of its rivalries with Britain and France in the Ottoman Empire. As these two processes unfolded, Russian officials on the ground in the Caucasus and Syria came to see these two regions as bound together, as a historical zone of interaction and exchange, largely due to the network of hajj routes that connected the two regions, and the pilgrim traffic moving between them.

In the end Russia did not open a consulate in Mecca, probably because the Ottomans resisted the idea. However, Russia did embrace Titov's idea of expanding Russian influence abroad through hajj networks. Over the second half of the nineteenth century, Russia opened a constellation of new consulates and facilities along major hajj routes that connected the empire to Arabia. Central to this emerging hajj support network was Russia's Jeddah consulate, founded in 1891, and located at the hub of sea traffic to Mecca. Much as Titov had envisioned, Russia's Jeddah consulate was first headed by a Muslim subject of the tsar—a trusted Tatar intermediary who had served the regime in Turkestan—who had access to Mecca and could act as an authority for Russia's hajj pilgrims within the holy city.

Over the next several decades, as Russia's hajj traffic grew apace with the rise of modern transportation, and as a result of its late nineteenth-century conquest of Turkestan, Russia would create a multiple-branch system of hajj patronage connecting the empire to Arabia. With branches connecting Tiflis to Damascus, Tashkent to Odessa, and Jeddah to Bombay, Russia's hajj infrastructure connected disparate places that had little or no previous relations or contact. This infrastructure was both riddled with internal tensions, as we will see, and integral to Russian imperialism in the late nineteenth and early twentieth centuries.

2

Mapping the Hajj, Integrating Muslims

During the second half of the nineteenth century the hajj became a mass phenomenon in Russia, due to Russian imperial expansion and the tsarist state's creation of modern transport networks. Russia's conquest of Turkestan increased the empire's Muslim population dramatically, adding some seven million new subjects. Muslims now were fifteen percent of the empire's total population, and Russia's second largest confessional group after Orthodox Christians.[1] Meanwhile, Russia's rapid construction of an empire-wide railroad network, and its new steamship service from the Black Sea, had the accidental effect of widening access to Mecca for Muslims across Russia and Eurasia. Russia may have built its modern transport system with economic and strategic goals in mind—to industrialize, foster commercial activity, integrate the empire's regions, and secure Russia's borderlands—but this did not prevent Muslims from putting the system to their own uses. In Russia as elsewhere Muslims embraced modern modes of transport as a new and improved way of getting to Mecca.[2]

By the 1880s tens of thousands of Muslims were making the pilgrimage to Mecca through Russian lands and Black Sea ports every year, having abandoned their old caravan routes through Ottoman, Persian, and Indian lands. Lured by promises of superior safety, comfort, and speed, these Muslims now took Russian railroads and steamships to get to Arabia and back. They hailed not only from Russian lands, but also from Bukhara and Khiva, Persia, Afghanistan, and China. In Odessa, Russia's chief port on the Black Sea, the sudden surge of Eurasian hajj traffic through the city was significant enough to attract the attention of the sharif of Mecca, in faraway Arabia. As the Ottoman official responsible for the Muslim holy cities and the annual pilgrimage, the sharif every year sent a fleet of professional pilgrim-guides out to cities worldwide that were transit points for hajj pilgrims—these included Najaf and Karbala, Baghdad and Bombay, Rasht and Constantinople, and, by the 1880s, Odessa.[3]

One of Russia's major modern migrations, and its largest pilgrimage, the hajj was inscrutable to most tsarist officials. They had a limited understanding of its religious meaning. Many confused Mecca with Medina, referring to it as the site where the prophet Muhammad was buried, and where pilgrims prayed at his tomb. They had little sense of Muslims' routes to Mecca, their itineraries, or their actions along the way. The hajj journey between Russia and Arabia largely involved foreign travel, much of it through lands where Russia had no historical interests or formal presence. The same was of course true of Russian Orthodox pilgrimage to Jerusalem, which involved travel along multiple, shifting routes through Ottoman lands, putting pilgrims beyond the reach of tsarist authorities. But the Jerusalem Orthodox pilgrimage was a familiar tradition to Russian officials, and they generally regarded it more positively.[4]

The rise of Russia's mass hajj traffic occurred at a time of growing European and Russian anxieties about Pan-Islamism as a threat to empire, when Russia was struggling to integrate millions of newly acquired Muslim subjects in Turkestan. In classic Orientalist fashion, and like colonial officials elsewhere, many Russian officials viewed the hajj as a clandestine, conspiratorial activity, and a symbol of Muslims' "fanaticism." Many also feared it, more so than any other migratory phenomenon, as a source of infectious disease, above all cholera. And so, as the hajj became a mass phenomenon, tsarist officials grew increasingly intent on bringing it under government supervision and control.

They began by trying to understand hajj pilgrims' routes and itineraries. In a tradition dating back to the eighteenth century, the tsarist state sought to capture, and co-opt, human movement within Russia's vast imperial expanses by envisioning it in terms of an itinerary, a set of stations and stops.[5] Russia approached the hajj similarly. To gather information on how Muslims were getting from Russia to Mecca and their stops along the way, Russia opened a network of new consulates abroad starting in the 1880s. It opened these at known transit points of Russia's hajj traffic, as gleaned from interviews with returning pilgrims—in Baghdad and Jeddah, Karbala and Mashhad, Constantinople and Bombay.[6] As this pattern of new consulates suggests, with one at Karbala and one at Mashhad (both important Shi'i holy sites), the hajj was not the sole Muslim pilgrimage central to tsarist interest and planning. But as the largest of all Muslim pilgrimages, it was the main focus of Russian state attention and intervention.[7]

As this chapter will show, Russia's creation of an external consular network for its hajj pilgrims illustrates how Russia's imperial project of managing, governing, and integrating diverse populations extended beyond the empire's formal borders by the late nineteenth century. Recently, historians have begun to explore important and long overlooked questions about the spatial dimensions of Russian history, focusing on, among other things, the processes (cultural, political, ideological, etc.) that produced the geographical space of the Russian Empire as we know it today. Scholars working along these lines tend to treat Russian empire-building as a process that took place within the bounded territory of the empire, reifying Russia's borders and the idea of empire as a kind of closed container.[8] But this is not quite right. Russia's imperial borders were porous and often less fixed in the minds of nineteenth-century contemporaries than they seem today. And as Russia's imperial populations moved across these borders with increasing ease and frequency during the late nineteenth century, they pushed the tsarist government to devise new policies and strategies of imperial governance. Migrations, in other words, shaped the geography of Russian imperial rule and tsarist administrative networks.

STUDIES of the hajj often focus on the ultimate destination of Mecca, treating it as a simple journey from one point to another and overlooking crucial questions about the process of getting there and back.[9] This approach perhaps makes more sense today in the twenty-first century, when the hajj is a highly streamlined affair under strict Saudi government control, and most of the world's Muslims (as many as three million a year) make the pilgrimage by plane, from their home cities directly to the Jeddah airport and then by air-conditioned bus to Mecca.[10] But before the era of air travel and mass transit, the pilgrimage to Mecca was more circuitous, and the voyage itself had more meaning. For many Muslims it was the journey of a lifetime, the only time they would ever travel far away from home. Much of the experience was about the physical journey, as well as the places and people they visited and encountered along the way.

In the eighteenth and nineteenth centuries most Muslims from Russian lands took their time getting to Mecca. Their routes and itineraries changed according to political events, weather, and contingencies along the way. They typically involved stops at many other important holy sites along the way, in Constantinople, Damascus, and Jerusalem above all, with time for sightseeing thrown in, and, in some cases, several months of study with religious scholars in major centers of Islamic learning, such as Cairo and Medina.

This multisite hajj itinerary is represented in art made by Muslim Tatars in late imperial Russia. Native religious paintings called *shamail*, popularized in the nineteenth century through mass-produced postcards and prints, depict images of the Meccan pilgrimage that are noteworthy for what they reveal about the growing centrality of Mecca and the hajj to Islam in modern Russia, as well as Muslims' hajj itineraries. One popular print depicts four holy sites within a single frame—Mecca, Medina, Jerusalem, and Damascus—with small lettering in Tatar identifying major tombs, shrines, and sites in and around each city. The kind of print that might have hung on the wall of a Tatar home in late

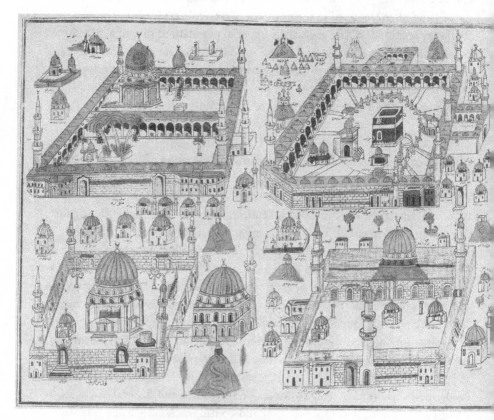

Figure 2.1. This *shamail* print captures the multisite itinerary that many hajj pilgrims from Russia adhered to in the early twentieth century. It depicts four cities and their Muslim holy sites, all located at the time in Ottoman lands. *Clockwise, from top left*: Medina, Mecca, Damascus, and Jerusalem. Notes in Old Tatar indicate tombs, shrines, and landmarks. Kazan, early 1900s. (*Tatarskii shamail: slovo i obraz* [Moscow: Mardzhani, 2009])

nineteenth-century Russia, it suggests the proximity of these places in the minds of Russia's Muslims, when modern transport had made them suddenly widely accessible. It also appears to be a map, something that one might have studied or even taken on the pilgrimage as a guide to the major sites in these four cities.

Similarly, hajj memoirs that Muslims began to produce in the modern era read like guidebooks for future hajj pilgrims, with exhaustive details on the logistics of getting to and from Mecca, people to avoid and places to see, and lists of the many holy sites and shrines to visit in Constantinople, Damascus, Jerusalem, and, finally, Mecca and Medina.[11] Unlike other kinds of modern travel writing, they were not written to entertain, but instead to offer practical and useful information on how to make the pilgrimage. As such they offer precious detail on Muslim itineraries to Mecca as well as changing experiences of the hajj in the modern colonial era.

The historian Barbara Metcalf has argued that written accounts of the hajj are a distinctly modern phenomenon. There are several famous examples of Arabic-language hajj travelogues from earlier centuries—including Ibn Battuta's fourteenth-century account that begins in Morocco—but, she notes, there is no continuous genre of hajj memoir-writing until the eighteenth century, when European imperial expansion into Asia increased possibilities for long-distance travel, and inspired more travel writing in general.[12] By the late nineteenth century, dozens of hajj accounts were being written in Russia. Most were unpublished and remain in manuscript form today. Scattered among private collections and libraries in former Russian imperial lands, these accounts are rich and largely untapped sources on Muslim experiences under tsarist rule.[13]

The earliest known hajj memoir by a Russian subject is the mid-eighteenth-century account by the Tatar merchant Ismail Bekmukhamedov.[14] He set out for Mecca in 1751 from Orenburg, Russia's chief military and commercial outpost on the Ural River and the empire's frontier with the Kazakh steppe. From Orenburg, Ismail and four companions took a trade route headed toward "the Kazakh region." After twenty-two days they reached the Silk Road city of Urgench (in today's Turkmenistan), where they joined a caravan that arrived in Bukhara twelve days later. From Bukhara, Ismail and his companions followed a circuitous route over land and sea, through Afghan, Persian, Arab, and Indian lands, before finally heading to the Holy Cities of Mecca and Medina. Next, he traveled north with a group of Crimean Tatars to the Ottoman capital of Constantinople, site of the some of the most majestic mosques in the Islamic world. He then spent twenty-five years in Constantinople, working in a shop to earn enough money to pay his way home.

Figure 2.2. First pages of a hajj memoir written by Muslim Tatars from the Volga-Ural region. In these opening pages they describe their departure, in 1886, from their home village near the Volga River, and travel by steamship and railroad to Odessa and on to Istanbul, where they stopped off for several days to visit Islamic tombs and shrines, and marvel at the magnificent Aya Sofya mosque (Haghia Sofia). (A1522, Manuscript Division, Institute of Oriental Studies, Russian Academy of Sciences, St. Petersburg)

Ismail's account is not typical. Many Muslims from Russian-ruled lands were surely able to make the round-trip journey within a year's time, particularly those who joined one of the Ottoman imperial caravans leaving from Cairo and Damascus. And there are fantastic and terrifying aspects to Ismail's account that strain credulity and have prompted some scholars to suggest that he made it up.[15] For instance, he describes his visit to a forest in India filled with "monkeys as big as horses" that were "bearded and mustachioed like men," and had human-looking hands and feet.[16] Yet Ismail's account is also consistent with patterns of the premodern hajj corroborated by other sources. His long-distance voyage was not singularly about the pilgrimage, but also about trade. And his itinerary involved visits to multiple holy sites, Mecca and Medina as well as Jerusalem (the third most holy site in Islam), Damascus, and finally Constantinople. His account also reveals a number of problems and contingencies that other hajj pilgrims from Russian lands would surely have contended with before the modern era—pirate attacks; wrong turns; long waits in cities abroad for caravans or ships headed in their direction; unpredictable winds at sea; corrupt Ottoman officials; a lack of Russian diplomatic presence to turn to for protection or help; and unanticipated expenses.[17]

Ismail's account usefully describes the hajj experience for Russian subjects prior to the late nineteenth century, before modern transport and Russian state intervention in the late 1800s transformed it. His account also captures the beginnings of European interactions and involvement with hajj pilgrims in Asia. More than once he describes turning to Europeans for help along the way. Under attack by pirates in the Arabian Sea, he and his companions are saved when a "European war ship" shows up, and they pay its captain to tow their ship to safety. And later, in Calcutta, they encounter another European ship and hire a soldier from it to help them set sail across the Indian Ocean.[18]

His account illuminates the informal Turkic networks that he and surely other Russian subjects relied on to make the hajj in the eighteenth century. Several times in the text Ismail relies on fellow Turkic-speakers from Russian lands, now living or traveling in Arab lands, to help him negotiate with the authorities, and navigate foreign cultures and long-distance travel. In addition to the "Uzbek" he meets in Afghan lands, who explains the strange behavior of the local women, a group of twenty Crimean Tatars escort him from Arabia to Constantinople, and the "Uzbek envoy" of the emir of Bukhara tracks him down in Constantinople to inquire about the estate case of one of his companions.[19] These informal networks are worth keeping in mind, as are the geographic visions of the hajj represented in the Muslim sources considered above, as we explore Russia's efforts to trace, uncover, and replace the networks and infrastructures of Muslims' hajj itineraries.

It would be hard to exaggerate the extent to which modern transport transformed the hajj experience for Muslims in Russia and other parts of the world. The changes were multiple and diverse, but three in particular deserve mention. The first was speed. For Muslims from Russian imperial lands, the hajj was a journey of thousands of miles. Railroads and steamships drastically shrank the time and distance involved in traveling between the empire and

Arabia. Previously, getting to Mecca from Russian lands typically took many months and, in some cases, years. By the late nineteenth century, Muslims from Russia routinely made the round-trip pilgrimage in a few months. In hajj memoirs from this period, Muslims marveled at the speed of railroads and steamships, noting that they could now get from Ufa to Constantinople (a distance of more than 3,000 miles) in a week, and from Jaffa to Odessa in just ten days.[20] The experience in 1880 of Shihabetdin Marjani, the well-known Tatar theologian and historian, was common. Traveling exclusively by railroad and steamship, he made the round-trip pilgrimage in just over four months. He left Kazan in early August and was home by late December, having stopped off several times along the way to sightsee, visit mosques and holy sites, and meet with religious scholars.[21]

Second, modern and more affordable methods of transportation made the hajj widely accessible for the first time in history. Across colonial contexts, railroads reached into rural areas and connected them with bustling port cities. By the late nineteenth century the hajj had been transformed from a small-scale phenomenon performed largely by elites of means and connections into a mass event dominated by the poor.[22] Finally, railroads and steamships reorganized the hajj along new routes, commingling people with little or no previous history of contact, and generating new itineraries. Over the second half of the nineteenth century, Muslims worldwide began to turn away from ancient land routes to Mecca, shifting to railroad and steamship routes. The opening of the Suez Canal in 1869 made it possible for Muslims coming from "northern" lands—North Africa, the Balkans, Russia, and Central Asia—to get from the Black and Mediterranean seas to the Red Sea directly by sea route. By the 1870s Russia's Black Sea ports of Sevastopol, Batumi, and Odessa had become centers of bustling hajj traffic, where pilgrims gathered to catch steamships to Constantinople and beyond to Arabia.

The rise of mass hajj traffic through Russia brought a profound conceptual shift in how tsarist officials thought about the Meccan pilgrimage. If previously they had seen it as a mysterious, ill-defined Muslim cultural phenomenon, they now began to see it as a concrete religious process and a highly visible annual event that raised new questions about how to manage Russia's Muslim populations, as well as the geography of Russian imperialism.

In recent years historians have created a robust scholarship on how European empires used ethnography and technologies of mapping and census-taking as "cultural technologies of rule." Scholars argue that these technologies were as important as "more obvious and brutal modes of conquests" in Europeans' creation of centralized, sustained rule over colonial populations.[23] Russia's efforts to map the hajj routes and itineraries of its Muslims should be seen as part of this larger phenomenon of creating "colonial knowledge" as a means to capture, control, and govern conquered territories and peoples. And yet, these efforts were also different in important ways from conventional colonial mapping and knowledge-production projects, as described in previous studies. First, they did not aim to understand and control peoples rooted in particular locales, but instead their processes of movement, and the infrastructures that supported that movement. And second, the goal of this hajj mapping project was not primarily to gather information to project onto a Cartesian map, but rather to reconstruct the cross-border system of nodes, or the main itineraries of the hajj from Russian lands. Put simply, this project was about mapping *movement through space* rather than the absolute space of a discrete territory. It was an attempt by Russia to conceptually capture and control human movement, rather than the physical landscape through which it crossed.[24]

Russia would begin its project of mapping the hajj only after first trying to restrict it. Twice in the late 1860s the Ministry of Internal Affairs ordered governors across the empire to limit the number of foreign passports to Muslims going to Mecca. Passports, first introduced in Russia in the early eighteenth century, had acquired new meaning in the second half of the nineteenth century. In this era of Great Reforms, Russia was rapidly modernizing its transport networks and Russian subjects had new opportunities for foreign travel, notwithstanding the regime's fears about its implications for the empire. In 1856 Tsar Alexander II had removed the hefty 250-ruble fee for foreign passports, and lifted the ban on travel to western Europe, with an eye toward encouraging economic and intellectual development, and fostering foreign trade. The tsar did this reluctantly. He shared with many other tsarist officials a fear that increased travel to western Europe would drain money from the empire, and introduce subversive political ideas to it, but opted to loosen travel restrictions all the same.[25] The hajj inspired similar worries, especially in the Ministry of Internal Affairs, but in this case the ministry attempted to restrict pilgrims' access to passports, even at the risk of upsetting Muslims and appearing to interfere in their religious practice.

Sanitary concerns played a large part in this decision. The ministry's first order to restrict the hajj in Russia came in 1865, the same year that a massive cholera outbreak that began in Mecca became a global epidemic, spread far and wide by dispersing crowds of pilgrims.[26] Within six months, the disease had spread to Europe and New York City, and more than 200,000 people had died in large cities worldwide.[27] This event terrified the European powers, and stoked fears of the hajj as a sanitary threat to Europe and its colonies. Europeans had only recently come to experience firsthand the dreadful disease of cholera. Long known to exist in Asia, cholera became widely known to Europeans only in the 1830s, when the first epidemic was recorded. A bacterial infection of the small intestine, cholera kills its victims quickly and painfully: the infected develop violent diarrhea and vomiting and die from dehydration, sometimes within twenty-four hours of infection. In 1865 it was not clear to scientists and physicians how cholera was spread, making outbreaks all the more horrifying. The European powers responded to the 1865 epidemic by drafting a series of new international sanitary rules to prevent the spread of cholera and other infectious diseases. They built new quarantine facilities at transit points of hajj traffic around the world, and intensified efforts to monitor the flow of hajj pilgrims between European-ruled lands and Arabia.[28]

But correspondence about the ministry's 1865 order reveals other concerns as well. The ministry issued it in response to reports that many Crimean Tatars were using the hajj as a pretext for emigration, getting passports to Mecca and using them to resettle in Ottoman lands. Russian officials in the Tauride region (today's Crimea and environs) would later explain this movement as Muslim flight from Russian military conscription, and fears of government restrictions on their access to Mecca.[29] Whatever the reason for this emigration, the tsarist government sought to stop it, primarily for economic reasons. Since Russia's late eighteenth-century conquest and seizure of the Crimea from the Ottomans, there had been a chronic labor shortage there, due largely to waves of Tatar emigration from the region. The most recent wave had occurred after the end of the Crimean War. Starting in 1859, the tsarist government had expelled and encouraged the emigration of millions of Muslims from the Crimea and the Caucasus, on the grounds of their loyalties to the sultan over the tsar. Soon thereafter, the regime regretted the decision to push out Crimean Tatars, and reversed the policy, to discourage their emigration from the empire. To rebuild the population, the Russian government began offering social and financial incentives in the 1860s to encourage colonists from Russia's central regions to resettle in the Crimea. Against this backdrop, the ministry's 1865 order appears, in large part, as an attempt to stop the exodus of Tatar emigration for the sake of regional economic development.[30]

Economic concerns also drove the second order by the ministry, issued in 1869. This order required Russian officials in Muslim regions to issue passports only to Muslim pilgrims who provided evidence that they had the means to pay the costs involved in the pilgrimage, and left a deposit of ten rubles as insurance, to cover any debts they might have left behind. This measure was intended to discourage poor Muslims from applying for passports, and thus limit the number going on the hajj overall. It was also intended to solve the serious and growing problem of poor Muslims who made the hajj from Russia without sufficient means, creating a serious economic drain on the empire's institutions, as well as on its foreign consulates.

Russia's efforts to restrict the hajj over the 1860s did not work. The hajj traffic kept growing in spite of these measures. As railroads expanded deeper into the empire's Muslim lands, the numbers of pilgrims increased. And, as had always been the case, many hajj pilgrims simply left Russia without ever applying for a passport, slipping across the border undetected. The business of selling false passports was booming in Russia in this period, and so others bought fakes, or simply bribed officials to get a Russian passport, in spite of the prohibition.[31] Criminal rings in Black Sea ports peddled fake Chinese and Bukharan passports at high prices.[32] In this sense, reform of passport laws had little practical meaning or effect on the flow of Russia's hajj traffic.

Much of what the Russian government knew about the empire's hajj traffic came from its foreign consulates in Ottoman lands. By the late 1860s the tsarist government knew that large numbers of its hajj pilgrims were showing up at Russian consulates abroad and begging for money to cover their travel expenses. The Foreign Ministry received numerous reports about this problem from its embassy in Constantinople.

There was nothing new in the late nineteenth century about Muslims from Russian-ruled lands making the hajj by way of Constantinople. Hajj memoirs and Ottoman documents reveal instances from the seventeenth and eighteenth centuries of hajj pilgrims from Russia and Central Asia passing through the Ottoman capital, even when it made for a more circuitous route.[33] There, they visited the tomb of Abu Ayyub al-Ansari, a close companion of the Prophet Muhammad, marveled at the city's majestic stone mosques, and often stayed for extended periods to study with religious scholars. Some came also to witness the sultan's hajj investiture ceremonies and the *surre* procession that left Dolmabahçe Palace for Kabataş harbor, and crossed the Bosporus by ship to Üsküdar (from which the imperial hajj caravan departed on its route across Anatolia to Mecca via Damascus). Many from Russia and Central Asia stayed in Constantinople's *tekkes*, lodging houses for pilgrims scattered around the city. Naqshbandi Sufis had established these lodging houses across Ottoman lands starting in the sixteenth century, to provide a support network for Central Asia's hajj pilgrims. Other pilgrims stayed in hotels run by Crimean Tatar émigrés.[34]

Figure 2.3. Hajj pilgrims from Central Asia at the tomb of Abu Ayyub al-Ansari (a close companion of the prophet Muhammad) in Constantinople. The landscape of the Ottoman capital was dotted with majestic stone mosques, and Islamic tombs and shrines, which many pilgrims from Russia and Central Asia included in their multi-holy-site hajj itineraries. Early 1900s. (*Hac, Kutsal Yolculuk* [Istanbul: Denizler Kitabevi, 2014])

What changed in the late nineteenth century was scale. Suddenly hajj traffic surged through Constantinople from Russian-ruled lands every year, as steamships became the preferred mode of travel. Many hajj pilgrims from Russia were educated Muslims, with the means and connections abroad to ease their journey. The hajj memoirs they wrote give us some sense of how these elites experienced the Meccan pilgrimage in these years, as well as their experience of Constantinople. What is perhaps most striking when glancing through the pages of these memoirs is the absence of problems: there are few mentions of shady brokers and crooks lurking in the shadows of Constantinople's streets, ready to pounce on hapless hajj pilgrims. Such mentions fill pages of reports on the hajj from the Russian embassy in these years. Perhaps this is due to a retrospective whitewashing of the journey. But it also surely reflects the unique experience of the city by Russia's Muslim elites, who were often educated and well traveled, sophisticated and multilingual, and, no less importantly, plugged into an extensive network of scholars and émigrés and their institutions in Ottoman lands. Many arrived in Constantinople with a list of names in their pockets, and had local contacts to guide and lodge them in the city. This shielded them from many of the unpleasant situations that their poor compatriots suffered; it also meant that elites rarely appealed to the Russian consular authorities for help abroad, and often evaded their detection and influence.[35]

But the vast majority of hajj pilgrims from Russia in these years were not elites. They were poor, illiterate, and traveling long distances for the first time in their lives. Not surprisingly, these were the types of pilgrims that most Russian embassy and consular officials encountered in the Ottoman imperial capital, thus contributing to their conflation of the hajj with poverty, disease, and disorder. Hajj pilgrims who showed up at the Russian embassy hailed from Muslim regions across the Russian Empire, with the greatest number coming from the Caucasus and Central Asia.

The Russian ambassador in Constantinople and his consul-general received scores of requests every year from poor Muslim pilgrims stranded in Constantinople. Many had been robbed and were staying in damp, dirty inns, where disease was rampant. Their desperate situation was an embarrassment for the embassy. Crowds of pilgrims gathered outside the embassy gates to beg. Russian consulates in other parts of the Ottoman Empire also reported begging by hajj pilgrims, most of them from the Caucasus. The viceroy in Tiflis regularly received correspondence from Russian consuls posted in eastern Anatolia (in Trabzon and Kars, Erzurum and Batumi) about hajj pilgrims who had come to the consulate to beg for help. Most of these pilgrims had been robbed or simply run out money, and many had no passports or papers to prove they were Russian subjects. Russian consuls spent large sums to get them home—they bought them steamship tickets, hired guides (*kavas*) to escort them along land routes, and bribed quarantine and customs officials on their behalf. They wrote to the Russian viceroy in Tiflis to ask for reimbursement.[36]

This problem was not unique to Russia. Increasingly over the second half of the nineteenth century, poor Muslims, most colonial subjects, were undertaking the hajj without sufficient funds. To cover their costs, some hired themselves out as servants to wealthy compatriots headed to Mecca; others took jobs along the way. But many also began to show up at European consulates to beg for money. This pattern suggests a certain resourcefulness on the part of Muslim colonial subjects, who had begun mobilizing their status as European subjects and taking advantage of the new diplomatic institutions and services available to them for support in making the hajj. Europeans faced the costly problem of repatriating poor pilgrims, who were stranded in the Hejaz with no money and no way to get home, and tried different strategies to address it.

In 1897, on the sixtieth anniversary of Queen Victoria's accession to the throne, British Indian Muslims in Jeddah set up the Jubilee Indian Pilgrims Relief Fund, a charity fund to help poor pilgrims, overseen by the British vice-consul.[37] Also in the 1890s, a disagreement developed between the French Ministry of Foreign Affairs and the colonial government in Algeria over who should cover the mounting costs of repatriating indigent pilgrims to Algeria.[38] The Ottomans' inability to control the Hejaz and secure routes for pilgrims opened up opportunities for Europeans to intervene. When in trouble, Muslims often asked for consular intervention. In the 1880s a group of twenty-eight Muslims from Singapore in Mecca wrote to the British consul, asked him to secure their route from Mecca to Jeddah, and said they were being extorted in Mecca.[39]

This was not what the European powers had had in mind in offering consular services to their Muslim subjects headed to Mecca. They had hoped to gain more supervision and control over the hajj traffic by getting pilgrims to register their passports with consulates. Instead, they were finding that pilgrims often showed up only to demand money. This drained the limited resources of foreign consulates, and created conflict within European governments about how to solve this growing problem.[40] As always, the European powers showed great caution when it came to intervening in the religious life of their Muslim subjects. Recent scholarship has highlighted the extent to which European colonial rule of Muslim populations was based on accommodating Islam and supporting Muslim institutions. This was perhaps especially true when it came to the hajj, which the European powers generally saw as a nonnegotiable form of Muslim mobility and religious practice, and which they increasingly supported as the nineteenth century went on.[41] They were loath to introduce new restrictions on the hajj, for fear of a Muslim backlash. But they were also losing a lot of money. In 1859 the Dutch had started to require that Muslims departing for Mecca show proof of adequate means, and other imperial powers followed suit.[42] Russia, which frequently looked to other European powers for ideas on how to manage the hajj, most likely modeled its 1869 measure on the Dutch precedent.

The hajj traffic continued to grow not only because of better transportation and informal networks and pathways for travel, but also because many Russian officials inside the empire resisted measures to restrict it. In the Caucasus, the 1860s orders prompted new discussions and debates about hajj pilgrims and access to passports. Just a few years before, in 1864, Russia had finally put down the decades-long Muslim anticolonial rebellions in the North Caucasus. The leading Russian official in charge of Dagestan in the late 1860s, M. T. Loris-Melikov, wanted to maintain this newfound regional stability. He did not deny that hajj pilgrims were an economic drain on Russia's consulates (his archives were filled with "copious correspondence" about Muslims from Dagestan who owed money to Russia's consulates abroad after making the hajj).[43] And yet Loris-Melikov refused to increase the passport fee because the local population would surely interpret it as "religious repression." He also noted that the proposed measure violated the passport law of 1857, which stipulated that both Orthodox pilgrims to Jerusalem and Muslim pilgrims to Mecca were to receive reduced-fee passports for just fifty kopecks (the cost of the paper form).[44]

Loris-Melikov's resistance to these orders reveals the extent to which he had embraced open access to Mecca as a way to appease Muslims, demonstrate Russia's promised toleration of Islam, and integrate Muslims into the empire. Other officials in the Caucasus shared his view. Some pushed for free passports to Mecca as a way for Russia to "communicate toleration" to the many "submissive" Muslims in the North Caucasus, and to hopefully prevent them from joining the side of the resistance.[45] At the very least, these records show that officials did not feel they could limit the hajj without upsetting Muslim populations.

As the hajj traffic from Russia continued to grow, despite attempts to restrict it, the Russian ambassador in Constantinople, N. P. Ignat'ev, became overwhelmed by the needs and demands of pilgrims. His complaints would lead to one final attempt to restrict the hajj. Ignat'ev, a conservative well known for his anti-Semitism and enthusiasm for Pan-Slavism, served as Russia's ambassador to Constantinople between 1864 and 1877. Historians writing about his tenure as ambassador have focused mainly on his meddling in the Balkans, which contributed to the outbreak of the Russo-Ottoman War of 1877–78. But Ignat'ev was also a key figure in the development of Russian policy toward the hajj.[46]

For years Ignat'ev had been complaining to the Foreign Ministry about problems surrounding the hajj traffic, but in 1871 he declared a crisis. That year Ignat'ev wrote to the ministry about the "extreme situation of Russia's Muslims in Constantinople," and urged it to take steps to "limit as much as possible" the number of Muslims making the hajj. Mindful of the need to proceed cautiously and avoid any appearance of violating Russia's policy of toleration of Islam, Ignat'ev did not call for an outright ban on the hajj. Instead, he proposed subtle economic pressure to discourage Muslims from embarking on the pilgrimage. Specifically, he suggested that the government increase the passport fee to Mecca to five rubles, and require that all Muslims leave a one-hundred-ruble deposit with Russian authorities before leaving the empire.[47]

Figure 2.4. This *shamail* print, produced in Kazan in the early 1900s, shows Mecca and Medina and major holy sites in and around the cities. (*Tatarskii shamail: slovo i obraz* [Moscow: Mardzhani, 2009])

The catalyst for Ignat'ev's proposal seems to have been no single event, but rather a series of events, and a general sense that the situation was growing out of control. The disappearance of a Circassian pilgrim named Tsuk Borenov in Arabia in 1870, his presumed death, and Ignat'ev's subsequent efforts to investigate his case and recover his property, had unearthed dreadful details about the acute housing crisis in Constantinople during hajj season and the suffering of Russia's Muslim pilgrims while in transit in the city. In response to requests from Borenov's family in Ekaterinodar (Borenov's home, just north of the Black Sea)—which they made through their local Russian officials and the viceroy in Tiflis—Ignat'ev sent consular agents out to Constantinople's tekkes to investigate the Borenov case, and track down his belongings. The agents returned to Ignat'ev empty-handed, and with awful accounts of the dilapidated, squalid lodging houses in which most of Russia's hajj pilgrims stayed.[48]

The Borenov case was not exceptional. By the early 1870s, Ignat'ev was inundated with requests to investigate and resolve cases involving hajj pilgrims in

Ottoman lands. Many of these requests came from Russian officials in the Caucasus, on behalf of Muslims under their rule; they asked Ignat'ev to investigate the whereabouts of their relatives who had made the hajj and never returned, and the fate of their estates. Estate cases for hajj pilgrims who died in Ottoman lands had in previous centuries been handled by Ottoman officials, and had historically been a source of lucrative revenues for corrupt officials. But Muslims who were Russian subjects, many of them recently minted subjects from the Caucasus and Central Asia, were increasingly turning to Russian diplomatic officials to resolve these cases, no doubt seeing them as more likely to succeed. This offered Russia opportunities to increase its involvement in the hajj, and to encourage Muslims to rely on Russian support and institutions in making the pilgrimage, but it also required enormous efforts and resources from the Constantinople embassy. One of Ignat'ev's main difficulties in resolving estate cases like Borenov's, he told the Foreign Ministry in 1871, was that he had no consul on the ground in Jeddah, where many of Russia's hajj pilgrims died.[49]

Ignat'ev also received requests for financial aid from Muslim pilgrims in other parts of the Ottoman Empire. One such petition came in 1871 from Suez, from a group of six Muslims from the Caucasus who found themselves penniless and stranded. Clearly revealing their interpretation of Russian diplomatic protection as in part an economic entitlement, they appealed in their petition to Ignat'ev's "well-known goodness" that extended without difference "to all Russians," and asked that he as "protector of Russians in Ottoman lands" pay their way from Suez home to Russia. This, too, was not an isolated incident, but rather part of a broader and increasingly burdensome pattern. Ignat'ev told the Foreign Ministry that hajj pilgrims were becoming a "drain on our consuls in the East," who were being forced to offer them financial help despite not having the necessary resources.[50]

In early 1871 Ignat'ev received a complaint from the Ottoman grand vizier about a group of 2,000 Muslim pilgrims from the Caucasus who had shown up in Constantinople on their way to Mecca. Ottoman officials had stopped them and found they were armed to the teeth with weapons—daggers, knives, pistols, and guns—that they planned to sell to cover their travel costs. Officials discovered that one pilgrim had three hundred guns. The grand vizier complained that this posed a security risk to the Ottoman Empire, and demanded that Ignat'ev pressure the Russian government to tighten its border control. If nothing else, this episode revealed to Ignat'ev the ease with which Russia's Muslims were moving across the empire's porous borders. It doubtless heightened his sense that the hajj traffic was unsupervised, unobstructed, and out of control.[51]

While grappling with these various problems, Ignat'ev also faced the acute crisis in 1871 of a massive cholera outbreak in Jeddah. Because of the outbreak, steamship companies canceled their service to Arabia, leaving thousands of pilgrims stranded in Constantinople, among them thousands of Russian subjects. Stuck indefinitely in a foreign city with no infrastructure in place to support them, they became easy targets for con men and quickly ran out of money. They also began to contact Ignat'ev and his consul-general for help; both panicked as they realized that the pilgrims' needs were too great for them to manage. Moreover, Ignat'ev soon discovered, almost none of the pilgrims contacting the embassy and general consulate carried Russian passports. He warned the Foreign Ministry that, left to their own devices, these pilgrims faced "serious dangers," and their plight deserved "the special attention of the imperial government."[52] There is every reason to believe that Ignat'ev's apparent humanitarian concern and pity for these Muslim pilgrims was genuine. Uprooted from home, poor, vulnerable, disoriented in a strange city, and trying to perform a major ritual of their faith under awful circumstances, the hajj pilgrims he met in Constantinople must have appeared grievously sad. Yet it is also clear that he saw the hajj as a growing threat to Russia's imperial stability, and that the Foreign Ministry took seriously his pleas to restrict it.

On the Foreign Ministry's urging, in 1872 the Interior Ministry once again ordered Russian officials in Muslim regions to stop issuing passports to Mecca. The official reason given was the cholera outbreak in Jeddah, and the ministry urged Russian officials in Muslim regions to frame the measure in humanitarian terms. They were to discourage Muslims from getting passports to Mecca by informing them of the outbreak and warning them about the serious dangers and discomforts they would face if they went on the hajj.[53]

The 1872 measure, like those before it, met widespread resistance from Russian officials in the empire's Muslim regions. K. P. von Kaufman, Russia's governor-general of Turkestan, where the Russian conquest was ongoing, refused to implement it. One of Kaufman's first decrees as governor-general, in 1870, had stipulated that "no restrictions" be placed on Muslims applying for passports to Mecca. Like colonial officials in Muslim regions elsewhere in the world, Kaufman supported open access to the Mecca pilgrimage as a matter of pragmatism, to win local Muslims' loyalties, and neutralize "fanaticism." Reasoning that the hajj was a ritual central to the Muslim faith, and open access to it symbolic of Russia's policy of religious toleration, Kaufman intended to avoid the appearance of any kind of government intervention or prohibition.[54] In the Caucasus, too, officials resisted the measure. Here, also, they generally opposed restricting the hajj in the interest of integrating Muslims, and maintaining stability in the region. They argued that government interference in it "could create rumors unpleasant for us" among Muslims in the North Caucasus about the "religious persecution of Muslims."[55]

In New Russia and Bessarabia—a broad swath of land north of the Black Sea, encompassing today's Moldova, southern Ukraine, and Crimea—the governor-general, P. E. Kotsebu, also resisted the measure. Kotsebu's position was in some ways the most complex. Not only did he rule large Muslim populations in his region, but also the northern shores of the Black Sea, where most of Russia's hajj routes converged. No other region of the empire saw as much hajj traffic at this time. He initially complied with the 1872 order, but refused to do so the next year, saying it was "inconvenient" to keep denying Muslims passports. By that time the cholera outbreak in Jeddah was over, steamships were running again, and passport requests to Mecca were growing. Increasingly, also, Muslims from Turkestan were showing up in Odessa, the Black Sea port under his jurisdiction, with documents from Kaufman, authorizing them to make the hajj. Kotsebu ordered his officials in Odessa to grant passports in such cases, clearly out of concern for maintaining order within his own region, and also to support Kaufman's ongoing colonization of Turkestan. To send them back to Turkestan, he told the Ministry of Internal Affairs, would "decrease their respect for local authorities that had allowed them to make the pilgrimage."[56]

Kotsebu saw the 1872 measure as counterproductive to his efforts to govern Muslims, and get them to adhere to Russian laws and institutions. "Every new restriction" on the hajj, he reported, "will only strengthen their desire to make the hajj, and give rise to new efforts to get around the law."[57] He also pointed out regional patterns in problems surrounding the hajj. Muslims from his own region were not the ones causing problems in Constantinople. Ignat'ev's complaints were almost exclusively about Muslims from the Caucasus, who were numerous and poor and "burdening consulates in the East." Hajj pilgrims from Kotsebu's region of New Russia, by contrast, were no trouble. Only small numbers of them made the hajj—about sixty to eighty annually—and they tended to be affluent elites, who had their own informal networks for assistance, and the means to make the journey, and therefore asked nothing of Russian consulates. He also disagreed with Ignat'ev's proposal to discourage the hajj by increasing the passport fee and requiring pilgrims to make a one-hundred-ruble deposit. Such a measure, Kotsebu argued, would have undesired effects. The fee was not enough to deter pilgrims, but would be seen as an attempt to "restrict their religion."[58]

Kotsebu's resistance to the 1872 measure, and concern for maintaining stability in his region, were surely tied to the broader problem of unrest in his region a result of growing anti-Semitism and anti-Semitic violence there. Just the year before, in 1871, a major anti-Semitic pogrom had erupted in Odessa, a city with a rapidly growing Jewish population. By the late nineteenth century Jews made up a third of Odessa's overall population. Odessa was also a main transit point for hajj pilgrims using Black Sea routes. Kotsebu's resistance to the 1872 measure was doubtless shaped by this experience, and perhaps a fear that anti-Semitic pogroms could spread into a broader disorder involving Muslim populations as well.[59]

The resistance of Kotsebu, Kaufman, and others illustrates one of the chief difficulties Russia would face in trying to control the hajj. The hajj was a multidimensional phenomenon, having religious, political, economic, and strategic dimensions. Russian officials necessarily saw it through the lens of their own local concerns and pressing agendas. This made it exceptionally difficult for tsarist officials to come to a consensus on what the hajj meant for the empire, or what kind of policies they should develop and apply. Clearly not all tsarist officials saw the hajj in wholly negative terms. Kotsebu, for one, in resisting state restrictions on the hajj essentially argued that there were opportunities for Russia in instrumentalizing the hajj, that by allowing and involving itself in this form of Muslim mobility Russia could in fact bring its Muslim populations more firmly under imperial influence and control.

And yet there was no agreement among tsarist officials on these points, beyond a consensus that the government could not ignore the hajj, and had to get involved in it somehow. These tensions, between the aims of regional officials and central imperial agendas, would persist and continue to complicate government efforts to involve itself in the hajj.

REALIZING that the hajj could not be stopped, and that Russian officials in Muslim regions of the empire were increasingly committed to keeping open access to Mecca in the interest of integration and governance, leading officials in the Ministries of Internal and Foreign Affairs began to discuss ways to bring it under state patronage and control instead. To do this they first needed to understand its basic geography, and the existing networks that Russia's Muslims relied on to get to Mecca and back.

They considered new facilities for hajj pilgrims abroad. The first idea, put forth by Ignat'ev in 1874, was to establish a "Russian caravanserai," a lodging house for Russia's hajj pilgrims in Constantinople. This would be modeled on the city's centuries-old tekkes, the Sufi-run lodging houses where many of Russia's pilgrims stayed, but on a much larger scale and with a different purpose. Ignat'ev envisioned the caravanserai as a facility where all of Russia's Muslims could find comfortable, affordable, and safe lodging under one roof during their extended stays in the city. He proposed the plan as a way to isolate Russia's Muslims from harmful influences abroad, and protect the empire from destabilizing influences. With suitable lodging in Constantinople, he reasoned, they would have no reason to venture into the city streets and "rub elbows" with "local mullahs or hodja" who had been filling their heads with "harmful ideas."[60] The proposal also reveals Ignat'ev's anxieties about the hajj as a political event, and his desire to redirect Russian pilgrims away from alternate institutions and support systems—and foreign influences—while in Ottoman lands.

Russia never built the caravanserai. Officials in the Ministry of Internal Affairs widely rejected the idea as infeasible. There was no guarantee that Muslims would actually use it, they argued, as they could not be forced to stay there. They might even see it as an attempt to interfere in their religious rituals, and avoid it altogether. Other officials worried that it would send a wrong signal to Muslims that Russia was trying to encourage the hajj, when in fact the opposite was true.[61]

But clearly Russia had to do something to address its external hajj traffic. In the mid-1880s, the new Russian ambassador to Constantinople, A. I. Nelidov, noted to the Foreign Ministry a "sharp increase" in Russia's hajj traffic through the city, and said he and his consul-general were "barely able to manage" pilgrims' needs and demands.[62] In reports to the Foreign Ministry Nelidov, like Ignat'ev, emphasized the serious sanitary problems of the hajj, and their potential threat to Russia. With no central lodging house to receive them in Constantinople, he reported, the many thousands of pilgrims who came from Russia stayed in "filthy" lodging houses, about fifty small places scattered around the city, which failed to satisfy their "most basic hygienic needs." Many pilgrims died of disease in these places, often without the knowledge of the Russian authorities. Of those who returned to Russia, many carried disease.

But Nelidov warned of yet another danger, also with potentially serious domestic implications for Russia. The "sad situation" of hajj pilgrims abroad, he argued, was damaging to the tsarist government's reputation among its Muslim populations, and might even be working against Russia's efforts to integrate Muslims into the empire. As things stood, it looked like Russia was failing to provide its Muslims with the diplomatic protection they were entitled to as subjects of the tsar. This perception, he argued, was only heightened by the parallel flow of Russian Orthodox pilgrims through Constantinople, who also stopped in the city to rest, sightsee, and visit the patriarchate before continuing on to Mt. Athos and Jerusalem. Muslim and Orthodox pilgrims often arrived in Constantinople from Russia on the same steamships, but they had starkly different experiences in the city after disembarking. "Well-known" and "trusted" Russians were there to greet the Orthodox on the quay, and whisk them away to comfortable accommodations to rest and pray. Muslims, by contrast, were left at the mercy of "shady brokers" and con men, most of them Muslim émigrés from the Caucasus, who robbed, cheated, and abused them. One common trick was to sell unsuspecting pilgrims a ticket on a nonexistent steamer; another was to take their passports for "processing," and then charge them exorbitant fees for meaningless stamps. The result, Nelidov warned the Foreign Ministry, was the appearance of a double standard, that Russia was supporting its Orthodox pilgrims but neglecting its Muslim ones.[63]

Nelidov had touched on a sensitive issue. Russian officials, like their European counterparts in other colonial contexts, worried a great deal about the hajj's potentially subversive political effects on Muslims. Specifically, many worried that the hajj, as a meeting of Muslims from all corners of the globe, would heighten Muslims' sense of solidarity as part of the wider Islamic community (*umma*) and undermine efforts to cultivate imperial identities and loyalties. A number of scholars have argued that in fact the opposite happened: that the mass hajj exposed Muslims for the first time to the diversity within their community, and in many cases heightened their sense of locality and national identity.[64] Nevertheless, fear of the hajj as a political threat was widespread among European colonial officials, and contributed to a large degree to Russia's efforts to bring it under government control.

To shield Russia's hajj pilgrims from foreign influences abroad, reinforce their identity as Russian subjects, and gain a better sense of their itineraries and activities abroad, Nelidov urged the Foreign Ministry to increase support and services for hajj pilgrims abroad. To add yet another reason for doing so, he noted that the Ottoman sultan had begun to take advantage of Russia's neglect of its Muslims, and was trying to cultivate their loyalties by offering free-of-charge steamships to Mecca.[65] "If we accept the hajj as something Russia cannot avoid," Nelidov wrote, "and that obstructing it or stopping it is out of the question—and not in our interests—then we can agree that sponsoring it is an opportunity to cultivate Muslim loyalties." Among other measures, he proposed opening a new Russian consulate in Jeddah, where the majority of pilgrims traveled after Constantinople. Here Russia could supervise its pilgrims, gather more information on their patterns of travel and behavior, and establish an outpost for the embassy by which to monitor the traffic, track down missing pilgrims, and resolve estate cases for pilgrims who died while traveling.[66]

Following Nelidov's suggestion, in November 1890 Russia petitioned the Ottoman government for permission to open a new consulate in Jeddah to serve its "numerous Muslims" who passed through Jeddah to "fulfill the holy pilgrimage" to Mecca.[67] Noting that "other states kept consuls" in Jeddah, and there was "no reason" to deny Russia's request, the Ottoman sultan granted it. Russia opened its Jeddah consulate in February 1891, appointing as consul one of its Muslim subjects, a fifty-year-old Tatar named Shakhimardan Miriasovich Ibragimov (known to Russian colleagues as Ivan Ivanonich). In Jeddah Ibragimov joined an already large group of European consuls: the British, French, Swedes, Austrians, Greeks, Dutch, and Spanish all had consulates there, which demonstrates the growth of European involvement in the hajj in the colonial era, as well as the emergence of Ottoman Arabia as an arena of international trade.[68] The Ottoman government was aware of the threat of this growing European involvement in the hajj and in Arabia. In 1882, for example, it had renewed a ban on the acquisition of land and property in the Hejaz by "foreign" Indian, Algerian, or Russian Muslims. It did this after local officials warned that if the government did not move to prevent the accumulation of property "by devious means in the hands of foreign Muslims" the situation would get to the point where "much of the Holy Lands have been acquired by the subjects of foreign powers" and that the powers would then use this situation, "as is their wont," to "make the most preposterous of claims."[69]

Russia's Foreign Ministry chose Ibragimov to serve as Jeddah consul for his extensive government experience, knowledge of Islamic culture and traditions, linguistic skills, and status as a trusted Muslim intermediary. A Tatar originally from Orenburg, he arrived in Jeddah from Tashkent, where he had spent two decades serving the Russian government as part of a circle of Muslim informant-administrators. From 1870 to 1880, Ibragimov and his twin brother worked as translators in the governor-general's office, and as editors of the Russian administration's official Turkic-language newspaper, *Turkistan wilayatining gazeti*.[70] In these years, Ibragimov wrote and published several important ethnographic accounts that tsarist officials relied on in developing an Islamic policy for the Kazakhs. He also performed diplomatic duties for the Russian governor-general, traveling to Khiva, Bukhara, Persia, and India to conduct talks with officials.[71]

As a Muslim, Ibragimov was able to serve Russia not only in Jeddah, where European merchants and diplomats were allowed to live within the city walls, but also in Mecca, which was closed to non-Muslims. This was not lost on local Ottoman officials in the Hejaz region, who noted with alarm that Ibragimov had rented a house in Mecca, and expressed concern to the Ottoman government in Constantinople that European powers were starting to use their Muslim colonial subjects as a way to penetrate the Muslim holy cities.[72]

Ibragimov's time as Russia's Jeddah consul would be brief. Within less than a year he was dead and buried in the cemetery outside the city walls, a victim of the 1892 cholera outbreak in Arabia, his grave marked with inscriptions in Russian and Arabic.[73] As it turned out, he would be the first and last Muslim subject to serve as Russian consul. After his death, the Russian Foreign Ministry appointed as his successor A. D. Levitskii, the first in a line of non-Muslims to serve as Russian consuls in Jeddah.[74]

The Jeddah consulate was supposed to help the tsarist government map Russia's hajj traffic through Ottoman lands. The Foreign Ministry hoped that by getting pilgrims to register their passports with the consulate, they could gain a better sense of the scale of the traffic, the logistics, the specific needs of pilgrims, and the networks they relied on for support. It hoped that by identifying these networks the Jeddah consulate could then displace them, redirect Russia's Muslims, and isolate them from the influence of foreign institutions, officials, and ideas in Arabia. It was one thing for Russia to open a Jeddah consulate for its Muslim subjects, however, and another to get them to use it. And getting Muslims to show up at the consulate and use its services was crucial to Russia's efforts to gather information on the hajj.

To understand how the tsarist government gathered data on the hajj, we must piece together scattered evidence. The archives of Russia's Jeddah consulate are missing. They may have been destroyed during World War I, during the fighting in Arabia. Fortunately, however, the history of this institution lives on, albeit in fragments, in other collections.

Soon after the Jeddah consulate opened, *Turkistan wilayatining gazeti* began to advertise its services through a series of articles. Most Muslims in Turkistan were illiterate. The readership of this weekly newspaper was surely small, perhaps several thousand, out of an overall regional population of some seven million Muslims. But since 1870, the year it established the newspaper, the Russian administration had been using it to convey important information to the local population. The historian Adeeb Khalid has explored some of the ways Russian officials used the paper as a colonizing tool, to communicate decrees of the new

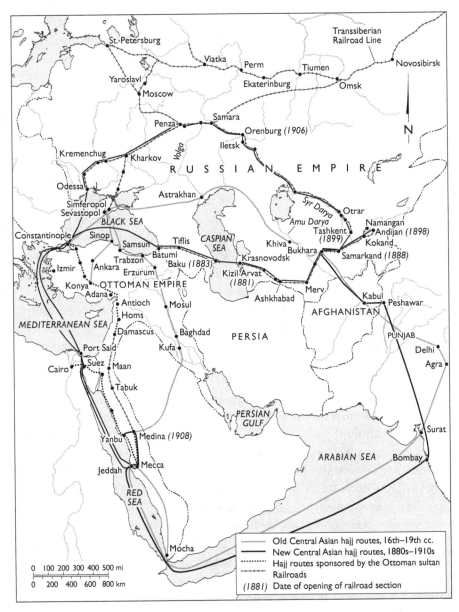

Map 4. Changing Central Asian hajj routes, 1880s–1910s

governor-general early on, and later to encourage intellectual debate and reading knowledge of Russian as part of a policy of "cautious enlightenment."[75] Articles from the early 1890s reveal that officials also used the newspaper to influence patterns of the hajj from Central Asia, by directing Muslims toward Russian institutions abroad.

The newspaper published a series of articles that encouraged Turkestan's Muslims to register with and use the services of the Jeddah consulate and other Russian consulates abroad while making the hajj.[76] The first articles appeared in March 1892, a few months before the scheduled annual hajj rituals in Arabia, at a time when Muslims in Turkestan would have been preparing to leave on the pilgrimage. That month the paper published "A Guide to Russian Consulates in Turkey for Russian Subjects Making the Pilgrimage to Mecca." This article emphasized the importance of Muslims using Russian consulates abroad to ensure that their rights were protected through Ottoman lands. It described procedures for filling out the proper documents required to make the hajj "legally" as Russian subjects, and in order to receive Russian consular support. It announced the recent opening of the Jeddah consulate and its importance for pilgrims as the closest Russian consulate to Mecca.

At the time, officials in Turkestan were increasingly eager to know the routes the region's Muslims were taking to Mecca, especially the purported "secret" routes through Afghanistan and India, where Russia had no consular outposts. The newspaper published several articles that were clearly attempts to encourage hajj pilgrims to make the pilgrimage through legal channels, by way of Russian railroads and steamships, and through its consulates, in order to facilitate supervision and to track the traffic. An article from 1895 is an example of this: it offered additional practical information to readers on how to make the hajj from Turkestan through official Russian channels. It covered how to properly fill out "hajj documents," Muslims' rights to consular protection abroad as Russian subjects, etiquette for riding trains and steamships, and the need to follow sanitary rules and pass through quarantine stations.[77]

Over the next few years, *Turkistan wilayatining gazeti* published several other articles showcasing the services the Jeddah consulate offered Russia's Muslim subjects. At first glance, these read like simple reports on new services. But more likely they were calculated attempts to lure pilgrims to the Jeddah consulate, and away from competing institutions organized around the hajj traffic. This was not, of course, simple benevolence on the part of the regime toward its Muslim subjects, as it was often presented in such articles, but part of the regime's agenda of surveillance, control, and rerouting of Russia's hajj pilgrims through legal channels. An 1895 article, for example, described how Muslims could leave their money and valuables at the consulate before heading to Mecca. There were local brokers who offered this same service in Jeddah, and had been doing so for centuries, but they charged high fees and were known for cheating pilgrims. Now, however, the Jeddah consulate offered this service for just five kopecks. The article recounted a happy story about how, in 1894, a group of twelve Muslims had left 3,000 rubles with the Jeddah consulate, and that "all of the money and property was returned to pilgrims" upon their return from Mecca. In addition, the article described the Russian consul's discovery in Jeddah of unclaimed estates of several deceased Bukharan and Russian subjects, for a total value of 2,500 rubles. In keeping with Islamic traditions, and with its role as protector of the rights of Russian subjects, the article noted, the Jeddah consulate had worked closely with the Ottoman authorities and Russian authorities back in the empire to deliver the estates to the proper heirs.[78]

It is difficult to judge the effectiveness of these articles in persuading Turkestan's Muslims to use the Jeddah consulate's services. It is clear, however, that in spite of them, many Muslims continued to rely on alternate sources of support in Arabia, and avoided the consulate. We see this in other articles that contain implicit warnings to would-be pilgrims about the risks of not using the Jeddah consulate, or ignoring official procedures in making the hajj. An 1895 article, for instance, reported that more than 3,000 Muslims had made the hajj from Russia by way of Jeddah the previous year, but only half had registered with the Jeddah consulate, presumably because they had no passports. The article highlighted the problems that cropped up for these pilgrims later, when they reached Constantinople and showed up at the Russian general consulate to request an entry visa into Russia. With no documents to prove they were Russian subjects, the consul-general denied their requests, and they ended up stranded in Constantinople.[79]

Histories of Russia's late nineteenth-century colonization of Turkestan often explore this process as it unfolded within the borders of this newly conquered territory. Framed in regional terms way, the cross-border dimensions of this process remain hidden. To see these, we must think of Russia's colonization of Central Asia differently, not as a process contained within hard borders but rather, following David Ludden, as a complex process influenced by local, regional, and global transformations that occurred within shifting "imperial circuits of space" and reflected efforts to control human resources and movement.[80] The articles considered above reveal close connections between Russian authorities in Tashkent and Jeddah, produced by and organized around the mass movement of hajj pilgrims between Turkestan and Arabia—a collaboration with the goal of colonizing Turkestan and integrating Muslims into the empire.

On the ground in Jeddah, Russian consul Levitskii attempted to bring the hajj traffic under his control and authority, among other means, by laying claim to the city's network of Central Asian tekkes. As noted earlier, Sufis from Central Asia had established these lodging houses across Ottoman lands in earlier centuries to support hajj pilgrims from Turkestan.[81] Levitskii's investigations turned up five such tekkes in Jeddah, and he visited them all within a year of his arrival. In an 1893 report to Russian ambassador I.A. Ivanov in Constantinople, he described them as "exclusively for Russian and Bukharan subjects," funded by Russian subjects, and generally in appalling shape. One of them, the "Bukharan tekke," was "extremely dilapidated," and the Ottoman subjects running the tekkes were overall of "extremely limited intelligence." "Given that these lodging houses were obtained by and for Russian subjects," he wrote in his report to the ambassador, "it goes without saying that with the opening in Jeddah of a Russian consulate, their supervision should become the domain of the consul."[82]

Levitskii's main argument for taking over the tekkes in Jeddah was sanitary. He insisted that he, as Russian consul, should oversee "the cleanliness of the tekkes and their hygienic condition," and that he or his secretary needed to make regular visits to these places in order to "preserve hajj pilgrims' health."[83] There is no reason to question Levitskii's sincerity on this point. There had been eight major cholera epidemics in Jeddah since 1865, and Levitskii wrote his proposal in 1893, in the midst of one of the worst ever. The 1893 epidemic killed more than 30,000 pilgrims in Arabia. That same year a cholera epidemic ravaged Russia. It began in Astrakhan, and was blamed on returning hajj pilgrims. The most deadly epidemic Russia experienced in the nineteenth century, it killed 250,000 Russian subjects empire-wide. In Russia, as elsewhere, the disease disproportionately afflicted the lower classes. Myths and legends swirled among them to explain the appearance of the "dreaded guest," including the idea that the government had created it to kill off poor people.[84] Levitskii would most likely have been aware of anxieties within the Russian government at this time about cholera as a threat to domestic order, and the role of the hajj in spreading it.

In Jeddah in 1893, Levitskii would have seen firsthand the horrors described by another eyewitness, a doctor employed by the Ottoman government named Oslchanictzki. He described Jeddah that year as a "vast cemetery," with dead bodies filling the caravanserais, mosques, cafés, houses, and public areas, and the city's workers and porters refusing to bury the dead. "Everywhere," Oslchanictzki wrote, "were the dead and suffering, the cries of men, women, and children, mixed with the roaring of the camels, in short, a terrifying scene which will never be blotted out of my memory." The epidemic lasted a full month, and the majority of the afflicted were colonial subjects. This epidemic transformed cholera in the Hejaz into a major international issue, and prompted the European powers to insist on their right to intervene directly in sanitary conditions in Jeddah, given the failures of the Ottomans to enforce international regulations in their own lands.[85]

In response to the devastating cholera epidemic in Arabia, as well as a plague scare in India, the European powers convened the first Sanitary Conference on the Mecca Pilgrimage. There they drafted the 1894 Paris Sanitary Convention, which focused largely on cholera, and marked stricter and more invasive controls over hajj traffic—these included, among other things, stringent medical inspections in pilgrims' ports of departure, and the establishment of a new quarantine station on Kamaran Island in the Red Sea, staffed by European and Ottoman, Muslim and non-Muslim medical officials.[86] The 1893 epidemic, in other words, led to a deepening of European involvement in the hajj in and around Arabia as well as in colonial locales. The Ottomans, seeking to regain control and authority over the mass hajj traffic, and to curb European influence over the pilgrimage, introduced their own series of measures after the 1893 epidemic. Among other things, Ottoman Sultan Abdülhamid II ordered the construction of a lodging house for poor pilgrims in Mecca, with a capacity for 1,400.[87]

But Levitskii's interest in taking control of the Jeddah tekkes was also about his authority over Russia's hajj traffic, and gaining control over the tekkes' financial and legal dealings. He sought both to eliminate barriers that blocked his access to pilgrims and to remove them from other sources of influence and authority. He told Ambassador Ivanov that he needed open access to the tekkes in order to resolve "judicial-estate issues" when pilgrims died. As things stood, Ottoman officials were trying to block him from the tekkes, for fear of losing their own authority over estate cases, which were for them a lucrative source of income. Levitskii asked Ivanov to get the Ottoman government to issue a decree to local officials, asking them not to "condemn" him for visiting the tekkes, or to obstruct his access.[88]

Ivanov hesitated to do this for fear of upsetting the Ottoman government. Scribbled in pencil in the margins of Levitskii's proposal is his response, in which he noted that the Ottoman government was already opposing Russian efforts to extend hajj patronage to Bukharans, who were not technically Russian subjects. They were subjects of the emir of Bukhara, which was a semi-independent protectorate of Russia, and therefore, according to Ottoman officials, fell under the patronage and authority of the Ottoman sultan-caliph. Ivanov proposed that Levitskii wait until the Jeddah consulate was "more established on legal grounds," and then let Muslims themselves ask for the consulate's assistance.[89] Ivanov's response reveals his embrace of caution over coercion. It also suggests his confidence that if Muslim pilgrims were offered superior services, they would eventually and voluntarily submit to the authority of the Jeddah consulate.

The tekke episode reveals two major challenges Levitskii and his successors faced in their efforts to establish authority over Russia's hajj traffic in Arabia. The first was ambiguity and sometimes disagreement over who, exactly, was a Russian subject and entitled to diplomatic protection through the Jeddah consulate. Central to this issue was the Bukharan émigré community in Arabia. European colonization of Muslim lands over the nineteenth century had set off waves of Muslim migration to Ottoman lands, among them Bukharans fleeing the Russian invasion of Turkestan. They had been living for decades in Ottoman lands, had long ago become Ottoman subjects, and some had resettled in Arabia, where they worked as merchants. But with the opening of a Russian consulate in Jeddah, some of these émigrés began to show up at the consulate, presenting themselves as Russian subjects and demanding diplomatic protection.[90]

There is no evidence that Levitskii deliberately tried to cultivate Bukharan émigrés and lure them to the consulate. Rather, it seems that Bukharan émigrés often came to the consulate on their own, seeking to claim extraterritorial privileges as Russian subjects to advance their own economic interests or escape prosecution under Ottoman laws. Two cases from the Ottoman archives, involving Ottoman subjects, illustrate this. In one, from 1891, a Bukharan resident of Arabia named Celal appealed to Russia's Jeddah consulate to secure his release from prison, after being arrested by the Ottoman authorities in Arabia for illegally selling slaves. In another, from 1898, a Bukharan merchant named Abdurrahman applied to the Jeddah consulate for Russian subjecthood soon after being charged merchant fees to enter Jeddah for trade.[91]

The second challenge Levitskii and his successors faced in Arabia was the resistance of Ottoman officials to their authority over Muslim pilgrims. The European consular presence in Arabia was relatively new, and unwelcome by Ottoman officials, who saw it as part of broader European efforts to meddle in

Ottoman legal affairs and undermine Ottoman control over the empire's populations. Some complained that the European powers had "invented" a cholera threat as an excuse to expand their presence into Ottoman Arabia.[92] Whether or not Russia's Jeddah consuls were actively recruiting Bukharan émigrés to become Russian subjects, this was how Ottoman officials perceived the situation, and it increased their resistance to the consulate's authority. Some apparently saw the Jeddah consulate as part of a broader strategy by Russia to erode Ottoman authority over its subjects. In the case of Celal, officials in the Hejaz noted that he also carried documents from the Russian consul-general in Constantinople, and they complained to the Ottoman government that the consul-general in Constantinople "considers all Bukharans to be Russian subjects."[93]

Ottoman resistance to the authority of the Jeddah consulate was an ongoing and frustrating problem for Levitskii, and would be also for his successors. Starting in 1895, he complained repeatedly to the Russian embassy in Constantinople that Ottoman officials were blocking him from resolving pilgrims' estate cases, partly for economic reasons. For centuries, these estate cases had been the exclusive domain of Ottoman officials, and an important source of financial enrichment both for them on an individual level and for state coffers. The Ottoman state's organization of the pilgrimage was an enormous and costly undertaking, and was funded in part by proceeds from unclaimed estates of deceased pilgrims, of which there were many.[94] There were also strategic reasons for this resistance. Since the 1880s, when European consulates began to proliferate in Jeddah, because of the rise of colonial subjects making the hajj and trading in Arabia, the Ottomans had introduced various measures to tighten their control over the region and the pilgrimage.[95]

But Levitskii was within his rights in seeking to resolve estate cases and other legal issues for Russian subjects. As Ottoman officials discovered in discussing his complaints, a little-invoked article of a 1783 Russo-Ottoman trade agreement gave Russian diplomatic officials authority over the estates of all Russian subjects who died while in Ottoman lands.[96] The Ottoman government had no choice but to order its officials in the Hejaz to stop intervening in these cases, with mixed results. Throughout the 1890s and early 1900s, Russia's Jeddah consuls would continue to complain about Ottoman officials interfering in their efforts to support Russia's hajj pilgrims, as numerous petitions of the Russian embassy to the Ottoman government attest.[97]

As Levitskii grappled with these challenges, he also worked steadily to compile data and intelligence on the hajj for the Foreign Ministry. As a Russian-speaker with limited knowledge of Islam or Arabia, he relied heavily on the

Muslim agents who staffed the consulate for help in doing this. These Muslim agents were often Russian subjects who had demonstrated their loyalty and usefulness to the Russian government as native informants and officials in Muslim regions of the empire.[98] As Muslims, they understood the rituals of the hajj and, no less importantly, were able to travel to Mecca and Medina. Their linguistic skills also allowed them to communicate with Russia's hajj pilgrims moving through the region. Officially appointed to the Jeddah consulate, as well as other consulates along hajj routes, as clerks, guards, and interpreters, these Muslim agents in fact took on much broader roles, spying and compiling detailed reports for the government on the hajj traffic.[99]

One such person was Shakirdzhan Ishaev. A Muslim Tatar who had served the Russian administration in Turkestan for many years, he arrived in Jeddah in 1895 to work at the consulate.[100] His appointment offers further evidence of a growing collaboration between officials in Jeddah and Tashkent to monitor and organize the Turkestani hajj traffic. The Russian ambassador noted that he was appointed to the Jeddah consulate because of his "intimate knowledge of life" in Turkestan, suggesting that he would primarily focus on pilgrims from that region of Russia.[101] Ishaev would work closely with Levitskii to encourage pilgrims to come to the consulate. He greeted pilgrims arriving in the city from Russia, speaking to them in their native tongue, and describing the Jeddah consulate's services. His efforts to get them to deposit their money and valuables with the consulate for safekeeping earned him the enmity of Ottoman "guides" (vekils) in Jeddah, who offered these same services for a fee, and jealously guarded their hereditary role in the local hajj industry.[102]

During his time at the Jeddah consulate, Ishaev researched and wrote a series of reports on the hajj, Arabia, and the Holy Cities of Mecca and Medina for the Russian Foreign Ministry. Other colonial governments had commissioned such reports—most famously Snouck Hurgronje's reports from the 1880s for the Dutch government in Indonesia—but Ishaev's were the first written by a Russian subject, based on firsthand travel and observations, for the tsarist government.[103]

At a time when the tsarist government sought to gather basic information on the hajj traffic from Russia—routes, logistics, and existing Muslim support networks—Ishaev's reports offered rich details as well as recommendations on how to reorganize the hajj under Russian authority, based on extensive interviews with hajj pilgrims from Russia passing through Jeddah, as well as his own pilgrimage to Mecca in 1895. That year he set out on the pilgrimage to Mecca from Jeddah with his wife and four-year-old son. He described the unenjoyable overland trek from Jeddah to Mecca, a distance of some fifty miles along a well-worn desert path, as a "deadly slow and tiring journey" made by a huge caravan of hundreds of people and camels—"desert ships"—across the desert, and many poor pilgrims on foot. The heat was unbearable, and he was appalled by the primitive conditions along the way. There were no caravanserais in which to rest, only shabby huts called "coffeehouses" every several miles, where pilgrims sat under awnings drinking overpriced tea and coffee, surrounded by stinking piles of human and animal excrement.[104]

Perhaps most useful to the tsarist government, Ishaev's reports identified existing networks in Arabia that Russia's Muslims relied on in making the hajj. He highlighted two above all. First, there was the tight-knit Turkestani émigré community living and working in Jeddah, Mecca, and Medina. This community was relatively small, but had grown a lot in recent years. It was a mix of families that had fled the Russian invasion and resettled in Arabia, and those who had stayed on after making the hajj because they had no money to get home. Ishaev counted forty such people in Jeddah, working as shopkeepers or peddling goods on the streets from trays and bins, and reported that many also lived in Mecca, where they worked in different trades and seemed to have settled permanently.[105] Many made their money off the hajj traffic from Turkestan. Indeed, many of the worst "exploiters" of Turkestani pilgrims came from this group, Ishaev noted, whose members used shared language and culture as a way to earn the trust of fellow Turkestanis and cheat them. A standard ploy was to agree to store money and valuables for pilgrims, and then disappear. Ishaev reported that he had "made a lot of enemies" by warning Turkestanis not to leave their valuables with these men, but to leave them instead with the Russian consulate in Jeddah. He drew up a list of "the most dangerous Central Asians," three men he charged with stealing pilgrims' money: Muhammadjan Mansurov, Kary Makhmut, and Zakir Effendi. He also accused them of working to discredit the Jeddah consulate among Russia's hajj pilgrims. He complained that in 1895, in the wake of an attack by local Arabs on the Russian consul and other European consuls, they had been spreading "false rumors" that pilgrims' deposits had disappeared in the attacks and Ishaev had "deliberately deceived them."[106]

The second network that Ishaev identified in his reports was the *dalil* system, the ancient institution of guides that largely controlled the pilgrimage in Arabia. He described in detail how this system worked. Appointed by the sharif of Mecca, the dalil position was hereditary, and the job was highly coveted in a region that had almost no industry besides the pilgrimage. The dalil system was also, according to Ishaev, hard to avoid: for reasons of safety and lack of knowledge of Arabic and local customs, pilgrims relied heavily on guides for support while on the hajj. "Official dalils" as well as private, freelance ones cruised around the Kaaba (the central site of the Meccan pilgrimage) looking for pilgrims to serve. The sharif of Mecca appointed dalils to groups of pilgrims based on their land of origin, and the volume of traffic from that region. For the Russian Empire and its protectorates of Bukhara and Khiva, Ishaev reported, there were nineteen dalils in Mecca. To help Russia's hajj pilgrims get from Jeddah to Mecca, the dalils relied on deputies (vekils) that they hired in Jeddah, many of whom were émigrés from Turkestan.[107]

Ishaev described the dalil system as corrupt and exploitative. "After the ordeals of the Hejaz," he wrote, "a pilgrim is lucky if he makes it home alive." He noted that dalils were authorized to handle estate cases when pilgrims died while in Mecca. They were supposed to inform the Ottoman authorities of the death, and take the deceased's property and money for safekeeping until it could be gotten to the proper heirs, but this did not always happen. The deceased's travel companions sometimes made off with the property, or the money stayed in the hands of the dalil.[108] Ishaev noted that elite pilgrims were treated much better by the dalils, who arranged everything for them in Mecca: apartment rentals, a samovar, bed linens, coal, and clothing. His own experience illustrated this. The head dalil for Russia, a sixty-year-old local Arab named Muhammad Ali Srudzhi, had greeted Ishaev when he arrived in Mecca and given him and his family a "very cordial welcome." He brought them sacred water from the Zam Zam well, and served them meals in his home.[109]

Ishaev's reports made clear that Russia's hajj pilgrims were suffering in many ways under the status quo in Arabia. Turkestani émigrés and dalils alike exploited them ruthlessly, and the Ottoman government was failing to provide adequate services and an infrastructure to accommodate the fast-growing hajj crowds showing up in Mecca. But Ishaev's reports also revealed that the existing system had its strengths, and that not all pilgrims were unhappy with it. Srudzhi emerged in his report as a particularly influential figure. As the head dalil for "all Tatars and Kirgiz from Russia," he wielded enormous authority, not least of all as the official responsible for handling estate cases for pilgrims who died in Mecca. He spoke perfect Russian—learned during a two-year stint in a Turkestani prison, after being charged with entering Russia illegally—and was "very well respected" among Russia's Muslims.[110] He had close ties to Muslims back in the Russian Empire. Ishaev reported that he knew all of the richest

Tatar merchants in Russia by name, and even knew the Tatar community in Turkestan better than Ishaev, who had been a part of it for years. Ishaev reported that Srudzhi had "entire volumes of lists of Russian Muslims," with whom he corresponded regularly, and he often sent students back to Russia with returning pilgrims to collect donations.[111]

Ishaev's reports confirmed that, four years after the founding of the Jeddah consulate, Russia still had much work to do in bringing the hajj traffic under Russian influence and control. He noted in particular the prevalence of "secret pilgrimage" by Russia's Muslims from Turkestan. By this, he meant the large numbers of pilgrims making the hajj without passports, along unsupervised land routes, and largely beyond the detection of Russian officials inside or outside the empire. He noted a recent "flood" of pilgrims from Turkestan into Arabia by "secret" routes, and attributed it to a lack of local oversight and control by the Russian authorities in the region, and ineffective passport registration. Through interviews with pilgrims, he learned that local Muslim spiritual authorities in Turkestan largely controlled the hajj. Generally, he reported, Turkestani Muslims did not leave on the hajj without the permission and blessing of these authorities. They gave departing pilgrims signed certificates to authorize their hajj, or sent them without any documents at all. And departing pilgrims honored these authorities before leaving for Mecca, inviting them into their homes and serving them a feast. Many were poor and ended up stranded and penniless in Arabia, leading a "pitiful existence."[112]

The archival trail suggests that Ishaev's reports were commissioned with a specific purpose in mind—namely, to help the newly established Russian administration in Turkestan understand and develop a policy toward the hajj. Russian ambassador Ivanov in Constantinople read Ishaev's reports closely, and forwarded them on to the Russian governor-general of Turkestan, A. B. Vrevskii, during the 1890s. They contained not only information and data on the Turkestani hajj traffic, but also recommendations for the governor-general on how best to control it and stop the problem of "secret pilgrimage." To remedy "secret" hajj departures, Ivanov in 1895 conveyed Ishaev's recommendation that Turkestanis without passports be sent home by steamship through Batumi, and the costs for travel paid by the state be collected from their home community.[113]

Muslim agents staffing the consulate, like Ishaev, studied the hajj and wrote reports, and the consulate hosted spies and agents sent into Arabia by the tsarist government on research missions. Like the British, Russia also sent in physicians to assess the sanitary situation in and around Mecca, and write reports.[114]

In 1897 and 1898 it sent two doctors, D. Zabolotnyi and D. M. Sokolov, to report on sanitary conditions along pilgrims' routes and in Arabia. Zabolotnyi took a route through India (popular among Turkestanis), while Sokolov took the Black Sea route. Both reports cited awful conditions that Russia's hajj pilgrims suffered on board steamships. Zabolotnyi described the garbage-strewn deck of his ship, where pilgrims fought with one another for space, and cooked and slept amid the ill. Both doctors noted a general lack of medical facilities for pilgrims in Arabia, to tend to the many sick and dying from disease.[115]

Also in 1898 Russia's minister of war, A. N. Kuropatkin sent a high-ranking Muslim officer, Staff-Captain Abdul Aziz Davletshin, to Arabia on a secret intelligence-gathering mission. A Tatar and trusted intermediary for the government, Davletshin had served an intelligence role under Kuropatkin in Turkestan in the 1880s, and wrote an extensive report on local legal customs.[116] The result of his 1898 mission was a 145-page report on the Hejaz region and the hajj, submitted to the Ministry of War, the first of its kind by a Russian subject for the Russian government. Divided into seven sections, Davletshin's report covered a wide variety of topics, including the flora and fauna of the Hejaz, pilgrims' routes in the Hejaz, climate, and the currency system.

One long section of Davletshin's report focused on "the hajj by Russian Muslims and the sanitary conditions of the pilgrimage." Much like Ishaev's reports, Davletshin's provided rich, ground-level detail on the logistics of the hajj for Russia's Muslims, the main institutions and individuals that organized and served the crowds of pilgrims from Russia, and data on those making the hajj, including numbers, their origins in the empire, sex, and age. A Turkic-speaker and a Muslim, Davletshin had access to pilgrims through a shared language, and to Mecca and Medina. He gathered information from interviews with pilgrims, whom he accompanied from Jeddah to Mecca and Medina. His account also included, tucked in the back, a series of detailed maps—one of the Haram-ı Sharif or Great Mosque in Mecca, one of the Great Mosque in Medina, and finally a map of the topography of Arabia and the main land routes pilgrims used to reach Mecca and Medina.[117]

THE work and reports from Jeddah yielded a geographic conception of Russia's hajj traffic, a "map" of sorts, that would guide the government's efforts to organize and co-opt the hajj over the next decade. Much like the maps produced by British colonial officials of "British India," these reports created an image of Russia's hajj traffic that purported to be accurate, but in fact missed a great deal, including the vibrant informal networks that many Muslims from Russia continued to rely on in getting to Mecca, and that would thrive well into the twentieth century. These networks fell outside the view of most tsarist officials doing the mapping.

In 1896 the Ministry of Internal Affairs produced a thirty-two-page composite document titled "On the Hajj, Its Meanings, and Measures for Organizing It," based primarily on reports from Russia's consulates in Jeddah, Baghdad, and Mashhad. The ministry sent it out to all of Russia's governors across the empire, and asked them to respond to the report and its proposed measures.[118]

The 1896 report, for the first time, mapped out the basic geography of Russia's hajj traffic. It identified three main routes that an estimated 18,000 to 25,000 Sunnis and Shi'is took as they made the hajj from Russia to Arabia. First, there was a land route from the Caucasus that traversed northern Persia and Mesopotamia, across the desert to Arabia. Shi'is in the South Caucasus preferred this route, as it allowed them to visit Shi'i holy sites in Karbala and Najaf on their way to Mecca. The second main route went by land from Turkestan, through Afghan and Indian lands down to Bombay, where pilgrims boarded ships to cross the Indian Ocean. Pilgrims made "secret" undetected pilgrimages along this route, as it passed through places where Russia had no consular outposts and pilgrims traveled undetected. The report showed how criminal rings operating in Black Sea ports facilitated these "secret pilgrimages." The third and most modern route was by railroad through Russian lands to the Black Sea, and onward by steamship through Constantinople and the Suez Canal to Jeddah.[119]

In addition to taking secret routes through Afghan and Indian lands, pilgrims routinely left without receiving passports. This posed public health risks for the empire. At a time of recurring global cholera epidemics, mostly related to the Meccan pilgrimage, the unregulated hajj traffic, largely beyond the view or authority of Russian officials, was dangerous.[120]

Echoing Ambassador Nelidov's idea from a decade earlier, the report proposed a pragmatic approach to the hajj, while also revealing a negative attitude. "We must agree that the hajj is harmful and undesirable," it concluded, "but it is also inevitable and a 'tolerated evil'; it must be limited and organized and the awful state of affairs for our pilgrims must be addressed."[121] Russia had to do something about the hajj. The volume of hajj traffic moving through the empire was increasing every year, and the unregulated and disorganized crowds were causing disorders along Russia's railways and in its Black Sea ports. There were political and security concerns as well. The awful conditions that Muslim pilgrims endured were becoming an embarrassment for the government, and seemed to call into question Russia's professed toleration for its Muslim populations.

STANDARD narratives emphasize how Russia ruled Muslims through violence, repression, and restrictions, and by trying to isolate them from contacts with foreign coreligionists. Here we see efforts to achieve this same goal through a different, ostensibly more positive exercise of power, by mapping patterns of Muslim pilgrimage to Mecca, as a way to expand the surveillance and regulatory capacity of the regime over its Muslims, and bring them more firmly within the Russian imperial orbit, even while abroad. After trying and failing to block the hajj, Russia tried a new tack, seeking instead to control and co-opt it as a mechanism of imperial integration. This strategy grew out of trial and error, and a general acceptance of the hajj as part of the Islamic inheritances that came with its conquests of Muslim lands, and as a network upon which to build new imperial pathways and agendas.

The mass movement of Muslim pilgrims between the empire and foreign lands, and tsarist officials' perceptions of this movement and its implications for the state and the empire, had dramatic consequences for Russia. As a phenomenon that lay at the intersection of Russia's foreign and domestic policy, the hajj demanded and produced new collaborations between officials in the Ministries of Foreign and Internal Affairs to draft policies and imperial agendas.

Mass migrations reshaped and expanded Russia's territorial attachments worldwide, opening up new arenas of Russian imperial activity and space that extended well beyond the empire's formal borders, and brought Russia into parts of the world where it had no prior history of involvement. By opening consulates to serve its hajj pilgrims, Russia was building upon the global networks of its Muslim populations, and quietly expanding its influence and institutional presence in the world. Mass migrations also restructured Russia's project of imperial governance, transforming it into a cross-border enterprise that in some cases required cooperation and collaboration between tsarist officials inside and outside the empire.

A focus on the hajj, furthermore, illuminates how empire building transcended Russia's formal imperial borders in the nineteenth century. Migrations effectively reorganized Russian state structures in this period, connected previously disparate places, and expanded and emboldened the imperial imaginings of tsarist officials. The hajj migration also shows how local and peripheral concerns played a crucial role in setting state policies, which, as this example illustrates, were not simply imposed from the center on the periphery. Sometimes they emerged from concerns about local traditions, the issues important to peripheral natural environments, and patterns of human movement.[122]

Historians of Russia are divided in their view of how the late imperial state managed Islam, whether it generally tried "ignoring" Islam, or in fact institutionalized and sponsored it. What scholars do agree on, however, is that the state worried about and tried to cut cross-border ties between its Muslims and their coreligionists abroad. But in the case of the hajj—by far the main conduit of transimperial Muslim movement and communication—Russia did not ultimately try to block cross-border Muslim mobility, or cut Muslim ties to foreign lands and peoples, although its first impulse was indeed to restrict the hajj. Instead, it tried to govern its Muslims through this mobility network, using it as an instrument of external surveillance as well as imperial integration. It institutionalized and began to sponsor the hajj, in the process facilitating movement and making the hajj more central to the practice of Islam than it had ever been before for Muslims in this part of the world.

As we have seen, Russia gathered enough data from its new consulates to compile a map of sorts, a description of Russia's hajj pilgrims' main itineraries, which would serve as a blueprint for further involvement in the hajj. No less significantly, by following Russia's hajj pilgrims into foreign lands, and creating an infrastructure along their routes to Mecca, tsarist officials effectively expanded the arena of Russian imperialism, and with it Russia's presence in the world.

3

Forging a Russian Hajj Route

Having mapped the basic geography of the hajj, Russia next turned to organizing it. In the 1890s Tsar Nicholas II ordered the Ministry of Internal Affairs to create a government "monopoly" of the hajj.[1] This plan fit the regime's broader efforts to control and co-opt Russia's mass migrations and channel them in ways beneficial to the state and the empire.[2] It was testimony to the growing consensus within the government that stopping the hajj traffic was impossible and that it must do something to regulate and manage it—and, that Russia could benefit from organizing the pilgrimage.

Russia's goals were ambitious. It wanted to redirect Muslim pilgrims' movement way from secret, unsupervised land routes and onto a state-sanctioned route, and have them adhere to a state-established itinerary that eliminated many popular stops along the way, including Constantinople, which tsarist officials saw as a center of Pan-Islamic activities. The government wanted pilgrims to register with Russian consulates in Jeddah and other key nodes abroad. With support from Russian railroad and steamship officials, tsarist officials envisioned speeding Muslim pilgrims through Russian lands to its Black Sea ports, and from there directly to Arabia and back.

Organizing the hajj, then, was ultimately about forging and streamlining a single Russian route to Mecca, keeping Russian-subject Muslims within the imperial orbit even while abroad. To attract pilgrims to this route, Russia would try strategies used by the Ottomans and previous Muslim empires to forge their own imperial hajj routes: ceremonies and pageantry, economic incentives, subsidized transport, and facilities along the route to enhance comfort and security. In other words, Russia would begin to sponsor the hajj.

Russia was not the only European power to do so. By the late nineteenth century the majority of the world's Muslims lived under colonial rule, and Europe's leading imperial powers all actively supported the hajj. Around the world colonial governments set up support systems for their hajj pilgrims along the major routes that connected their colonies to Arabia, complete with consulates, provision stations, lodging houses, and medical posts, and seasonal, subsidized transport on railroads and steamships. Russian patronage of the hajj was modeled in large part on the examples of other colonial powers. Tsarist officials frequently looked to other colonial settings for ideas and policies to copy, and the Foreign Ministry sometimes asked its consular officials posted in French Algeria and elsewhere to investigate colonial hajj policies, and submit detailed reports on them.[3] At the same time, Russia also clearly borrowed ideas and models from the Ottomans.

Much like the Ottomans, Russia attempted to streamline its hajj traffic along a state-sanctioned route, largely for economic reasons. At a time when Russia was rapidly modernizing and seeking to increase passenger traffic along its new and expensive railroad and steamship lines, many tsarist officials began to see economic opportunity in the hajj. They saw in the mass, circular movement of hajj pilgrims between Russia and Arabia not just potential threats to public health and imperial stability, but also passengers for Russia's railroads and steamships, and thus a source of state revenues.[4]

To organize the hajj, Russia could have simply adopted the model it had developed in 1889 for the Russian Orthodox pilgrimage to Jerusalem, as a leading official in the Ministry of Internal Affairs indeed proposed.[5] Tsar Alexander III officially endorsed the Imperial Orthodox Palestine Society (IOPS) to support the pilgrimage to Jerusalem. With state funding and the public support of the royal family, the IOPS established a network of services and facilities for Orthodox pilgrims along their routes through Russian and Ottoman lands, including hostels in Odessa and IOPS branch offices in regions across the Russian Empire. The centerpiece of this Russian Orthodox pilgrimage infrastructure was the complex of buildings that the IOPS built in Jerusalem, just outside the old city walls. Still standing today and called the Russian Compound, this complex included barracks to house pilgrims, a hospital, a refectory, a small church, and an ecclesiastical mission to house Russian Orthodox clergy.[6]

But Russia did not do this. Many officials strongly resisted the idea of treating the hajj like Orthodox pilgrimage. By offering the same support to Muslim and Orthodox pilgrims, they warned, the government would send a dangerous message—that Russia was trying to encourage the hajj, or, even worse, that it was starting to privilege Islam over Orthodoxy.[7] They feared a backlash from the Orthodox Church, which enjoyed preeminent status in the empire, and was a crucial source of institutional support for the regime. At the same time, they worried that Muslims might resent government involvement in the hajj as an attempt to restrict the practice of their faith.

These concerns and complexities around the hajj illuminate a much larger problem for Russia: How could it reconcile its identity as an Orthodox state, and the historically privileged position of the Orthodox Church within the empire, with the diverse confessional makeup of its internal populations, and the need to integrate and effectively govern these diverse populations? How could it harness the economic and other benefits of the hajj, without appearing to control or interfere with it?

Ultimately, the government never created or endorsed the equivalent of the IOPS for the Muslim pilgrimage, nor did it build an elaborate complex for its hajj pilgrims in or around Mecca. Most strikingly, as this chapter describes, Russia never officially announced its support for the hajj or its plan to organize it. The plan was never centralized in a single ministry or institution, but was instead carried out in a decentralized manner, in semisecrecy.

THE idea to forge a state-sanctioned hajj route was first proposed in 1896, in the Ministry of Internal Affairs' comprehensive "Report on the Hajj, Its Meaning, and Measures for Organizing It." In addition to providing data on Muslims' patterns of travel in making the hajj—and identifying the three main routes that Russia's Muslims took in getting to Mecca—this report stressed the urgent need for the government to organize the hajj, for sanitary, political, and economic reasons. It offered specific proposals on how best to do this, based on data compiled by Russian consuls abroad, above all in Jeddah.

The report proposed that Russia redirect its hajj traffic along the Black Sea route. This was not, in fact, a single route but rather a set of Russian railroad routes that converged in the sea's main Russian ports of Sevastopol, Batumi, and Odessa. From these ports hajj pilgrims continued on by steamship to the Arabian ports of Jeddah and Yanbu. According to estimates by Russian consular officials, the Black Sea route was growing in popularity among Russia's Muslims by the 1890s, but still attracted the fewest numbers of pilgrims overall—about 2,000 to 3,000 a year, while twice as many took land routes through Afghanistan and India, and almost 15,000 took land routes through the Caucasus.[8] The modern railroad-to-steamship routes through the Black Sea were ideal for organizing the hajj, tsarist officials widely agreed, for two reasons. First, they ran through

Russian lands and points abroad where Russia already had consulates, and thus would be easiest to supervise. Second, streamlining the hajj along this route would bring much-needed passenger traffic and revenues to Russia's railroads and steamships.[9]

The report argued that organizing the hajj was imperative from a political and sanitary standpoint. Unsupervised abroad, officials feared, Russia's Muslims were exposed to both subversive political ideas and infectious diseases that threatened the empire's internal stability. Tsar Nicholas II was sufficiently concerned about the sanitary threat. In 1897, after reading the report, he established the Commission on Measures for Prevention and Struggle against the Plague, Cholera, and Yellow Fever (KOMOCHUM). Among other things, KOMOCHUM set up medical observation posts in well-trafficked Black Sea ports and popular crossing points along Russia's borders to study disease and prevent its import into the empire. Also in 1897, Russia established a nearly 200-mile-long quarantine cordon of manned observation posts along its southern borders, to intercept caravans traveling long-distance routes.[10]

The report also stressed economic incentives for hajj organization. It made a striking claim: Russia's hajj traffic generated three to five million rubles in transport revenues every year, very little of which enriched Russia. Most of this money flowed abroad, to the detriment of Russia's domestic economy, enriching foreign governments as well as the foreign steamship companies that dominated Black Sea transport.[11]

To attract hajj pilgrims to the Black Sea route, and capture transport revenues, the report proposed that the tsarist government mobilize Russia's two largest steamship enterprises: the Russian Steamship Company (ROPiT) and the Volunteer Fleet. Both were heavily subsidized by and extremely costly to the state, notoriously inefficient, and always looking for passenger cargo. They had been created after the Crimean War, mainly to develop Russia's foreign trade, and, in light of the postwar prohibition of Russian naval forces in the Black Sea, to have a fleet that could serve as an auxiliary naval force in a future war.[12] Russia's modest foreign trade, compared to other European powers, put both fleets at a disadvantage in global competition for cargo and passengers. Even with steady infusions of generous state subsidies, the fleets charged higher rates than other European fleets.[13]

The main architect of this plan was the Russian consul in Jeddah, A. D. Levitskii. The report included his detailed ideas on how to organize the hajj along the Black Sea route, based on his firsthand observations and experience over many years in Arabia. He cautioned that the hajj should be organized not by force but by suasion, using "friendly" measures to attract pilgrims to the intended routes with promises, and delivery, of superior services and security. The timing could be synchronized, with hajj passports issued a few months before the Feast of the Sacrifice (the Muslim holiday that marked the end of the hajj rituals in Mecca). Levitskii proposed that the government make an agreement with one of Russia's steamship companies to provide direct, round-trip hajj service to Jeddah. Finally, he argued that the government should appoint guides and companions to the hajj crowds "from among trusted Muslims who do not work for the government."[14]

Levitskii pointed out that other European powers had undertaken similar measures with success, including the provision of special hajj steamships to their Muslim subjects. And he cited the economic and administrative benefits that would come from such measures. By providing steamships that gave Muslims a "safer, cheaper way" to make the hajj and perform their religious duties, the Russian government could both capture some of the hajj revenues of which Russia had been deprived, and also help with Russia's efforts to "supervise" the hajj traffic. At the same time, he added, these measures would help reassure the local population (in Arabia) of Russia's good intentions.[15]

To organize Russia's hajj traffic within Arabia itself, Levitskii suggested that the Foreign Ministry expand Russia's consular apparatus there, appointing agents in Mecca, Medina, and Yanbu, with Ottoman approval and "from among the Russian Muslims living in the Hejaz." It should also cover the costs of travel for Muslims stranded in the Hejaz, by charging a fee upon issuing passports or by organizing charitable donations from among departing Muslims (there were a lot of stranded Muslims from Russia, and not all of them were poor or illiterate). Finally, it should petition the Ottoman government to restrain the Bedouin population of the Hejaz.[16]

Levitskii's proposal, which effectively called for Russia to facilitate and capitalize on Muslim mobility, was not unusual. The plan took shape during the era of Sergei Witte, Russia's minister of finance from 1892 to 1904, who famously sought to industrialize Russia rapidly as a matter of imperial strength and survival. Witte focused in particular on the modernization and expansion of Russian railroads and steamship networks, as a means of building industry and developing capitalism in Russia, and also knitting together the different regions of the empire to foster economic growth and imperial unity.[17]

Levitskii's plan fit with Witte's broader efforts to encourage and profit from passenger traffic along the empire's new rail network. During Witte's tenure as finance minister, the government invested heavily in railroad construction and expansion, including the building of the trans-Siberian railroad. It also gave generous subsidies to develop and expand steamship transport. In 1894 Witte had launched efforts to increase passenger traffic on Russian railroads and steamships, most of which were state owned or heavily subsidized by the state. Witte believed that the empire's economic wealth depended upon mobility, and stressed the urgent need for more of it, in order to enhance "the economic and moral bonds among the various geographical regions of the country." Russia's railroads had far less passenger travel than other European countries. To develop industry, Witte argued, it was important that workers take rails instead of pedestrian land routes, and bring revenues to the railroads. Russia's railroads under Witte began to offer special discounts for workers and peasant-settlers migrating to Siberia and Central Asia, and for Orthodox pilgrims going to Jerusalem.[18]

Scholars have so far explored Witte's efforts to expand Russian transport within the borders of the empire, paying less attention to their considerable external dimensions. In the early 1900s, for example, when Britain's preoccupation with the Boer Wars in South Africa detracted its attention from the Persian Gulf, Witte was emboldened to persuade the State Council to fund the creation of new steamship service between Odessa and Basra on ROPiT ships. In 1901 ROPiT introduced its "Persian Line," which provided direct service between Odessa and the Persian Gulf. At the same time, the Foreign Ministry opened new Russian consulates in the Persian Gulf, in Basra and Bushehr, to help expand trade in the region and explore opportunities to build Russian railroads linking Russian Central Asia with southern Persia.[19]

Russia never built railroads across Persia, but this plan is nevertheless significant for what it reveals about the Russian imperial vision and agendas in the early 1900s. We tend to hold a picture in our minds of Russia circa 1900 as a massive and fixed entity. This was the peak of the empire in territorial terms, and Russia would not, in the end, expand its borders any farther. But in the minds of many Russian officials at this time, the empire's borders were more fuzzy and temporary than fixed. Russia was competing with Britain for influence and territories in weakened Ottoman and Persian states, and many tsarist officials envisioned further Russian expansion into Persia as well as Arabia, which had also emerged as a focus of imperial interest and colonial commercial activity.[20]

As the creation of the "Persian Line" reveals, Witte's plans to use railroad to develop Russian industry and strategic interests were not confined within the empire's borders. It is unclear if Witte had a direct hand in developing the plan to use Russian transport to organize the hajj, but it seems likely that he would have supported it. Not only did this plan fit his vision of mobility as essential to economic growth for the empire, it was also consistent with his view of Russia's non-Orthodox peoples as economic resources, and the need to selectively push—most notably in the case of Russia's Jewish populations—to lift restrictions on their mobility, social and otherwise, so that they could contribute to the empire's economic development. Witte's support for the rights of Russia's non-Orthodox peoples often put him at odds with other officials within the government, many of whom were committed to preserving Orthodox privilege in the empire and suspicious of non-Orthodox political loyalties.[21]

IN the end the tsarist government embraced Levitskii's proposal to streamline the hajj along the Black Sea route. Starting in the 1890s officials in the Ministries of Internal Affairs, Trade, and Transport began to draft plans to get more Muslims to take Russian railroads and steamships in making the hajj. But how could Russia, an Orthodox Christian state, persuade its Muslim subjects to adhere to state-sanctioned routes in making the hajj, and abandon their traditional land routes? As Russian officials saw it, they had two options. One was to essentially force pilgrims onto the Black Sea routes by blocking access to the alternate land routes. Many officials in the Ministry of Internal Affairs liked this idea as an efficient way to curb the spread of cholera and other infectious diseases into the empire. But Russia's foreign consuls strongly advised against this approach. They warned that it would not work and might even provoke a Muslim backlash. Hajj pilgrims' land routes crossed a wide open Russian southern border that was thousands of miles long. The Russian consul in Baghdad made the important point that Russia was in many ways at a disadvantage in terms of knowledge of the terrain, and would therefore have to tread carefully. Although they were not known to Russian officials, the secret land routes that pilgrims used to get to Mecca were varied and well known among Muslims through word of mouth. The informal Muslim guides (*cavus*) who led caravans of hajj pilgrims from the Caucasus and Central Asia knew the terrain intimately, and were always able to forge new routes in response to prohibitions or contingencies, such as political unrest or war. Russia's Baghdad consul had seen evidence of this from his posting: hajj pilgrims continued to stream through the city in spite of government bans in years of cholera epidemics, and often without passports.[22]

The second option was to attract pilgrims to the Black Sea routes by improving travel conditions along the railroads and aboard Russian steamships, and offering superior services and incentives for using these modes of transport. The government had been trying this model since the 1880s, with limited success, to control patterns of peasant migration within the empire to Siberia, and channel it along a set route.[23] Russia's consuls in Baghdad and Jeddah, the two main sources on Russia's external hajj traffic, also recommended this approach of using "friendly measures" rather than force to persuade Muslims to take the Black Sea routes, through the establishment of an "open pilgrimage" along them. They suggested that the state introduce new domestic policies such as easier access to passports and special facilities, services, and discounts to make these the easier and more appealing routes. Only in this way, they argued in their reports to the Foreign Ministry in the 1890s, could Russia pull its Muslim pilgrims away from the land routes and onto state-supervised railroad and steamship routes.[24] The second option prevailed. Starting in the 1890s, the Ministry of Internal Affairs asked both companies to develop new service for hajj pilgrims through Russia's Black Sea ports.

ROPiT took the lead and began posting flyers in railroad stations across the Caucasus and Central Asia in 1899 advertising new "combination tickets" for Muslim pilgrims heading to Mecca. It sold these exclusively during hajj season, and offered pilgrims round-trip service from their home regions to Arabia and back. These tickets were designed to offer pilgrims more convenient, direct service. "Combination" referred to the merging of rail and steamship service: tickets were sold at a flat rate, for service on both means of transport, with the trains scheduled to sync with waiting steamships in Black Sea ports. They were modeled on similar ROPiT tickets for Orthodox pilgrims heading to Jerusalem. To accommodate a variety of itineraries, ROPiT ships were scheduled to leave from Batumi, Odessa, and Sevastopol.[25]

ROPiT officials had good reason to expect to profit handsomely from hajj transport. They had over a decade of experience transporting Orthodox pilgrims to Jerusalem. And ROPiT had set up a network of agencies across Ottoman lands, many in places where routes to Mecca and Jerusalem overlapped, such as Constantinople, Izmir, and Beirut. And theoretically the hajj should have been easier to organize than the Orthodox pilgrimage: it was performed once a year at a set time, making it highly predictable, and its obligatory nature made it reasonable to expect consistently high numbers of pilgrims. ROPiT had also wisely created its new hajj service by building upon existing Muslim networks, and recruiting Muslims active in the hajj industry in Russia's Black Sea ports to work as its agents. In Odessa, for example, it hired the city's mullah, Sabirzhan Safarov, as its broker. As the leading Muslim official in the city,

Safarov had been working for years with foreign steamship companies to organize transport for hajj pilgrims. He had the know-how that ROPiT needed to get its service started, and also claimed to have connections to Muslim communities that would allow him to advertise this new service. ROPiT hired him to recruit pilgrims to its ships in exchange for a percentage of each ticket he helped sell.[26]

But while ROPiT's service promised hajj pilgrims comfort and speed, it glossed over many logistical and cultural issues. ROPiT could not have been expected to know about conditions along the railroads, or to have the capacity to deal with them. The Ministry of Internal Affairs, however, was well aware of the hajj pilgrims' problems on the railroads, from decades of reports from governors across the empire. It had a good sense of the scale of the hajj, and the multiple problems associated with it, as with any form of mass human movement, especially one involving mainly poor people, inexperienced with travel. The ministry was naïve to think that ROPiT's new service alone could entice pilgrims to these routes.

Global histories often portray the modern shift of hajj traffic away from traditional land routes and onto railroads and steamships as sudden, total, and permanent.[27] But in fact the situation was not so simple. The flow of hajj traffic persisted along the old land routes well into the modern era, waxing and waning for many reasons. In Russia, this had a lot to do with poor travel conditions along Russia's railroads. Russia's railroads were notoriously unregulated and uncomfortable, and the trans-Caucasian and trans-Caspian lines—those created in the 1880s across the Caucasus and Central Asia, and used by most Muslim pilgrims—were no exception.

For Russia's Muslim pilgrims, the vast majority of whom spoke no Russian and were poor, illiterate, and traveling long distance for the first time in their lives, the journey along these routes could be exceedingly difficult, even frightening and dangerous. Piecing together firsthand accounts of the railroads gives a general sense of what this experience was like for Muslim pilgrims, and the unique difficulties they faced compared to their Orthodox counterparts.

Some hajj pilgrims complained of being harassed by "infidels" along their routes through Russia. In a memoir of his railroad journey from Central Asia to the Black Sea, one Turkestani hajj pilgrim described an awful scene in the Rostov railway station, where the local Russians mocked pilgrims for their turbans and for praying openly in the station, and a fight broke out with the conductor when the pilgrims could not communicate to him their destination. The police arrived and locked up the hajj pilgrims in an empty room in the station.[28]

Figure 3.1. View of the Merv station along the trans-Caspian railway. 1899. (General Research Division, The New York Public Library, Astor, Lenox, and Tilden Foundations)

Thieves abounded on the trans-Caucasus line, according to a Persian notable named Hosayn Farahani who rode the line in 1885 to get to Mecca. He was part of a new trend of Persians taking a more circuitous route to Mecca through the Caucasus and the Black Sea, lured by promises of speed and comfort on the new railroads and steamships. He was shocked by much of what he experienced along Russia's railroad across the Caucasus. He complained of the uncouth and drunken Russians he met along the way, from Baku to Batumi. He found the ride to be something of a shock culturally, and was dismayed by how unaccommodating the railroads were to Muslim religious customs and cultural norms. The rail cars were not sex segregated, and men and women, Muslims and "infidels," sat side by side. The train lacked clean, fresh water on board for drinking and ablutions. Farahani described with disgust how the only drinking water on board was in a huge barrel, made impure by non-Muslims scooping from it with their dirty cups.[29]

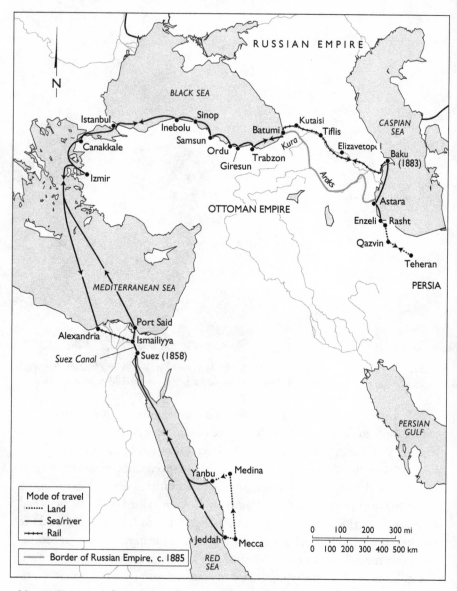

Map 5. Hajj route through Russian lands followed by Persian subject Hosayn Farahani, 1885–1886

Along the trans-Caspian line, a military railroad manned entirely by soldiers, things were not much better. Terrifying, whip-wielding Cossacks walked the platforms at stops to keep order. Their "principal duty," according to a British observer named George Dobson, who traveled the line in 1888, seemed to be to shout at Muslims who jumped off the train to fill their water pitchers from tubs sunk into the ground, or to perform their ablutions at the station's fountain. Those who did not heed their shouts to hurry back onto the train were simply "thrashed over the head."[30] This line was built largely across desert, where flash floods and sandstorms were common. Trains were often delayed, either because floods had washed away parts of tracks, or because locomotives' engines were gummed up with sand. Stations were not always located near stops. Inconveniently, the station for Uzun Ada (the original Caspian Sea terminus for the line) lay a quarter mile away from the landing place for steamships, so passengers had to "trudge ankle-deep through the hot sand to get to

Figure 3.2. Geok-tepe station along the trans-Caspian railway. 1899. (General Research Division, The New York Public Library, Astor, Lenox, and Tilden Foundations)

the platform."[31] Provisions were also scarce along the way. Most stations had a buffet run by Armenians, selling warm seltzer, lemonade, beer, wine, rye bread, hard-boiled eggs, and cucumbers. But only at the half-dozen larger stations, Dobson complained, could a "well-served substantial meal" be gotten. At a station called Peski (Sands) two railroad cars propped in the sand, with ladders up to the doors, served as a restaurant and kitchen.[32]

Having suffered numerous indignities along Russia's railroads, hajj pilgrims faced further difficulties upon their arrival in Odessa, Sevastopol, and other ports. Many complained about the government's new sanitary facilities, seemingly expressly for Muslims. At these new facilities in Black Sea ports Muslims were subjected to medical examinations that at best humiliated them, and at worst delayed them, causing them to miss the hajj rituals in Mecca. On the quay in Odessa and other Black Sea ports, hajj pilgrims would be separated from the Orthodox, and subjected to "disinfection," which meant different things at different times—it could involve being forced into a steam-disinfection chamber and having one's belongings seized and doused with foul-smelling disinfection powder. Or it could mean a rough and cursory examination on the

Figure 3.3. Odessa, view of the quarantine port. Early 1900s. (Author's collection)

quay, before boarding a steamship bound for the Red Sea.[33] It was also not lost on Russia's Muslims that the Orthodox pilgrims who traveled alongside them were not subject to the same intrusive rituals of screening and examination in Russia's ports. Several Muslims, in their written accounts of the hajj, noted bitterly the division of Muslim from Orthodox pilgrims on the quay in Odessa, and saw anti-Muslim and discriminatory overtones in medical screening.[34]

Firsthand descriptions from the early twentieth century capture the disorientation and misery that many Muslims experienced as part of new medical inspection and disinfection procedures in Russia's Black Sea ports. One account, by a Russian journalist on the ground in Sevastopol during hajj season that year, described how police forced a large crowd of angry pilgrims from Central Asia to line up on the quay for examination before they boarded the ship. None of these pilgrims spoke Russian, the ship's horn was blaring in the background, and the scene was chaotic. There were only three doctors for nearly 2,000 pilgrims; the doctors were overwhelmed and rough with the pilgrims, rushing to examine them all in just an hour and a half. The medical examination consisted of the doctors asking pilgrims, one by one, in Russian, "Do you feel well?" Any sign of fatigue or illness, pilgrims knew, could get them yanked from the line and barred from entry onto the waiting ship. And so the sick tried to conceal their illnesses, and others refused to answer the questions and just kept moving, with overwhelmed doctors letting them slip past.[35] While thousands of Muslims were taking Russia's railroads to get to Mecca by the 1880s and 1890s, many continued to avoid them. And Russian officials suspected, no doubt correctly, that rumors of chaotic scenes like this reached Muslims by word of mouth, frightened them, and kept them traveling the old land routes.

Unsurprisingly, given these problems along the railroads, ROPiT's hajj tickets sold poorly. It sold only a couple thousand tickets a year from 1899 to 1901. In the end, it was stuck with piles of unsold ticket books for hajj pilgrims.[36] ROPiT's chairman would later say that this was a result of the perceived high cost of ROPiT's combination tickets. Overall the round-trip tickets were cheaper than what pilgrims paid, all told, to make the multileg round-trip journey. But the lump sum seemed large to them, he argued, and deterred many from buying the tickets. Price may indeed have been a factor, but it seems likely that the cultural issues and logistical problems discussed above also played a key role. Another issue that ROPiT had not anticipated surely also contributed to poor sales. The combination tickets, which offered fast, nonstop, direct service between the Black and Red seas, did not fit typical multistop itineraries between Russia and Mecca.

Два мусульманина — паломника,
возвращающіеся изъ Мекки въ Ташкентъ.
За отсутствіемъ средствъ, онипробираются
изъ Одессы въ Ташкентъ пѣшкомъ. Сни-
мокъ сдѣланъ на ст „Одесса-Застава".
(Фот.-люб. М. Я. Сидорчукъ).

Figure 3.4. Two Central Asian hajj pilgrims at the Odessa train station, on their way home from Mecca. The caption in Russian reads: "Two Muslim Pilgrims returning from Mecca to Tashkent. For lack of funds, they will go on foot from Odessa to Tashkent." 1913. (*Odesskiia novosti*)

There was still another factor that probably contributed to ROPiT's poor sale of tickets to hajj pilgrims in 1899 and the early 1900s. Oddly, the Ministry of Internal Affairs, while encouraging ROPiT to get involved in hajj transport, also introduced measures that worked against ROPiT's new service. Every year between 1897 and 1900, Russia's ministers of internal affairs, I. L. Goremykin and D. S. Sipiagin, had announced a ban on the hajj, because of cholera outbreaks in Arabia.[37] By all accounts, these bans did not stop the flow of hajj traffic out of Russia, but only pushed more Muslims to the land routes, where they could slip across the border undetected. Adding to this, the Foreign Ministry effectively increased support for hajj pilgrims along the route through Afghanistan and India that the Ministry of Internal Affairs was trying to shut down. In 1900 the Foreign Ministry opened a Russian consulate in Bombay to intercept and assist its Turkestani Muslims passing through the port city. Citing Russia's "numerous hajj pilgrims" who traveled through Bombay as one of its "interests" in need of "protection" there, the ministry got permission from the British to open the consulate.[38] The diplomatic record shows that this institution was partially conceived as an intelligence outpost to keep Russia informed about goings-on along the border between Russian-ruled Turkestan and British India. In secret instructions, the Foreign Ministry ordered the Bombay consul general, V. O. Klemm, to interrogate the "large numbers of Muslim pilgrims and traders" coming down through Afghanistan and northwest India from Russian-ruled Turkestan, and to cultivate among them "reliable correspondents" and "intelligence agents."[39] Officials in the Ministry of Internal Affairs were upset about the opening of the Bombay consulate. They argued that it undermined their efforts to centralize the hajj traffic, and that it was increasing the empire's exposure to deadly cholera. Klemm, in response, defended the consulate as an important strategic asset in Russia's ongoing competition with the British in Persia and Central Asia.[40] He urged the Foreign Ministry to increase services in Bombay for "the many poor pilgrims from Turkestan" who passed through, as a way of demonstrating "the benevolence of the Russian government" toward India's Muslims and of cultivating their allegiance. "Every 'friend' we make in the Muslim population in northern India will be a help to us," Klemm wrote to the Foreign Ministry in 1905.[41]

This is a perfect example of how a lack of centralized leadership complicated Russia's efforts to organize the hajj, and even resulted at times in tsarist officials working at cross-purposes with one another. It also suggests that the government was internally divided over the hajj, and that not every minister supported the idea of organizing it. This would not be surprising, given the unstable political situation in Russia, which was certain to cause rapid turnover in the leadership of the Ministry of Internal Affairs (two ministers would be killed by revolutionary assassins in this period, one in 1902, and another in 1904).

As ROPiT struggled to find ways to attract hajj pilgrims to its ships, the Ministry of Internal Affairs also asked the Volunteer Fleet to develop its own hajj service. The Volunteer Fleet ranked with ROPiT as one of Russia's leading maritime shipping companies. It had been founded in the 1870s through donations (hence its name), as a fleet to develop Russia's foreign trade, and was later nationalized by the government. It was under the authority of the Naval Ministry, and heavily subsidized by the government.[42] For decades it had been involved in passenger traffic, mainly transporting colonists, convicts, and troops to Russia's Far Eastern territories on the Pacific Ocean. Now, it too sought new opportunities for transporting hajj pilgrims and capturing revenues.[43]

It would have made a lot of sense for the Ministry of Internal Affairs to have ROPiT and the Volunteer Fleet collaborate to develop new hajj service. But for whatever reason, it did not do this. Instead the Volunteer Fleet developed service in direct competition with ROPiT. In the early 1900s Volunteer Fleet agents in Russia's Black Sea ports and abroad began to gather information on the possibility of entering the market for hajj transport, largely by looking at ROPiT's activities. On orders from the Committee of the Volunteer Fleet, its agents in Black Sea ports wrote a series of reports that answered basic questions about pilgrims' routes, the most popular Black Sea ports among Muslim pilgrims, the hajj calendar, pilgrims' itineraries, the kinds of ships they preferred to take, typical rates charged by steamships, and so on.[44]

Foreign Ministry officials were closely involved in helping the Volunteer Fleet develop service for hajj pilgrims. The ministry ordered the Russian ambassador in Constantinople to inform arriving hajj pilgrims of the superior services offered by the fleet's ships, essentially getting him to work as an agent of the fleet. And Russia's consul in Jeddah, V. V. Zimmerman, played a key role. He corresponded directly with members of the Committee of the Volunteer Fleet in St. Petersburg starting in the early 1900s, and urged them to develop new service for Muslim pilgrims from Russia's Black Sea ports. In 1901 the committee wrote to Zimmerman to assure him that its agents were researching the opportunities available to the fleet.[45]

Within a year, in 1902, the committee had gathered a picture of the situation in Russia's Black Sea ports from its agents there. They were not very optimistic about the opportunities. They had gathered extensive data on the hajj traffic by canvassing the ports and interviewing hajj pilgrims as they passed through, as well as various officials involved in organizing transport and other services for pilgrims. They found that about 18,000 hajj pilgrims would pass through Sevastopol and Batumi that year, and each would pay one hundred rubles for steamship service. In Sevastopol, the city's Ottoman consul and local mullahs largely controlled hajj transport. For the Volunteer Fleet to break into this market, agents noted, it would have to collaborate with a local company already organizing the transport. They also suggested that the fleet study the IOPS's services for Orthodox pilgrims. Agents noted that Odessa had much less hajj traffic than the other two ports (only about 800 to 2,000 pilgrims a year). The city had no infrastructure to support the hajj traffic, and the local mullah, Safarov, dominated the organization of this small-scale hajj transport. Finally, they noted that the Volunteer Fleet would have trouble competing for hajj pilgrims' business with ROPiT, which charged much lower rates.[46]

Zimmerman kept the pressure on the Volunteer Fleet. He wrote back to the committee, urging it to introduce service to replace the awful service that ROPiT was providing pilgrims. Writing from the vantage point of Jeddah, Zimmerman seems to have based this judgment on firsthand encounters with and eyewitness observation of pilgrims who arrived in Jeddah after taking ROPiT ships. Zimmerman reported that as many as 16,000 Russian hajj pilgrims passed through Jeddah every year, most of them having taken ROPiT ships to Alexandria, and from Suez, Egyptian steamers to Jeddah. Zimmerman reported that ROPiT was allowing pilgrims to stop in Constantinople for several days but doing nothing to protect them: they were fleeced mercilessly by their compatriots in the city, expat Tatar and Turkestani communities that had organized to prey on the traffic. The ROPiT ships were bad: they didn't have enough space, were poorly ventilated, filthy, and lacked adequate provisions. Pilgrims traveled for days without food. The ROPiT ships took pilgrims only as far as Alexandria, where pilgrims were greeted by local ROPiT agents (the one in Alexandria was a local Greek named Prasinos) who escorted them to the train station for passage from Alexandria to Suez. The train ride was hell: pilgrims were put on open platforms, and made to endure hot sun or punishing rains during the ten- to fifteen-day trip, which took a long time due to numerous stops. They next boarded "filthy, slow" ships from Suez to Jeddah. These ships were in constant danger of crashing; the English ship captains steering them were often drunk. Zimmerman told the committee that he had reported all of this to ROPiT in St. Petersburg, but it had done nothing to improve conditions for pilgrims.[47]

In 1903, Zimmerman urged the Volunteer Fleet to take the leading role in organizing hajj transport for Russia's Muslims. This made some practical sense, given that the fleet was looking for passengers to fill its ships. In 1903 the trans-Siberian railroad had opened, and the fleet had lost much of its passenger traffic to the new rail route.[48] Both Zimmerman and Russia's city-governor in Sevastopol pointed out that the fleet had ships standing idle in Sevastopol, and urged it to use them for transporting hajj pilgrims. In response to this "agitation," the fleet's committee relented. It ordered two of its ships returning empty from the Far East, the *Petersburg* and the *Saratov*, to pick up pilgrims on their way back through the Red Sea; as it happened, their return coincided with the end of the hajj rituals in Arabia, so the timing was right. Things did not go smoothly, however. The *Saratov* got tired of waiting for pilgrims in the port in Jeddah and left without them. The *Petersburg* took 2,000 on board, and then the problems began. There was a huge backup of ships in El-Tor for quarantine, and the *Petersburg* got delayed; it should have gotten from Jeddah to Odessa in one week, but instead it took three weeks.

In August 1903, the head of the Committee of the Volunteer Fleet, Rear-Admiral P. Iur'ev, wrote a long, exasperated letter to the Naval Ministry to explain why the fleet could not do as the Jeddah consul had proposed and organize Russia's hajj transport. "It is not possible to name all of the numerous reasons why" the fleet could not do this, he wrote, but he laid out the main ones. They were logistical and economical. The committee, he wrote, had "long ago come to the definitive conclusion" that it did not fit the "usual operations of the fleet in transporting passengers and freight to the Far East to also transport pilgrims." To send reserve ships filled with hajj pilgrims to the Red Sea was "completely absurd" from an economic standpoint: with their colossal navigational costs, without freight, and with deck passengers only for the return trip, and the need to pay, for each trip, around 30,000 rubles in fees for use of the canal, not including the fee per passenger, meant huge losses.[49] Iur'ev was pointing out what European officials elsewhere were also discovering: it was very difficult to profit from hajj transport, given the demands and complexities of the journey, and the added pressures of sanitary screening.[50] Not only did steamships need to pay high fees for passing through the Suez Canal, and risk long delays in quarantine, but there were complications because of the timing of the hajj.

The logistics of the hajj made it impossible for the Volunteer Fleet to make money from transporting pilgrims round-trip, Iur'ev insisted. Only steamships operating in the Red Sea could afford to do this: they picked up pilgrims in Suez (where they had gone by train from Alexandria), took them to Jeddah, and then back to Russia. They were much bigger than Volunteer Fleet ships, and could engage in local trade during the month-and-a-half wait for pilgrims to finish their rituals in Mecca and Medina.[51] As Iur'ev's letter made clear, Russia was at a disadvantage compared to other imperial powers, above all the British, who had trade networks and economic interests in and around the Red Sea that made hajj transport not only feasible but profitable for British shipping companies.

There was also the problem of the powerful syndicate that had existed in Jeddah since the 1880s, which controlled steamship service for hajj pilgrims. It blocked outsiders from transporting pilgrims.[52] The only way to get around the syndicate, Iur'ev explained, would be for the Volunteer Fleet to transport pilgrims who already had return tickets, as the Jeddah consul proposed. But the fleet could not possibly organize such a huge undertaking, Iur'ev objected. It would require selling and issuing tickets to Muslims all across the vast empire.

Iur'ev argued that transporting hajj pilgrims would require special steamships and hefty government subsidies, and the government should take it upon itself to organize the transport of pilgrims on Volunteer Fleet ships.[53]

CLEARLY the job of organizing the hajj was too great for the Volunteer Fleet or ROPiT to manage on its own, or even together. In 1903, then minister of internal affairs V. K. Pleve acknowledged as much. That year he submitted to the State Council a proposal titled "Temporary Rules for the Muslim Pilgrimage."[54] This was the first formal proposal for government involvement in the organization of the hajj. It was also the latest in a series of ministry initiatives to manage Russia's migrations by the introduction of new laws and policies.[55] It called for broad government patronage of the hajj, through incentives and privileges, and organization of services.

Pleve had been made minister of internal affairs in 1902, after serving in several other leading roles in the ministry, including head of the Police Department. From this work he would have been well aware that the hajj was an internal issue for the empire. And his concern for organizing the hajj no doubt was informed by a broader concern for imperial stability and the need to manage the various peoples of the empire. 1903, the year Pleve proposed the new "Temporary Rules for the Hajj," was also the year of the Kishinev Pogrom, one of the most deadly and destructive episodes of anti-Semitic violence in modern Russian and Jewish history—a sign of growing anti-Semitism in the empire. The pogrom revealed popular Russian intolerance for Jews, against a backdrop of upheaval and revolutionary violence in the empire. An assassin had killed Pleve's predecessor, Sipiagin; and Pleve would soon come to a similar end. In July 1904 socialist revolutionaries threw a bomb into Pleve's carriage in central St. Petersburg and killed him.[56]

Pleve is perhaps best known for repression of radical political groups, his resistance to liberal measures (which put him at odds with Witte many times), and his anti-Semitism.[57] But in this case we see him trying to ease Muslims' access to Mecca by way of the Black Sea routes: in effect, facilitating their cross-border movement and improving the conditions of their travel. His proposed rules tacitly acknowledged that conditions along the Black Sea routes needed improvement, and that more needed to be done to entice Muslim pilgrims to use them. To do this, Pleve proposed three measures.

The first was that Russia provide free, easily accessible passports to its Muslims who wanted to make the hajj. This was a special privilege that had also been extended to Orthodox pilgrims, to encourage more of them to go to Jerusalem, and to make the journey legally, with the support of the IOPS. In the case of the hajj, Pleve hoped it would put a stop to illegal pilgrimage. Both the Baghdad and the Jeddah consuls had reported that most of Russia's hajj pilgrims traveled abroad without passports, mainly because it was inconvenient and costly to get them.[58] Laws introduced in the 1840s, and still on the books, required hajj pilgrims (as well as their Orthodox counterparts) to obtain passports only in Russia's Black Sea ports. This was supposed to prevent them from "wandering" aimlessly in the empire, under the aegis of pilgrimage. But it had become a hardship for many, as it added layers of bureaucracy to the pilgrimage, complicated and slowed down their journey, and surely pushed many to avoid the Black Sea routes altogether.

By authorizing Russian officials across the empire and at various levels (governors, regional heads, city-governors, and district heads) to issue passports to hajj pilgrims, Pleve hoped to end illegal pilgrimage and nudge pilgrims to the Black Sea routes. Recent work has explored how Russia, like other modernizing states, embraced passports in the nineteenth century as a tool for documenting and policing populations, and controlling mobility.[59] Here we see how, and to what ends, the state tried to use passports as an instrument for policing Muslim pilgrims. Pleve proposed free passports largely to allow Russian officials to compile more detailed data on patterns of Russia's hajj traffic. The "Temporary Rules" stipulated that Russian officials would keep detailed logbooks with lists of Muslims who applied for passports, including information on their places of origin, age, social estate, and intended route to Mecca. All of this information would also be recorded on the passport itself; the third page of the passport would provide space for the official to record the detailed itinerary, as well as a list of places that the passport holder intended to visit along the way. At the same time, Russian officials were to use the face-to-face encounter with Muslims to influence their route. Together with passports, officials were supposed to give pilgrims a copy of "Temporary Rules," printed in both Russian and Turkic languages, with instructions from the ministry regarding sanitary rules necessary to observe during travel; the locations of Russian consular representatives in Ottoman and Persian lands; and the penalties for violating quarantine laws.[60]

Pleve also proposed the recruitment of Muslim leaders to help the government organize the hajj. There was nothing new about Russia co-opting Muslim intermediaries to help with the work of governing the empire's Muslim populations.[61] In this case, Pleve was proposing that Russia's Muslim clergy be asked to appoint trusted leaders to organize large groups. The idea here was to concentrate pilgrims into large groups that would depart at scheduled times, to make the hajj easier for the state to manage. At the same time, these Muslim leaders would help ensure that pilgrims made the hajj legally, by getting passports, and adhering to their intended routes. This proposed measure is interesting for what it reveals about the ministry's reluctance to put Russian officials in charge of the hajj and hajj pilgrims, and its goal instead to recruit Muslim leaders to put a Muslim face on a state project. Correspondence suggests complex reasons for this plan: Russian officials did not want to anger Muslims by appearing to intervene in their rituals, nor did they want to upset the Russian Orthodox Church by appearing to favor Islam and Muslim pilgrims.

Finally, Pleve called for increased and coordinated involvement of Russian officials across the empire in the organization of the hajj. This activity was to take place to some extent behind the scenes—again, to avoid the appearance of government intervention. To this end, Russian governors and officials under their authority were to arrange food, lodging, and medical aid for hajj pilgrims. They were also to coordinate with one another to ease pilgrims' travel by forwarding lists of pilgrims to officials in other regions, to forewarn them of their arrival and allow them time to arrange provisions and services. They were also to contact railroad authorities and alert them to the impending arrival of crowds.[62]

Pleve's plan was ambitious if also vague on how exactly it could be implemented. How would Muslim leaders be identified? Why would they perform these duties on behalf of the government? And how exactly could pilgrims be made to travel the routes dictated by the government? Pleve's proposed rules sparked immediate resistance from all parts of the government. The members of KOMOCHUM rejected them outright, on the grounds that they would stimulate greater hajj traffic and increase the sanitary threat to the empire.[63] The minister of justice, for his part, objected that the rules violated existing passport laws, and so also rejected them.[64]

The strongest objections came from Russia's foreign minister, V. N. Lamsdorf. He objected that Pleve's proposed rules amounted to government sponsorship of the hajj, and special "privileges" for Muslims. He dissented that the measures, which basically aimed to make travel through Russian lands less expensive and easier with the support of special services, might give Muslims the "false impression" that the government wanted to sponsor and encourage the hajj. He also objected that Pleve's rules went beyond simple sanitary issues to offer Muslim pilgrims privileges that not even Orthodox pilgrims enjoyed. Expressing a concern that was widespread among officials, if not universal, the minister objected to any measures that might increase the numbers of hajj pilgrims, for fear of increasing "fanaticism" among Russia's Muslims. Citing a cliché of the time, one that appears to have little empirical foundation, Lamsdorf warned that the hajj radicalized Muslims, and that they returned to the empire "hostile to everything Russian" and more intent on "religious-political isolation." Returning hajjis had influence over other Muslims of a kind that was not desirable from the point of view of the government.[65] Lamsdorf's objections illuminate two of the most difficult issues tsarist officials faced in trying to organize the hajj: the need to do it without damaging the prestige and standing of the Orthodox Church in the empire, and the fear that organization might look like encouragement, and increase the volume of hajj traffic, which would create even bigger problems for the government.

Unsurprisingly, the State Council rejected Pleve's proposal, on the grounds that it would give hajj pilgrims the same privileges the state offered its Orthodox pilgrims, and because it "looked like encouraging Muslim pilgrimage."[66] This was in fact what Pleve had sought to avoid in designing the rules, particularly by suggesting that Muslim leaders be co-opted. In fact, Ministry of Internal Affairs officials would later describe the proposal as an attempt to "provide Muslims themselves with power by giving them the right to help their co-tribesmen" and without establishing "protective measures for the pilgrimage itself."[67] In response to the State Council's rejection, Pleve revised his proposal, resubmitting a much stripped-down version of his rules. The State Council passed these in June 1903.[68] The new rules are noteworthy for two reasons. First, they did not include any special privileges or incentives for Muslims. And second, they indicated a shift from suasion toward coercion, with the state essentially trying to dictate pilgrims' routes and forbid travel along the land routes. This, in turn, suggests that some officials, Pleve among them, had begun to embrace a different, forceful kind of model for organization.

The 1903 measure passed by the State Council introduced special "pilgrim passports" for Muslims heading to Mecca as well as Mesopotamia and Persia (with their important Shi'i holy sites). There was no mention of a reduced fee. These passports would be small booklets with pages in which Russian officials were supposed to record detailed itineraries of pilgrims' planned routes, based on what pilgrims told them upon applying for a passport, and provide stamps proving that pilgrims had undergone sanitary inspection at border checkpoints. Russia's governors were required from now on to issue such passports to all Muslim pilgrims.

The new rules also set restrictions on hajj pilgrims' routes. They required Muslim pilgrims to return to Russia only through those Black and Caspian ports and border spots mandated by the Ministry of Internal Affairs, all of

Figure 3.5. Hajj passport. Created in 1903 by the Ministry of Internal Affairs for Muslims making the pilgrimage to Mecca. In five languages: Russian, French, Persian, Tatar, and Ottoman Turkish. (Courtesy of kasanof.livejournal. com)

which were equipped with medical-inspection stations to screen them for disease before their reentry into the empire. The minister announced approved points of reentry: on the Black Sea, the Feodosiia quarantine and Batumi maritime medical-inspection station; on the Caspian Sea, the Baku maritime medical-inspection stations; and on the border of the trans-Caspian region with Persia, the medical-inspection station in Gaudan. Finally, the new rules required governors to inspect pilgrims' passports upon their return. Those found to be without a stamp from border sanitary officials were to be subjected to medical screening by local authorities.[69] In November 1903 Pleve sent out a circular to all governors in the Russian Empire that informed them of the new laws governing Muslim pilgrimage, and ordered them to apply them.[70]

✦✦✦

HAVING established new laws that aimed to organize and document the hajj traffic along the Black Sea routes, Pleve next returned to the important issue of transport. In late 1903 he created a special commission to discuss the organization of transport of Muslim pilgrims to the Hejaz on Russian steamships. The commission was chaired by the ministry's Medical Department, indicating its sanitary concerns with relation to the pilgrimage.[71] The commission met, and the members agreed on a number of issues. One was that government assistance should not involve force or restrictions. They agreed that local Russian authorities should help steamship companies advertise their services, and that railroad and steamship companies should once again coordinate to link their services and provide direct travel. This, again, amounted to covert government intervention that put transport officials in front of government efforts to organize the hajj.[72]

At a conference convened by the Ministry of Internal Affairs in 1904, tsarist officials gathered to draft plans to organize the hajj. The conference brought together representatives of Russian railroads, ROPiT, and the Volunteer Fleet, as well as the Ministries of Trade and Internal Affairs. A concrete goal laid out by the 1904 conference was to concentrate Russia's hajj traffic on the railroads and through Russia's Black Sea ports. While officials widely agreed on this goal, they disagreed on how best to achieve it. The records of this conference reveal the extent to which officials continued to disagree on a way forward. The group acknowledged that as many as 10,000 Muslims made the hajj from Russia every year. Most took Turkish, Egyptian, British, or Greek ships. Tsarist officials lamented that the sea transport of hajj pilgrims was "passing by" Russia's steamship companies, just as the transport of Jewish émigrés to America had.[73] The Ministry of Internal Affairs proposed trying combination tickets again. But many officials from Russia's state railroads opposed this. They said it had not worked in 1899, and that they could not give out any more discounts (they already gave discounts to Orthodox pilgrims and the blind, among others).[74] But officials realized that something had to be done: as things stood, the market rates were not attracting hajj pilgrims to the railroads or to ROPiT's service.

The government responded by providing a generous subvention to its railways and steamship enterprises to subsidize hajj transport. In 1904 it created a tariff for the transport of hajj pilgrims that set an artificially low rate for tickets on Russian railroads and steamships. This tariff was not widely advertised, doubtless out of concern about a backlash such as that provoked by Pleve's original measures, since it amounted to a secret incentive granted by the government to Muslim pilgrims.

A 1904 ministry circular to Russia's governors revealed comprehensive and ambitious plans for the hajj transport. It also revealed that the ministry had joined forces with the Ministry of Transport to address many of the logistical issues along the railways. The circular announced special seasonal hajj transport, with supplemental rolling stock to accommodate the anticipated crowds. Hajj pilgrims traveling in large groups by way of the Black Sea would be transported in special cars outfitted with green "Hejaz" signs to make them easy to spot. Inside, the cars would be outfitted with schedules and information about which stations provided hot water, all of this in Russian, Turkic, and Persian. Every year before hajj season, Russia's rail lines would be responsible for confirming with the Ministry of Transport their need for additional rolling stock, their preparedness, and their adherence to government regulations.

The results of these measures were immediate and dramatic. In 1904 ROPiT announced regular, seasonal service for hajj pilgrims aboard "Hejaz Steamships," providing direct service between the Black Sea ports of Sevastopol and Batumi to the Red Sea port of Jeddah. ROPiT also built a *khadzhilar-sarai* in Sevastopol—a full-service lodging house for hajj pilgrims on the pier, complete with a prayer room (*masjid*), shop, kitchen, and sleeping quarters, and served by a special railway line.[75] It advertised this service widely in Muslim newspapers across the empire, and in brightly colored posters hung in railroad stations across the empire's Muslim regions and Black Sea ports.

A poster advertising ROPiT's new service gives a sense of what it offered. Printed in four languages (Russian, Turkish, Persian, and Sart, the Turkic lingua franca in Turkestan), this large poster on bright green tissue paper would

Figure 3.6. ROPiT advertisement in Turkestan's main newspaper, offering "Hejaz steamship" service for hajj pilgrims, by way of Sevastopol. 1910. (*Turkistan wilayatining gazeti*)

have been pasted up on the side of a building (in the early twentieth century the poster emerged as a new genre, and Russian towns were plastered with colorful advertising signs and announcements). At the top was a sketch of a steamship flying a flag with a crescent moon and star, over which was written in nineteenth-century Tatar, and in the Arabic script, "Hejaz Steamships" (Hijaz vapurları). It described these as "established for the comfort and convenience of esteemed hajjis" and specially outfitted and furnished to suit their "traditions." It announced that that year (1904–5) ROPiT would be running three Hejaz steamships from Sevastopol to the Hejaz and back, and one from Batumi.

Clearly reflecting an effort to accommodate pilgrims' itineraries while also keeping pilgrims under state supervision and control, the poster noted that the ships would make a five-day stop in Constantinople. There, pilgrims would be allowed to leave their belongings on board, disembark and visit the city, and come back at night to sleep on the ship. To appeal to a wide range of plans and schedules, ROPiT offered varied service on four ships: the *Tsaritsa*, the *Kornilov*, the *Iunon*, and the *Odessa*. Two would provide one-way service, and the other two would offer return service. The ships would depart between December 1 and 25, and make stops along the way not only in Constantinople, but also in Izmir, Beirut, Jaffa, Alexandria, Port Said, Suez, Yanbu, and Jeddah, with pickups on the way back from Yanbu and Jeddah. The trip from the Black Sea to the Red Sea would take about two and a half weeks, and the return trip only ten to twelve days. The poster gave detailed information on departure and return times, and the return itinerary: from Yanbu and Jeddah, stopping at El-Tor, and back to Feodosiia. Those wishing to leave ahead of the scheduled Hejaz steamships, in order to spend more time in Constantinople, Beirut, Jaffa or Alexandria, could buy tickets in November on ROPiT postal ships for the cost of a "pilgrim ticket," and could then join the Hejaz steamship when it arrived in those ports to continue on to the Hejaz.

On board, special services for Muslims would be extensive. The ship would have a tea- and coffee-seller (*çaycı-kahveci*) and space for performing ablutions. Free hot and cold water would be offered five times a day. The ship would also sell hot, affordable food (native dishes such as lamb and rice pilaf) as well as *ihram*, the simple white garments that pilgrims must don to perform the hajj.[76] Ticket prices were 250 rubles for first class, 200 rubles for second class, and one hundred rubles for third class. In each class pilgrims would be provided with comfortable accommodations, including a berth, free cold and hot water, a hot plate for cooking, permission to use a grill to cook hot food, and space for washing.

Disembarking in Jeddah, pilgrims could leave their baggage and money on board while they performed the hajj.

"For the convenience of pilgrims," the ROPiT poster announced, "direct tickets to the Hejaz" were being sold in railroad stations across the Russian Empire—in Cheliabinsk, Tiumen, Omsk, Petropavlovsk, Tomsk, Moscow, Riazan, Kazan, Nizhnii Novgorod, Tambov, Ufa, Samara, Simbirsk, Penza, Batraki, Perm, Orenburg, and Tsaritsyn—as well as in stations along the Central Asian railroads. Ticket holders riding in both directions would be offered separate train cars for hajj pilgrims. Round-trip tickets were heavily discounted. For more information, pilgrims could contact the ROPiT agency in Sevastopol or the office of the newspaper *Perevodchik* in Bahcesarai.[77]

If these advertisements promised superior speed, comfort, and affordability for hajj pilgrims, Russia had other goals as well. One was to revise pilgrims' itineraries and prevent them from making stops along the way. The advertisements listed several stops, but in fact ROPiT's ships often passed through Constantinople without stopping, angering many pilgrims intent on visiting holy sites and mosques in the city. Some of these were foreigners who deliberately followed itineraries through Russia to visit the Ottoman capital, and were outraged to be prevented from visiting it. In 1906 a group of Kashgar hajj pilgrims from the Qing Empire complained to the Ottoman government that the Russian government was not letting them travel the routes they wanted, blocking them from

Figure 3.7. ROPiT advertisement in Turkestan's main newspaper, offering "esteemed hajj pilgrims" service aboard "Hejaz steamships" from Sevastopol. 1910. (*Turkistan wilayatining gazeti*)

visiting Constantinople and interfering with their religious rituals. The group wrote that in order to "increase their devotion and loyalty to the caliphate," they wanted to visit Constantinople on their way to Mecca via the Black Sea. But Russian officials were very careful about taking pilgrims from Odessa, Sevastopol, and other Russian ports and sending them on steamships straight to Jeddah. And on the return they stopped only in Yanbu, Jeddah, and Jaffa, where they met guides who were interested in them only as passengers, not as religious pilgrims. Russian steamship company agents in these ports were also doing the same, using force to send pilgrims directly to Sevastopol, for the sake of order. The Kashgar pilgrims also complained that the agents did not allow them to rest, and that people had been complaining about this for a long time. The pilgrims objected that without any formal political relations, the Russian consul was putting visas in their passports and holding onto them for weeks, leaving the pilgrims begging outside of the embassy gates for the return of their passports.[78]

THE full effects of Russia's organizational efforts were apparent during the hajj season of 1907–8. In Sevastopol a Russian-language newspaper captured a ceremony on the pier to send off the first of that year's Hejaz steamships. ROPiT's Sevastopol agent, A. I. Mlinarich, had organized the ceremony. It began with a Muslim prayer service led by a naval *akhund* (Islamic official) by the name of Zamaletinovyi, and held just outside the khadzhilar-sarai.[79] Attending the ceremony, in addition to Mlinarich and Zamaletinovyi, were Muslims and non-Muslims involved in various aspects of the hajj: the Ottoman consul to Sevastopol, local police and officials from the city-governor's office, and a large group of hajj pilgrims. Afterward, Mlinarich invited his fellow officials to breakfast at a local hotel, while Zamaletinovyi ushered pilgrims into the lodging house for a ceremonial meal. Several days earlier, with the help of ROPiT and local sanitary officials, these pilgrims had undergone "disinfection" in preparation for the pilgrimage to Mecca, and in line with new international sanitary rules. Now they ate and relaxed in the lodging house, waiting to board the next steamship bound for Jeddah.[80]

In Odessa the effects were particularly visible and dramatic. Thanks to the opening of the Orenburg-Tashkent railroad line in 1906, which connected Tashkent directly by rail to Odessa, the city saw the largest hajj crowds ever in 1907. More than 10,000 hajj pilgrims arrived in Odessa over a period of three months, most of them from Central Asia.[81] Their numbers may well have been increased by the Volunteer Fleet's advertising efforts. In June 1907, just ahead of hajj season, the fleet had placed ads in Central Asia's major newspapers, announcing its new service. That fall, nearly all of the hajj pilgrims who passed through Odessa left for Arabia on Russian steamships, mainly those of the Volunteer Fleet.[82]

Figure 3.8. Volunteer Fleet advertisement for "Hejaz steamships." The text describes onboard accommodations for Muslims, including plenty of water, kitchens, and open space on deck to grill food. 1910. (*Turkistan wilayatining gazeti*)

Following ROPiT's lead, the Volunteer Fleet in 1907 had introduced its own direct service to Jeddah aboard Hejaz steamships that left mainly from Odessa. The Volunteer Fleet had done this largely on the advice of Russia's new Jeddah consul, who noted that there was no direct service from Odessa, and correctly predicted that the opening of the new Tashkent-Orenburg line would create a surge of hajj traffic through the city. He also reported that the Volunteer Fleet "had the best reputation among hajj pilgrims," and that ROPiT continued to provide awful service to pilgrims.[83] Among other things, he complained that ROPiT ships were "rejecting weak and feeble pilgrims," even if they didn't look sick. He described the experience in Jeddah as horrible for old and poor pilgrims.[84]

The Volunteer Fleet carefully planned its new hajj service with the help of locals involved in the small-scale hajj industry in Odessa, getting their advice and relying on their expertise and connections. Two individuals were especially important. One was Safarov, who had been working for ROPiT on hajj transport for several years. And the other was Petr Gurzhi, a local retired ship captain, who had also been involved in the hajj industry for years, chartering foreign steamships for pilgrims. The fleet invited both men to St. Petersburg to confer with officials on the creation of new hajj service. During that visit, Gurzhi also conferred with the Ministry of Trade about the organization of railroad service for pilgrims. Among other things, Safarov suggested that the fleet advertise its new service widely in Muslim newspapers across the empire. Safarov signed an agreement with the Volunteer Fleet to "spread among pilgrims" information about the services offered by the fleet for hajj pilgrims. In return, the fleet promised him a commission of ten percent of the cost of each ticket he sold.[85]

In the fall of 1907, Gurzhi offered his services to the Volunteer Fleet with a comprehensive plan for that year's hajj season. His plan covered the sale of railroad and steamship tickets, lodging in Odessa, and efforts to get as many pilgrims as possible onto the fleet's ships. He hired Safarov to work with him, and, with permission from Odessa's city-governor, I. N. Tolmachev, created a company called the Central Odessa Office for Shipping Muslim Pilgrims to Jeddah by Steamship.[86] The Volunteer Fleet accepted his proposal.

Working together with Safarov, Tolmachev, local hoteliers, city sanitary officials, and both the Volunteer Fleet and ROPiT, Gurzhi organized lodging and transport for the more than 10,000 pilgrims who came through Odessa that fall. His plan was modeled in part on the Ottoman example. He reserved a certain number of free tickets for the poor, "just like the sultan does."[87] He arranged for hajj pilgrims to stay in a cluster of low-end hotels in the center of the city, halfway between the train station and the port: the New York and the Bellevue, the National and the Strasbourg.[88] In these hotels, the office's two doctors, Dr. Chorba and Dr. Balteron, visited pilgrims daily to examine them, and wrote daily reports on pilgrims' health.[89] Gurzhi organized a team of Muslim guides to help pilgrims navigate the city and accompany them by ship to Mecca.[90] He also wrote up a list of rules and instructions and sent them out to local officials involved in hajj transport in Odessa: the Persian and Ottoman consuls general; leading customs and port officials; police officials; the Odessa mullah Safarov; and the Ministry of Foreign Affairs agent in Odessa.[91]

At the end of December 1907, with the organization of hajj transport finished for that year's season, Gurzhi sent Tolmachev a final report on how things had gone. He reported great success overall. The sanitary measures had been thorough, and there had been no cholera outbreaks. His office had registered more than 10,000 pilgrims, and transported nearly all of them on ROPiT and Volunteer Fleet ships (an overflow of 560 had been sent on a Greek ship). Russian steamship companies had made nearly a million rubles in profits. His central office in Odessa had set up outposts all over Central Asia, the Volga region, the Caucasus, and Black Sea region. And with Safarov's help, the office had organized proper burials of the dead in the city's Muslim cemetery.[92]

And yet, at the same time, Gurzhi noted that a great deal more needed to be done to bring the hajj under state control and to solve the various problems and disorders that surrounded it. There had not been enough Russian steamships or doctors to accommodate the crowds that year. A centralized facility for hajj pilgrims was desperately needed in Odessa, to make arrangements easier logistically and to contain disease. Gurzhi proposed a "Pilgrimage-Sanitary *Khadzhikhane* (Lodging House)," a 3,000-person facility he envisioned building down in the port, near the standing point for steamships headed to the Red Sea.[93]

By the end of the 1907–8 hajj season it was clear that the government had not succeeded in forging an imperial hajj route or in organizing the hajj. The government had not achieved a monopoly on hajj transport or services, and many pilgrims continued to travel alternate land routes. Disorder and problems persisted along Russia's railroads. Much to the embarrassment of the government, Russian press coverage in early 1908 described the just-ended hajj season as disastrous by many measures, including a cholera outbreak in Russia that inspired more fear about the hajj. Officials in Russia's Black Sea ports drafted emergency rules for quarantining hajj pilgrims in the event of future outbreaks.

Some petitioned the Ministry of Internal Affairs, asking that their port be closed to hajj traffic.[94] Newspaper articles especially detailed the problems Russia's Muslims faced along the new Tashkent-Orenburg rail line.[95]

The government was well aware of the persistent problems of the hajj. In 1907, while hajj season was still ongoing, Russia's minister of internal affairs, P. A. Stolypin, oversaw the creation of new rules to govern the transport of hajj pilgrims between the empire and Arabia. Now more than ever the government was determined to organize the hajj. A revolution had broken out in the empire in 1905, set off by widespread, if uncoordinated, uprisings against the government. Tsar Nicholas II had been forced to issue the October Manifesto, which promised broad civil liberties and a constitution for Russia, and marked the end of absolute monarchy. In spite of these concessions, revolutionary activity and upheaval persisted, and the regime worried about the stability of the empire in the face of growing resistance. It also worried more than ever before about the hajj as an unregulated phenomenon, and focused with renewed energy on streamlining the traffic along the Black Sea routes.

Figure 3.9. Samarkand railway station, end of hajj season, c. 1900. Crowds of relatives and friends gathered on the platform to greet a train carrying *hajjis* returned from Mecca. (*Hac, Kutsal Yolculuk* [Istanbul: Denizler Kitabevi 2014])

To this end, in 1907 Stolypin drafted, and got the Senate to ratify, "Rules on the Transport by Ship of Muslim Pilgrims from Black Sea Ports to the Hejaz and Back." These rules described the cramped and unsanitary conditions pilgrims had long been suffering aboard steamships. The new rules required that ships provide adequate drinking water and food, access to clean toilets (at least one toilet per hundred passengers, and sex segregated), an onboard disinfection room and fully equipped medical clinic, ventilation and regular cleaning of below-deck space, and at least 1.5 square meters of space per pilgrim.[96]

Besides imposing new restrictions and requirements on steamship companies, the 1907 rules greatly expanded the role of Russian officials in Odessa in regulating hajj traffic, by establishing the city as the main port of exit for Muslim pilgrims leaving Russia (Feodosiia, which already had an established quarantine system, was made the port of return), and creating a Port Pilgrimage Commission in Odessa. Headed by Tolmachev, the commission included local sanitary, trade, and customs officials and Russian steamship company representatives, and its basic duties were to set ticket prices on steamships carrying Muslim pilgrims, ensure their sanitary screening in the port, inspect and issue certificates to steamships approved for hajj transport, and appoint doctors to hajj ships.[97]

Perhaps most significantly, the new rules limited the ports hajj pilgrims could use to depart the empire each year. They stipulated that, in consultation with the Ministry of Trade, the Ministry of Internal Affairs would name the designated ports of departure in the Black Sea and announce them six months ahead of the scheduled hajj rituals, in newspapers across the empire, so that pilgrims could plan their journey.[98] The 1907 rules were the first of two major measures that Stolypin would introduce to finally organize the hajj in Russia. His next move would be to appoint a hajj leader for the empire.

4

The Hajj and Religious Politics after 1905

In 1908, Russia's minister of internal affairs, P. A. Stolypin, appointed a hajj director for the empire. This was a major turning point in Russia's efforts to organize the hajj. The task of the new position, as described in the ministry's announcement to fifty-three governors and city-governors across Russia, was a formidable one: to "solve the many existing problems" associated with the hajj, and organize it inside Russia. The tsar had made the organization of the hajj a government priority since the late nineteenth century, which resulted in the creation of new laws, institutions, and commissions. But never before had the government put a single institution or individual in charge of the pilgrimage. No less strikingly, Stolypin appointed a Muslim to this important job—a Tashkent native named Said Gani Saidazimbaev.[1]

A major political figure in late imperial Russia, Stolypin was both prime minister and internal minister from 1907 to 1911. He is best known for cracking down on revolutionaries and introducing peasant land reforms to stabilize the empire after the Russian Revolution of 1905. He also tried to increase government support for Russia's non-Orthodox faiths. In so doing, Stolypin was following through on promises for reform issued by the tsar in the October Manifesto, following the revolution. Among other things, the manifesto promised greater religious equality in the empire, and the creation of a legislative body (the Duma) with multiconfessional representation. And as prime minister, Stolypin would push a broad program for religious reform in 1908 and 1909, bringing before the Council of Ministers (the upper chamber of the Duma) no fewer than fourteen bills to expand the legal rights of Russia's non-Orthodox communities.[2]

Though he would later shift to a more conservative position, in 1908 Stolypin was part of a cohort of tsarist officials who championed non-Orthodox rights as a matter of imperial preservation and stability. (This group included Sergei Witte, who had overseen Russia's industrialization and who had authored the October Manifesto in 1905). By supporting Russia's non-Orthodox peoples and accommodating them, Stolypin hoped to neutralize dissent and cultivate broad support for the regime. This agenda often put him at odds with the Russian Orthodox Church, which saw in it the erosion of the church's privileged position in the empire, as well as with the tsar himself, who relied on the church as a crucial source of institutional support for the monarchy.[3]

In this tense post-1905 context of political flux and contestation over religious policy, the hajj posed a particular challenge to Stolypin. To ignore it was out of the question. The disorders of the 1907–8 hajj season, and the fears they stoked within the regime about sanitary and political threats to the empire, had made the need to organize the hajj more urgent than ever. At the same time, as Stolypin saw it, organization offered a chance for Russia to ingratiate itself with its twenty-million-strong Muslim population, to demonstrate its policy of religious toleration and support for Islam, and to win Muslim loyalties at a critical moment. Political revolutions in 1908 in both the Ottoman Empire and Persia had only deepened tsarist officials' concerns about Muslim loyalties. The Young Turks' overthrow of the Ottoman sultan, in particular, and their propagation of Pan-Islamism and Pan-Turkism alarmed officials in Russia and made many more intent on establishing state control over the hajj.[4] And yet, just as Stolypin was under increased pressure to solve the problems associated with the hajj, he was also more restricted in his ability to increase government support for it.

And so Stolypin was doubtless pleased in early 1908 to receive from Saidazimbaev an ambitious plan to organize the hajj. The two met in Stolypin's office in St. Petersburg that February, in a meeting arranged by Muslim Duma representatives.[5] Saidazimbaev must have seemed to Stolypin like someone he could work with: he spoke excellent Russian, wore Western-style clothes, came from a family closely tied to the Russian administration in Turkestan, and had glowing recommendations from Muslims in the Duma. Saidazimbaev presented himself to Stolypin as an altruistic Muslim concerned about the suffering of his coreligionists, and the interests of the empire. He stressed the urgent need for the government to appoint a "trusted leader" to guide them, and offered his services to reorganize the hajj in Russia.[6]

Saidazimbaev's plan was comprehensive, and spanned the whole empire. He claimed to have the connections and experience necessary to carry it out, and to own land in Odessa and Tashkent, where he was already building transit facilities for hajj pilgrims. He had just signed an exclusive deal with the Volunteer Fleet to transport pilgrims between Odessa and Jeddah during the upcoming hajj season. He insisted that only a Muslim could lead the hajj in Russia, given that most pilgrims were unsophisticated and suspicious of outsiders, and believed that "one of their own, according to Islamic law, would never deceive them." Moreover, Islamic law had so many restrictions and requirements, he argued, only a Muslim could keep them straight.[7]

Much of what Saidazimbaev told Stolypin and others in the Russian government was untrue. He lied about owning land in Odessa. And he had no previous experience organizing the hajj or with a business venture of this scale. Nor was he well liked among Muslims in Turkestan. Had Stolypin looked into his background, by contacting Russian authorities in Turkestan, he would have discovered that Saidazimbaev had a long record of failed businesses, debts, and lawsuits against him, and a reputation as a drinker who liked dancing and Russian women. He also would have learned that Saidazimbaev had tried, and failed, to get elected to the Second State Duma the previous year.[8]

Stolypin did not do this. Instead, he naïvely took Saidazimbaev at his word, and hoped that Muslims would trust him as a coreligionist and a member of the elite, and follow his plan. His hasty appointment of Saidazimbaev, without any kind of inquiry into his past or his story, suggests the depth of his concern about growing Muslim discontent with conditions along hajj routes through Russia, and his eagerness to solve the problems of the pilgrimage and bring it under state control. The story of Saidazimbaev's appointment as hajj director, and the execution of his plan in the key transit point of Odessa, reveal how political discussions about the hajj and the government's handling of the pilgrimage changed after 1905.

As this chapter will demonstrate, the struggle over Russia's post-1905 religious order occurred not only within the Duma. Alongside his well-documented efforts to legislate religious equality and accommodate the needs and demands of Russia's non-Orthodox groups within the Duma, Stolypin also tried other, quieter strategies. In this example, he experimented with the co-optation of a self-declared Muslim "leader" to solve the problems associated with the hajj. Stolypin saw in Saidazimbaev a chance to solve a seemingly impossible situation: a way for the government to finally organize hajj in the empire without appearing to intervene in it directly, while appeasing Muslims and without exacerbating tensions between the state and the Orthodox Church. What looked like an elegant solution on paper would prove impossible to achieve, however. Saidazimbaev's plan would not, in the end, succeed in organizing the hajj, but would instead provoke a backlash from many sides, above all from Muslim pilgrims, for whom the hajj had become a major focus of debate within the newly expanded Muslim press, and an indicator of their status as Muslim subjects.

BEFORE being appointed hajj director, Saidazimbaev was largely unknown in Russia outside Turkestan. Some would later complain that Stolypin had hired him solely on the recommendation of Muslim deputies from the Duma.[9] One Russian official described him as "the American type," shrewd and enterprising. Saidazimbaev succeeded in gaining this powerful and lucrative position for three reasons: his family connections, the comprehensive character of his plan, and his astute ability to play to the multiple motivations animating government interest in the hajj.[10]

Saidazimbaev came from the Muslim elite class in Turkestan, created by the Russians from among those who helped them conquer the region in the late nineteenth century. His father, Said Bay, one of Tashkent's wealthiest merchants, had welcomed the conquest and served the Russian administration in

Figure 4.1. Said Gani Saidazimbaev. Note the many Russian medals pinned to his chest, attesting to his status as an elite and a trusted intermediary of the Russian colonial administration in Turkestan. Early 1900s. (Courtesy of www.medalirus.ru)

Turkestan as an interpreter and intermediary.[11] In his account of Turkestan under Russian rule, the American diplomat and writer Eugene Schuyler described Said Bay's "peculiar" position in Turkestan after the conquest. Russian officials believed that he had "vast influence" over the local population, and they relied on him as a trusted intermediary. His own people, however, detested him for meddling.[12] The tsar rewarded Said Bay for his support and loyalty by conferring on him the status of "hereditary honorable citizen," which brought special legal privileges, including exemptions from taxes and military conscription.[13] Saidazimbaev inherited this title and status from his father, along with a small fortune and political connections. He worked in family businesses and dabbled in local politics in Tashkent before exploring new opportunities beyond Turkestan.[14]

Saidazimbaev was not the only person to approach the government in this period with a proposal for organizing the hajj, but he was the most ambitious.[15] He proposed to streamline Russia's hajj traffic through the single port of Odessa, using exclusively Russian railroads and steamships. He would build a string of multipurpose facilities for hajj pilgrims along the rail routes between Tashkent and Odessa, sell single, "direct" tickets to hajj pilgrims in rail stations across the empire, and provide multilingual guides to help pilgrims navigate Russian-speaking regions, all at cut rates. Facilities would offer lodging and other services free of charge. They were to be erected in both Muslim and non-Muslim regions, more or less along the new Tashkent-Orenburg-Odessa rail route, which had opened in 1906. He proposed facilities in, among other places, Samara, Penza, Kharkov, and Odessa, and a "reliable person" to head each outpost.[16]

Globally the mass hajj traffic in the early twentieth century was dominated by poor Muslims, most of them traveling long distances for the first time in their lives, and Russia was no exception.[17] Russia's pilgrims were by and large "unsophisticated," Saidazimbaev argued, and easy targets for predatory brokers and "guides" who preyed on them along their routes, especially in Russia's Black Sea ports, where pilgrims' needs were greatest. His focus on Odessa was timely: the opening of the new Tashkent-Orenburg-Odessa line had suddenly connected the port city directly to Central Asia, turning Odessa overnight into a major hub of Russia's hajj traffic. Odessa had no infrastructure to support the hajj traffic; many pilgrims ended up sleeping on the streets, and the police were besieged with reports of crime. Here, as elsewhere along pilgrims' routes, Saidazimbaev's proposed his facilities as a way to "rescue" pilgrims from dishonest people, provide for their various needs, and solve problems of disorder and crime.

Saidazimbaev's proposal, which he would shop around to tsarist officials across the empire in 1908, painted a dire picture of the Muslim experience of the hajj through Russian lands, particularly for those traveling from Central Asia. Difficulties had beset pilgrims along the Tashkent-Orenburg line in the 1907–8 hajj season. Stations along their routes were often nothing more than a sign posted in the ground. Pilgrims sat beside the tracks for days waiting for a train, with no access to food, shelter, or water. The railroads were not adding enough rolling stock during hajj season, and trains were overcrowded. Penza and Samara were two of the worst stations. There, the new trans-Siberian railroad intersected with many other rail lines, and large crowds gathered to board trains that often arrived already full. As many as sixty passengers piled into cars built for forty, and people lay on floors, luggage racks, and passageways between cars, or were forced to stand. Men and women were packed together in miserable conditions for as long as two weeks. On board, Muslims found filthy toilets and no water to perform their daily ablutions, or open space to pray.[18]

Transfers had been especially difficult. Because most Muslim pilgrims could not speak Russian, they often ended up on the wrong train, or stranded in a station far from home, unable to communicate. Between home and Constantinople—the entire journey through Russian lands—Muslims had almost no access to their native foods, and for religious reasons they refused meat products offered at Russian train stations and stops along the way.[19] Many went hungry. Others carried a month-and-a-half's worth of food in their sacks, much of which spoiled and decayed, which created a stench in the train cars and cases of food poisoning.[20] Whenever people got sick, disease spread quickly. On the steamships they boarded in Russia's Black Sea ports, pilgrims again suffered crowded conditions, lacked access to water, and were charged exorbitant prices for food and drink—fifty kopecks for a roll and forty kopecks for a cup of tea.[21]

To address problems on Russia's railroads, Saidazimbaev proposed working with the Ministry of Transport to create special "hajj cars" tailored to Muslim traditions and needs. These would include sex-segregated space and bathrooms; access to water to perform their daily ablutions before prayer; open space for them to perform their prayers during travel; and a Muslim conductor to guide them. He would also work with the ministry to manage the complicated logistics of pilgrim transport during hajj seasons, and arrange for extra rolling stock.[22] He planned to assign Muslim guides to steamships to accompany and assist pilgrims on the long journey, and to subsidize and dispense a certain number of free steamship tickets to poor pilgrims.[23]

In its comprehensive scope and design, and its stress on comfort, efficiency, and affordability, Saidazimbaev's plan owed much to the "package tour" invented in the late nineteenth century by Thomas Cook, the legendary English-man and founder of the eponymous travel agency.[24] This was not a coincidence. Cook's organizational model was simple and easily replicated, and had spurred the growth of a modern travel and tourism industry worldwide, including Russia.[25] As an entrepreneur who traveled extensively around the empire, Saidaz-imbaev would surely have been exposed to Russia's burgeoning travel industry through advertisements, and seen firsthand the various services offered to trav-elers in cities and railroad stations across the empire. Saidazimbaev may even have modeled his plan in part on Cook's late nineteenth-century effort in India to centralize the hajj under a single agency (it failed).[26]

But Saidazimbaev's plan also differed from conventional package tours in significant ways. It aimed not only to organize and capture the profits involved in mass movement of people—pilgrims, in this case—but also to ensure that they underwent proper sanitary procedures before leaving Russia. Hence, the facility he proposed for Odessa would not only provide pilgrims with lodging and provisions, but would also have a specially outfitted "steam chamber" where they would undergo mandatory "disinfection," in line with international sanitary rules for the hajj.[27] There was also a charity dimension to his plan, insofar as it offered free lodging, and reserved a number of free steamship tick-ets for the poor. In this sense it resembled the Ottoman system of hajj organiza-tion, which was in part intended to demonstrate the sultan's generosity and largesse toward his most needy Muslim subjects.[28]

Saidazimbaev used his money and connections to gain support for his plan, and secure himself the job of hajj director. He began at home in Tashkent. Mobilizing contacts within the Russian administration there, he met with the Tashkent railroad authority in April 1907 to request a plot of land next to the city's main railroad station. He proposed leasing the land to build a facility—a "Muslim station" (musul'manskii vokzal)—to house and feed the growing num-ber of hajj pilgrims who used the city as a transit point, coming to Tashkent from across the Turkestan region as well as from Afghanistan and China.[29]

The railroad authority approved Saidazimbaev's request. It gave him a twelve-year lease on a plot of land, and he drafted a plan for a two-story, multi-purpose building to serve the needs of pilgrim-travelers. The building was to contain sex-segregated waiting rooms; a teahouse; a shop selling provisions and goods; a barbershop, cafeteria, and dining room (for elites); a ticket office sell-ing steamship tickets; space for performing ablutions; and a mosque in an outdoor courtyard.[30] Saidazimbaev would later describe his investment in this facility as charity on his part, to help the many hajj pilgrims coming to Tashkent who needed shelter and food while they waited for trains.[31] But as an entrepreneur, Saidazimbaev surely had economic interests top of mind. This is suggested by the design of the building as an all-purpose facility, which aimed to provide for all of pilgrims' needs; in other words, to sell them everything they needed, under one roof.

Like other major world pilgrimages, indeed, other forms of cyclic, mass human mobility, the hajj had always generated economic activity along the major routes to Mecca, as industries emerged to cater to pilgrims' many needs during their travels.[32] For many centuries, important cities along these routes (Damascus, for one) had economies based almost entirely on the seasonal hajj traffic.[33] With the rise of railroad and steamship travel worldwide over the second half of the nineteenth century, hajj routes shifted, which generated economic activity and business opportunities in new places, such as Tashkent and other cities in the Russian Empire, including Kharkov and Odessa.

Saidazimbaev's plan showed great resourcefulness and vision on his part: he understood that the Tashkent-Orenburg-Odessa rail line had opened up a new, major hajj route through Russia. He sought to monopolize the large profits to be made along this new route by building an infrastructure along it. As a Muslim, he was no doubt familiar with the historical tradition of Muslim imperial rulers sponsoring caravans to Mecca along fixed, fortified routes, for economic, political, and strategic purposes. His plan was a version of this: it called for the construction of an empire-wide infrastructure providing security and superior services to centralize the traffic along a single channel. But it was one thing for him to gain support for his plan in Tashkent, where Russian officials knew and trusted him. It was something else entirely to gain the trust of Russian officials in the central government, and in other parts of the empire. His genius in selling his plan lay in his ability to promise all things to all people, in one person and plan.

IN early 1908, Saidazimbaev sought support for his plan in St. Petersburg. Acutely aware of the multiple interests surrounding the hajj traffic in Russia, and the unseemliness of seeking to profit so blatantly from a major Muslim ritual, Saidazimbaev carefully played to these various interests. He started with Muslim representatives from the State Duma. In February he met with a small group of past and present deputies at the St. Petersburg home of Shakhaydar

Syrtlanov, a Bashkir from Ufa, who had recently served in the Second Duma.[34] To this group, he described his ideas for organizing the hajj, and improving travel conditions for pilgrims through Russian lands with his facilities. One of those present later recalled how Saidazimbaev had presented himself as motivated "solely by a noble and pious goal, of protecting pilgrims from exploitation," and how nearly everyone was "moved by the benevolent goals of Saidazimbaev," and his willingness to spend tens of thousands of rubles to help his fellow Muslims make the pilgrimage.[35]

With the help of Muslim Duma deputies, Saidazimbaev next arranged a meeting with the Committee of the Volunteer Fleet. As noted in chapter 3, the Volunteer Fleet was one of Russia's two main state-sponsored steamship lines. Along with ROPiT, it was trying to expand its operations in Russia's Black Sea ports, where European shipping companies dominated transport. Both were heavily subsidized by the Russian government, which controlled their boards. Both had been involved, to varying degrees, in hajj transport in the Black Sea since the late nineteenth century, with ROPiT taking the lead.[36]

In this meeting, Saidazimbaev played to the commercial interests of the fleet, offering to help it break into the lucrative business of hajj transport in the Black Sea. Saidazimbaev proposed an exclusive deal whereby he would "attract pilgrims" to the fleet's ships "in the largest possible numbers," in return for a cut of every pilgrim ticket he sold. To get pilgrims to choose Volunteer Fleet ships over its competitors, he proposed building ticket offices to sell the fleet's tickets in railroad stations across the empire, starting with the station under way in Tashkent. He claimed to also own a plot of land in Odessa, where he proposed to build a large, multipurpose hajj complex where all pilgrims would stay while in the city.[37]

In proposing this deal, Saidazimbaev was surely aware of the fleet's ongoing financial troubles and desire to break into new markets. Since the opening of the trans-Siberian railroad in 1903, the fleet had lost much of its business ferrying tea, colonists, soldiers, and convicts between Odessa and the Far East. It suffered further losses after the Russo-Japanese War broke out in 1904, and trade between Odessa and the Far East came to a standstill.[38] Searching for new ways to fill its ships, the fleet had become interested in hajj transport, especially out of Odessa, which had only just become a major hub of the traffic.[39]

Saidazimbaev's proposal offered the Volunteer Fleet a chance to make millions of rubles by monopolizing the traffic in and out of the Black Sea. He claimed to have the know-how and legitimacy to get pilgrims to take the fleet's ships. He also had the endorsement of Duma deputies. Downplaying his own financial interest, he instead emphasized his desire to direct profits to Russia's national fleet, and away from foreign steamship companies, for the good of the empire. He told the committee that he envisioned making the hajj "more orderly and less expensive," and ending the "awful exploitation" his fellow Muslims faced along their routes, "especially by foreigners."[40]

Saidazimbaev's plan agreed with the "commercial ethics" of the Volunteer Fleet, so the committee signed an exclusive three-year contract with him, naming him general agent. It promised him specially outfitted steamships to transport pilgrims between Odessa and Jeddah over the next three years, and a fifteen-percent cut of each pilgrim ticket he sold. It also gave him a 50,000-ruble interest-free loan to build a Volunteer Fleet ticket office at his "Muslim station" in Tashkent. In return, Saidazimbaev promised to deal only with the Volunteer Fleet, and build ticket offices selling its tickets in railroad stations across Russia's Muslim regions.[41] Finally, Saidazimbaev promised to finish construction of the "rail station" he claimed to be building in Odessa in time for the 1908–9 hajj season, which would begin in the early fall. The contract made clear that the agreement was provisional: if by September 1908 Saidazimbaev had failed to realize his plans, the Volunteer Fleet could nullify the contract.[42]

Within weeks of signing his contract with the Volunteer Fleet, Saidazimbaev presented his plan in a private meeting to Stolypin. Just as Saidazimbaev had played to the altruistic, religious interests of his fellow Muslims and to the commercial interests of the Volunteer Fleet, he presented the hajj, and the need to organize it, in political and humanitarian terms to Stolypin. He played to Stolypin's concerns about social unrest in the empire, sketching a dire picture of the uncomfortable, humiliating, and at times dangerous conditions pilgrims suffered during their travel through Russia that also sometimes made it impossible for them to observe their religious traditions and rituals. Echoing details from Russian newspaper coverage, which he clearly had followed closely, Saidazimbaev described the hellish experience along Russian railroads during the 1907–8 hajj season as a major source of disappointment for Russia's Muslims. They had abandoned their old land routes, hoping to find in the railroads a faster and more comfortable way to get to Mecca, but these hopes had "largely been dashed."[43]

None of what Saidazimbaev described would have been news to Stolypin. As minister of internal affairs, he was the main official responsible for managing domestic conditions surrounding the hajj. As described in chapter 3, in 1907, in an attempt to establish some government regulation of steamships, Stolypin had gotten the Senate to ratify "Rules on the Transport by Ship of Muslim Pilgrims from Black Sea Ports to the Hejaz and Back."[44]

But the 1907 rules focused mainly on steamship issues, leaving many others unaddressed. And in his report, Saidazimbaev implicitly warned Stolypin about severe consequences if he did not address these other issues. A key issue Saidazimbaev raised was public health. He described the inadequate lodging for pilgrims in Odessa, and the sanitary dangers for the city and the empire. He described a typical "hotel" situation in Odessa as a breeding ground for disease, with pilgrims crowded several to a room for as long as two weeks, with no ventilation, unwashed bodies lying on filthy linens, the stench of rotting food, and people preparing food and eating on the same dirty floor where they prayed and slept.[45]

Saidazimbaev also warned that if terrible travel conditions through Russia continued, pilgrims would start reverting to their old land routes.[46] Already, he claimed, rumors were circulating about the "rewards" offered by the Persian government for pilgrims who took routes through their realm, and some pilgrims were returning to these routes.[47] This point certainly would have made an impression on Stolypin. Since the late nineteenth century, the government had been trying to encourage Russia's Muslims to take state-sanctioned routes through Russia, along Russian rail lines. This was both for economic reasons—to channel the profits of hajj transport into state coffers—and for reasons of security and imperial stability. Russia had no way of monitoring pilgrims along land routes through Indian and Persian lands. Russian officials referred to this as secret pilgrimage, one that they had steadily tried to discourage, because they worried that it would have negative sanitary and political effects on the empire.[48]

Documentation of Stolypin's response to Saidazimbaev and his plan is spotty in the historical record. We know that Stolypin embraced the plan, because he appointed Saidazimbaev hajj director and authorized him to carry it out. But nowhere did he fully explain his motives. The existing evidence suggests that Stolypin was secretive about the appointment, treating it as an experiment to try out before going public. This would make sense, given the tense political atmosphere of the time.

By 1908 Stolypin was two years into his tenure as prime minister, and under fire in the government for pushing for "an expansion of the limits of 'religious freedom,'" as promised in the tsar's October Manifesto of 1905. Stolypin had a utilitarian view: he believed that the expansion of government support for Russia's non-Orthodox faiths, and the achievement of "full religious toleration" for all in the empire, were central to guaranteeing imperial stability and preserving autocracy.[49] His support for religious reform was ultimately part of a broader agenda to remove "causes of social discontent" in the empire, and thwart the growth of revolutionary groups.[50] But many disagreed with his vision. His reform program caused open conflict between the state and the Orthodox Church, which fought his measures in the Duma, fearing an erosion of its privileged status in the empire. And the tsar, who feared losing the support of a crucial imperial institution, was growing increasingly worried about Stolypin's proposals for religious reform.[51]

And yet the risks of the government doing nothing about the hajj were great as well. Saidazimbaev had covered most of them in his report. If the government ignored the miserable state of the hajj, and the growing Muslim appeals for help, it might call into question the government's commitment to expanding religious toleration in Russia. This was a central promise of the October Manifesto, and failing to deliver on it could endanger Russia's relationship with its Muslim populations. In this context, Stolypin's appointment of Saidazimbaev appears to be an attempt to increase support for the hajj by reliance on a trusted Muslim subject, to avoid the appearance of direct government support and further controversy. This plan was in keeping with Russia's centuries-long tradition, like that of other European empires, of turning to its Muslim subjects for help managing and governing its Muslim populations.[52] To manage the hajj, Russia had used Muslim subjects as consuls and spies. But Saidazimbaev was to be more than an intermediary. His plan put him in charge of organizing and overseeing all aspects of the pilgrimage. And he was to have broad, empire-wide authority. The Ministry of Internal Affairs ordered Russian governors and city-governors across the empire, and local authorities under their control, to provide Saidazimbaev with "all necessary assistance," within the boundaries of the law.[53] Stolypin envisioned that pilgrims would "naturally" flock to Saidazimbaev's facilities. He stressed that pilgrims needed to decide on their own, under conditions of competition, to use such facilities, based on word of mouth about their comfort and affordability, but under no circumstances should they be forced to use them. Perhaps most remarkably, Stolypin apparently accepted Saidazimbev's professed charitable intentions, and later expressed indignation when it became clear that his motives were, in fact, largely economic.[54]

AFTER his appointment, Saidazimbaev began his ambitious plan for the fast-approaching hajj season. Pilgrims would start gathering in Odessa in September, and he had a lot to do in a short period of time. That year the Feast of the Sacrifice, the festival marking the end of the hajj, fell on a Friday, so crowds were expected to be larger than usual—Saidazimbaev estimated at least 15,000. With construction of his "Muslim train station" already under way in Tashkent, in April he traveled to Samara and Penza to negotiate with local authorities to construct similar facilities there.[55] In early June, he returned to St. Petersburg for a meeting with Russian railroad representatives. At this meeting, organized by the minister of transport, he got the representatives to designate 1,000 third-class train cars for use as hajj cars along the fourteen different rail lines Russia's hajj pilgrims typically used. He also worked with them to develop a plan and a schedule for "direct"—transfer-free (besperesadochnyi)—service for pilgrims, to make transport faster and more orderly.[56]

Arriving in Odessa later that month, Saidazimbaev faced obstacles to his plan. Contrary to what he had told the Volunteer Fleet back in February, he did not have a building already under construction in Odessa to lodge hajj pilgrims, and did not even own land there. In fact, it seems likely that Saidazimbaev had never been to Odessa before. He had no political connections in the city, was completely unknown, even within the small Muslim community, and seems to have been unfamiliar with its already established and complex local hajj industry. His efforts, with the backing of the Ministry of Finance, to lease a plot of land in the port immediately caused controversy among local officials, both because they had no idea who he was and because there was already a project under way to build a hajj complex.[57]

Odessa's city-governor, I. N. Tolmachev, either had not received the announcement about Saidazimbaev's appointment as hajj director or had chosen to ignore it. Whatever the case, in June 1908 he was busy helping the local businessman and retired ship captain Petr Gurzhi build a facility for hajj pilgrims in Odessa's port. Gurzhi was an obvious choice for this job. For several years he had been involved in chartering ships to transport pilgrims. The previous year, in response to the sudden surge of hajj traffic through the city, Tolmachev had put him in charge of organizing lodging and transport for hajj pilgrims. More than 10,000 pilgrims had flooded the city in the fall of 1907, the highest number ever reported, all arriving within a three-month period.[58] Gurzhi had managed to house nearly all of them in city hotels and private homes, but city sanitary officials struggled to track them down to screen them for disease. To recall, at the end of the season, Gurzhi urged Tolmachev to support construction of a special building for hajj pilgrims in the city. Centralizing pilgrims in a single facility, he argued, would reduce the risks of a cholera epidemic in Odessa.[59]

In mid-June, at a special meeting of local officials, Tolmachev announced that the city had assigned Gurzhi a plot of land in the port for his hajj complex. The plot lay along the Old Quarantine Jetty, alongside public bathhouses and customs warehouses, and close to the stopping place for the Volunteer Fleet and other fleets with service to the Red Sea. A special rail line ran alongside the plot, and would provide direct service to the complex.[60] The spot was clearly chosen with sanitary concerns in mind: the idea was to deliver hajj pilgrims directly from their trains into the complex, bypassing Odessa's train station, and from there board them onto steamships.[61] This design followed a recommendation that sanitary officials in Odessa had made several years earlier, to prevent a cholera epidemic in Odessa by "not allowing Muslims into the city."[62] Tolmachev's support for the plan suggests how closely he, too, associated the hajj with deadly cholera, and viewed Muslim pilgrims as a source of disease and disorder in Odessa.

Within days of this decision, Saidazimbaev mobilized his ties to the Volunteer Fleet to undo Gurzhi's project. Eager to preserve their lucrative deal with Saidazimbaev, fleet officials in St. Petersburg immediately telegrammed Tolmachev, urging him to support the economic interests of the fleet—and, by association, of Russia—by transferring the plot of land to Saidazimbaev. They pointed out that Gurzhi had no agreement with any of Russia's steamship companies.[63] A. G. Niedermiller, chair of the fleet's committee, wrote Tolmachev directly to tell him that Saidazimbaev had been recommended by several Duma members, and seemed to have altruistic intentions.[64] In Odessa, the manager of the fleet's local office, L. F. Kompanion, also pressured Tolmachev to support Saidazimbaev, reminding him that Stolypin had just named him hajj director, and arguing that his plan was better for Russia overall because it spanned the whole empire, whereas Gurzhi's focused only on Odessa.[65] Meanwhile, fleet officials in Odessa also intervened with local representatives of the Ministry of Trade, which owned the plot of land in question, pressuring them to transfer the plot to Saidazimbaev.[66]

Saidazimbaev approached Tolmachev in the meantime to sell his plan. Writing to Tolmachev on official letterhead that announced his multiple impressive titles (Director of the Muslim Pilgrimage from Russia to Mecca and Back; Appointee of the Ministry of Internal Affairs; General Agent of the Volunteer Fleet; Hereditary Honorable Citizen), Saidazimbaev reprised the arguments he had made to Stolypin. He argued that only a Muslim could effectively organize the hajj, given the required cultural knowledge and sensitivity, and pilgrims' suspicions about non-Muslims' interference in the practice of their faith.[67] He also stressed the broad government support that he had as hajj director and his unique ability to bring order to the hajj traffic.[68] He assured Tolmachev that his comprehensive plan would solve the problems of railroad and steamship travel for pilgrims, and that with it the hajj would "finally happen as it should."[69]

The controversy surrounding the hajj complex in Odessa is noteworthy for several reasons. It reveals the limits of Stolypin's influence as minister of internal affairs, insofar as Tolmachev did not immediately heed his order to recognize and support Saidazimbaev as hajj director. Surely this happened in other parts of the empire as well, where local officials had their own concerns and agendas with regard to the hajj traffic through their regions or cities, and might have resisted deferring to an outsider on a matter of such importance. It is also clear that resistance among officials in Odessa to Saidazimbaev was tinged with anti-Islamic sentiment. Gurzhi, who saw Saidazimbaev as a threat to his business, tried to discredit him by resorting to stereotypes, referring to him as an "untrustworthy 'Sart,'"—the latter was a general term used by Russians to refer to settled Muslim peoples in Central Asia, but Gurzhi's usage seems less than neutral, if not a slur. Other Odessa officials also used this term to refer to Saidazimbaev, and rumors swirled that he sought land in the port so that he could "sell it to other people."[70] These reactions suggest anxiety on the part of some city officials about the sudden influx of Muslims into Odessa, one of the empire's most cosmopolitan cities, but also one marked by growing intolerance for its large Jewish population, and with little historical experience with Muslims.[71]

Interestingly, Tolmachev yielded to the pressure. He put Saidazimbaev in charge of organizing the hajj in Odessa, and forced Gurzhi to turn his blueprints for the hajj complex over to him. He also ordered Gurzhi and the personnel who had worked for him the previous hajj season to work for Saidazimbaev.[72] Tolmachev did not, however, have the authority to transfer the plot of land in the port to Saidazimbaev. It belonged to the Ministry of Trade, and negotiations over it continued to drag on. By July the Council of Ministers in St. Petersburg was considering the case, and it was unclear when the matter would be resolved.[73] With the first trainloads of pilgrims set to arrive in the city in two months, Saidazimbaev was eager to get started on preparations. Already telegrams were coming from Turkestan, asking about the readiness of the hajj complex. He and Tolmachev decided it was time to find an alternate spot to house the hajj complex.[74]

Subsequent developments, and Tolmachev's correspondence with other officials in the Ministry of Internal Affairs, shed light on why Tolmachev changed his mind and backed Saidazimbaev. With Tolmachev's help, and for the large sum of 7,500 rubles, Saidazimbaev rented the Alexander III House of Industry to house his hajj complex. Located in Peresyp, an outlying suburb about five miles from Odessa's city center, this building was a large, two-story stone structure, flanked by one-story wings. It was a work-relief institution, built by the government in the late nineteenth century to house and feed unemployed workers, but now standing mostly empty.[75] Saidazimbaev got use of the building from August through December, the projected hajj departure season, with the condition that a bakery continue to operate in one wing of the building.[76] The building was not ideal. It was located in a drab, industrial neighborhood that was a long walk from the train station and the passenger port. It was far from the 200,000-ruble complex Saidazimbaev had planned to build down in the port, with space for 3,000. This building had space for only 1,400. It also required extensive renovations, which Saidazimbaev commenced immediately.[77]

OVER the next two months, Saidazimbaev transformed Odessa's House of Industry into an elaborate hajj complex, based on Gurzhi's plan. The finished facility was captured in a photo essay published that fall in *Odesskii listok*, one of the city's most popular newspapers. Twenty-nine photos and accompanying text took readers on a tour of the complex, through immaculate sleeping quarters and a well-stocked pharmacy, "Japanese-style" steam disinfection chamber, small mosque, bakery, teahouse, and separate men's and women's hospitals staffed by uniformed nurses. Exterior photos showed makeshift structures housing a halal butcher and a barber; tents pitched in a courtyard for "Kirgiz pilgrims," and open fire pits for pilgrims to cook their native dishes. Several photos captured large crowds of bearded Muslim men in turbans and belted robes, standing alongside Russian police officers and city officials in bowler hats and overcoats, for ceremonies that marked the end of Ramadan, a major Muslim holiday. Standing at the center of this group was Saidazimbaev, identified in captions as the "creator of Odessa's hajj complex," and the hajj director for Russia, appointed by the Ministry of Internal Affairs.[78]

The photo essay would have comported with Stolypin's vision for the hajj, as an occasion to showcase the government's toleration of Islam and build loyalty among the empire's Muslim population, for political motives of imperial stability. In line with Stolypin's vision of the Odessa hajj complex as a "refuge, specially outfitted to serve the needs and demands of pilgrims," that would attract pilgrims because of its superior features, these photos showed a clean, efficient, multipurpose facility, with contented Muslims mixing easily with Russian officials.[79]

Figures 4.2, 4.3, 4.4, 4.5. Photographs from Odessa Russian-language newspaper, showcasing the *khadzhikhane* that Saidazimbaev built in the city to house crowds of hajj pilgrims. 1908. (*Odesskii listok*)

Figure 4.3. (Continued)

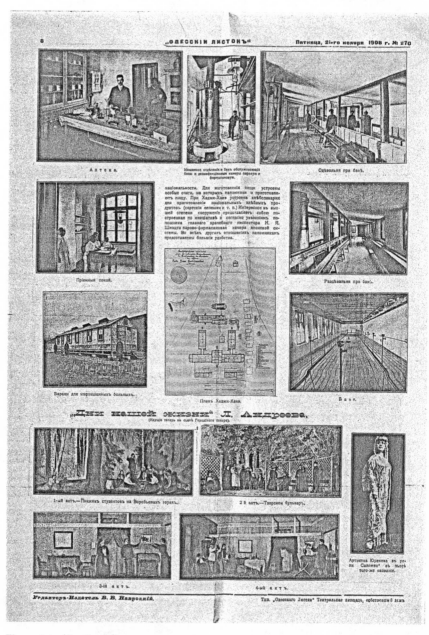

Figure 4.4. (Continued)

138

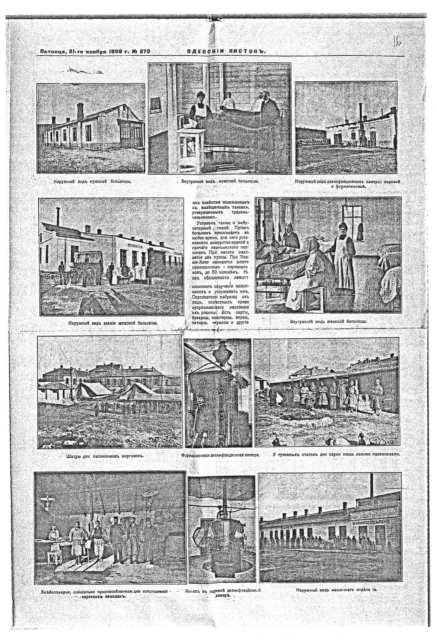

Figure 4.5. (Continued)

Important aspects of the hajj complex were not captured in the *Odesskii lis-tok* photos, however. Surrounding the entire complex were high iron gates, and the sole entrance was locked and manned by round-the-clock guards. And many, if not most, of those pictured were probably not there of their own voli-tion. This was because Tolmachev had made it mandatory for all hajj pilgrims to stay in the complex. In August 1908, he had issued "Instructions for Hajj Pilgrims," which was published in Muslim newspapers across the empire. Cit-ing the need to "prevent a cholera epidemic," Tolmachev outlined a nine-point procedure for hajj pilgrims during their time in Odessa. Punitive and threaten-ing, these instructions were supposed to apply only when cases of cholera had been reported in the city, as an emergency, preventive health measure. They stipulated that Muslim pilgrims were allowed to arrive only at Odessa's main railroad station (the city had two others), where police officers would be waiting on the platform to escort them directly to the hajj complex. Hajj pilgrims were permitted to stay only in the complex, where they would undergo "disinfec-tion," and would remain there until their steamships departed. No outsiders or unauthorized brokers were allowed inside the complex, and pilgrims were not allowed to walk around the city. The penalty for violating the instructions was severe: up to three months in jail or a 3,000-ruble fine.[80]

Whereas Stolypin viewed the hajj principally through the lens of religious reform and imperial politics, Tolmachev viewed it through the lens of disease, as his instructions demonstrate. From the vantage point of Odessa, Tolmachev's view made some sense. Cholera and other infectious diseases were a perennial threat to the city, whose bustling trade port exposed it to Near Eastern and Asian countries where these diseases were commonly thought to originate. By the early twentieth century, several global cholera epidemics had been traced back to crowds dispersing from Mecca, which created widespread fear of hajj pilgrims as carriers of disease.[81] Tolmachev had become worried enough that the hajj traffic might cause a cholera epidemic in the city to ask the Ministry of Internal Affairs in early 1908 to close the city to pilgrims. When the ministry rejected his request, he sought instead to contain the traffic, apparently seeing Saidazimbaev's plan as the best way to do this.[82]

There was yet another reason for Tolmachev's determination to centralize hajj pilgrims in a single complex, and isolate them from the city. On the issue of the hajj, Tolmachev's fear of disease converged with his anti-Semitic views. Odessa was one of the most Jewish cities in the Russian Empire. In the early twentieth century, Jews comprised one-third of the city's population of 400,000.[83] Scholars have argued that in the aftermath of revolutionary activity and social upheaval during the 1905 Revolution in Odessa—including the worst anti-Jewish pogrom in the city's history, which killed 400 people—Tolmachev largely blamed the city's Jewish population for the disorder, and made anti-Semitism "de facto city policy."[84] His backing of Saidazimbaev and the hajj complex appears to be an example of this.

In correspondence with the Ministry of Internal Affairs' director of the police, N. P. Zuev, Tolmachev blamed the disorder around the hajj in Odessa on "mostly Jewish" agents and brokers who owned hotels and rented rooms to pilgrims and exploited them terribly. Their exploitation began in train stations just before Odessa, where they went to "catch" pilgrims and lure them to their places in the city, often robbing them and leaving them with no money. Indigent, homeless pilgrims were a growing problem for city officials in Odessa, and were "costing the government money." In an effort to "order" the hajj in Odessa, Tolmachev told Zuev, he was supporting Saidazimbaev's plan. The city's Jews, he told Zuev, were "storming and raging" (*rvut i mechut*) over the plan and new measures, because it was putting an end to their moneymaking schemes and exploitation of pilgrims.[85]

And yet while Tolmachev aimed to establish order around the hajj traffic, his measures instead created greater disorder and new problems. His instructions provoked a backlash from all sides. Locals who made a living off the hajj traffic were among the first to resist. They included people like Rylka Zekhtser, precisely the type Tolmachev hoped to put out of business by supporting Saidazimbaev. A young Jewish widow with seven children, Zekhtser had supported her family for the past fifteen years by renting rooms to Muslim pilgrims during hajj season. In August she wrote Tolmachev, assuring him that she was not a "swindler," and that the local mullah, Safarov, could vouch that she had "always dealt honestly with pilgrims." She described the twenty rooms she rented to pilgrims as "light-filled and clean," and begged him to let her continue her business, which was her "only source of income" for her family. Zekhtser, like many others, was forbidden to rent rooms to pilgrims that fall.[86]

ROPiT also complained that the exclusive deal between Saidazimbaev and the Volunteer Fleet was unfair, and a threat to its business interests. ROPiT had a longer and more successful history in passenger transport out of the Black Sea. It owned the railroads to Odessa, had helped build the elevated railway connecting to the Quarantine Harbor, and leased large plots of land from Odessa's port authority for its offices, warehouses, and permanent piers for its ships. It also had a shipbuilding yard there.[87] But it did most of its business transporting hajj pilgrims from Sevastopol, where it also had extensive facilities and a large shipyard. ROPiT officials complained that Saidazimbaev was sabotaging their efforts to transport hajj pilgrims. Saidazimbaev had sent agents into Kharkov and other stations deeper in the empire, where they harassed ROPiT agents, preventing them from selling tickets to hajj pilgrims or even getting near them. To route pilgrims through Odessa and onto Volunteer Fleet ships, Saidazimbaev's agents were spreading lies about cholera and plague outbreaks in Sevastopol, urging pilgrims to avoid it that year.[88]

Although Stolypin had hoped that Saidazimbaev's plan would build imperial affection and loyalty, in execution the plan was consolidating discontent instead. In St. Petersburg, the Ministry of Trade had begun to complain to the Ministry of Internal Affairs on behalf of ROPiT. From Odessa, Tolmachev wrote a frantic letter to Zuev, saying that ROPiT was refusing to collaborate with Saidazimbaev in transporting hajj pilgrims and was trying to "sabotage" the plan to "order" the hajj by threatening to open a second, competing hajj complex in Odessa.[89] Meanwhile, from within the hajj complex, there were reports of pilgrims rioting and assaulting staff. Pilgrims were enraged over not being allowed to leave the complex and being forced to buy Volunteer Fleet tickets at rates higher than those charged by other fleets.[90]

Worse still for Stolypin, by October a backlash against the Odessa hajj complex had started in the press. What had looked like a beautiful, antiseptic facility, on paper and in photographs, and to certain people, looked and functioned like an instrument for Muslim oppression and exploitation to others. One of the first articles to criticize Saidazimbaev's hajj complex appeared in the liberal Kadet newspaper, *Rech'*, published in St. Petersburg. Titled "Khadzhikhane: Letter from Odessa," the article reached both Russian and Muslim readers—it was translated into Tatar and published also in the major Kazan daily *Vagit*. It accused Saidazimbaev and Tolmachev of violating Muslims' civil rights. It claimed that Tolmachev was "using" the threat of cholera and the premise of "protecting" Odessa from disease to force pilgrims into the hajj complex, to enrich both Saidazimbaev and the Volunteer Fleet. It was strange, the writer noted, that only in Odessa—the end point of a long journey through the Russian Empire for many Muslims—was such a facility established.[91] This article suggests the extent to which the issue of the hajj was becoming associated with questions about Muslims' civil rights in Russia, not only among Muslims, but also among liberal-minded Russians.

The most damning critiques of Saidazimbaev and his hajj complex appeared in the empire's Turkic-language newspapers, and were written by Muslims. Saidazimbaev would later dismiss these articles as the work of jealous "enemies" determined to undermine his plan for their own economic motives, but this seems unlikely.[92] The same complaints appeared in a variety of newspapers, and overall they suggest the extent to which Russia's Muslims had internalized ideas about religious reform, come to see in the hajj issues relating to their civil rights as Russian subjects, and become emboldened to demand change. They show that many Muslims had embraced the new medium of newspapers, which had spread throughout the empire after the 1905 revolution, as a way to express their dissatisfaction, and reject new measures regarding the hajj.

This point is worth emphasizing. Muslim representation in the State Duma had declined since the First Duma in 1906, as the government scaled back plans and promises for reform and pushed Muslims and others out of the Duma. There had been thirty-six Muslim representatives in the Second Duma of 1907, but by the end of the year, with the creation of the Third Duma, there were only ten. Standard narratives of post-1905 Muslim political activity often focus on a narrow group of Muslim elites and their emigration from Russia, above all to Turkey, where they worked to promote Pan-Turkism and Pan-Islamism (both projects failed).[93] But the vast majority of Russia's Muslims did not emigrate from the empire, and as discussions about the hajj in Muslim newspapers reveal, Muslims continued their struggle to advance their civil rights inside the empire after 1905, through the Duma and the popular press. By speaking out against what they deemed invasive and prejudicial policies and practices under Saidazimbaev's hajj regime, Muslims who wrote to these newspapers revealed their willingness to rely on institutions of the imperial state—above all, the Duma—to protect their rights as "citizens" in the Russian Empire, in which civil rights were being actively debated and were in flux. At the very least, this example suggests that some Muslims in the post-1905 era put stock in the October Manifesto's promise of religious equality in the empire, and begin to imagine themselves as "'citizens' in an empire with a highly contested rights regime."[94]

Many Muslims who wrote to the empire's newspapers likened the hajj complex to a "prison" and complained about being detained in it against their will. Writing to *Vagit* from within the hajj complex in October, Omar Ishkakov, a Tatar pilgrim from Astrakhan, described how police officers and gendarmes stationed at the gates of the complex scared away outsiders by yelling

"Go away!" whenever they approached the gates.[95] In another account, published in *Nur*, a group of Central Asian pilgrims described how they were "surrounded by police and gendarmes" at the Odessa train station, and forced to go directly to the hajj complex, where they were forbidden to leave. After managing to escape, they headed to the port in search of steamship tickets but were surprised to be apprehended by Saidazimbaev's agent Gurzhi. He had followed them from the hajj complex and got police officers to force them back to the "prison."[96]

Pilgrims reported shabby treatment and high prices rather than comfort and affordability at the hajj complex. They complained about its location in "one of the bad parts of the city," and their being packed into it "like herrings." Inside, a tin teapot sold for forty kopecks, more than twice what it cost in a regular shop, and meat sold at fifty percent higher than market rate. Pilgrims complained most bitterly about being forced to buy Volunteer Fleet steamship tickets in the hajj complex for twice the price charged by foreign steamship companies. Agents inside the complex pressured them to buy round-trip tickets, and they resented what they saw as an attempt to exploit them and achieve a monopoly over the traffic. "If you figure that 20,000 hajj pilgrims pass through Odessa every year," wrote one angry pilgrim, "you can begin to understand the motivations behind those who built the hajj complex." Told by Gurzhi they were not allowed to buy one-way tickets, "extremely outraged" Muslims began to protest, which ignited a riot. The police arrived, hauled off the leader of the protest to the precinct, and arrested eleven others.[97]

Many pilgrims also picked up on the obvious overlays of racism and contagion around the hajj complex, and accused Russian officials in Odessa of discrimination against Muslims. This came from their firsthand observations of how differently Orthodox pilgrims were treated in the city. Odessa was also a center of Orthodox pilgrimage to Jerusalem at this time, and hajj pilgrims often arrived in the city on the same trains with Orthodox pilgrims.[98] In *Vagit*, one hajj pilgrim described how his Orthodox traveling companions were free to stay "wherever they wanted," and walked freely off the train and into the city. They "were not escorted by gendarmes, and were not each charged fifteen rubles for 'sanitary costs.'" He, like others, also resented the identification of hajj pilgrims with cholera. As soon as the authorities understand you are a pilgrim, he wrote, they look at you like a "cholera microbe."[99]

Abdürreşid Ibrahim, a leading early twentieth-century Tatar intellectual, would make the same charge in his travel memoirs, based on a visit to Odessa in 1908. He described with indignation how ships arrived in port filled with "hundreds of dirty and sloppy Russians" coming from Jerusalem, who strolled off the ship and into the city, while Muslims were all forced to undergo quarantine in the hajj complex, even the "gentlemen" and first-class passengers.[100] In this respect, Saidazimbaev's plan had unintended consequences for Russia. By centralizing much of the hajj traffic through the single port of Odessa, his plan inadvertently revealed to Muslims the disparity between how they were treated in comparison to Orthodox pilgrims, which generated new complaints about discriminatory policies toward the hajj. Ironically, an approach intended to demonstrate an enlightened accommodation with the empire's Muslims had brought into sharp focus the regime's radically different treatment of its Orthodox Christian and Muslim subjects, and gave rise to complaints about state-sponsored prejudice against Muslims.

Muslims used newspapers to air their grievances about the Odessa hajj complex and their treatment there, and to redirect Muslims away from it. *Vagit* published several telegrams sent by pilgrims out in the field, like this one from mid-October 1908, when many pilgrims were on their way to the Black Sea: "We ask you to post a note to pilgrims that currently in Sevastopol there are ships waiting to depart for Yanbu and Jeddah. These are well-equipped ships that also carry returning passengers. One ship is leaving October 25, a second on November 15, and a third on November 20. We ask people not to believe it if they are told at train stations or by agents of Saidazimbaev that it is impossible to leave from Sevastopol (there are rumors that Saidazimbaev has dispatched a bunch of agents to ensure that pilgrims travel through Odessa and not Sevastopol). In Sevastopol pilgrims do not experience any oppression."[101]

These letters reveal Muslims mobilizing their newfound political representation in the government to demand change. Many ended with a plea to Muslim deputies in the Duma to "listen to the voices of pilgrims" and send someone to Odessa to save them from Saidazimbaev.[102] "Respected Duma members!" wrote one, "Give some attention to the situation of your coreligionists. . . . Rescuing us from this situation is the duty of Duma deputies. With tears in their eyes, pilgrims are addressing you."[103] "We are asking the Muslim faction of the Duma to conduct an investigation into this sad matter, to liberate the unfortunate pilgrims from this situation, and to tear them from the hands of several exploiters, and to improve the situation for tens of thousands of pilgrims."[104]

With a full-blown scandal developing in the press, and a bitter dispute erupting between ROPiT and the Volunteer Fleet, an outraged Stolypin wrote to Tolmachev in November to stop all use of force against hajj pilgrims in the city. He reprimanded him for introducing his instructions at a time when there was "no cholera in Odessa," and ordered him to cancel them.[105] He also forbade him to force pilgrims onto Volunteer Fleet ships, ordering that pilgrims be allowed to freely choose from among the steamships approved by the Port Pilgrimage Commission.[106] Reluctantly, Tolmachev canceled his instructions, and announced that hajj pilgrims were once again free to choose where they stayed in the city, provided that the lodgings had passed inspection for sanitary conditions.[107] Pilgrims were also now free to choose their steamships. However, he warned Stolypin that these reversals would revive all the old problems: if pilgrims were allowed to stay wherever they wanted, they would continue to choose cheaper options, and once again be exploited by shady hoteliers and agents of foreign steamship companies.[108]

But Stolypin was unswayed. By now it was clear that Saidazimbaev's appointment had been disastrous. Apart from the problems in Odessa, there were also reports from the head of the Tashkent railroad that Saidazimbaev had failed, as promised, to help with the transfer and transport of pilgrims on the special "hajj cars" headed directly to Odessa. Pilgrims had been suspicious of efforts to herd them onto the special cars, and many had refused to take them, which had caused disorder and delays.[109] In the meantime, the Tashkent railroad authority had shut down Saidazimbaev's "Muslim station" within weeks of its opening for sanitary reasons, after five pilgrims mysteriously died in their sleep.[110] Perhaps most distressing to Stolypin, he learned that Saidazimbaev had made a secret deal to send pilgrims on Egyptian steamers, pocketing a huge advance and violating his promise to Stolypin, and the Volunteer Fleet, to use only Russian ships to transport pilgrims.[111]

In late November the Ministry of Internal Affairs cut ties with Saidazimbaev. Across the empire, fifty-three governors and city-governors received a telegram from the director of the Department of Police, announcing that there had been an "error" in the wording of circular #29653 about the "appointment of Saidazimbaev as director of the pilgrimage" and that the circular "did not authorize any special authority for him."[112] When confused governors wrote to the ministry to ask for clarification, Stolypin claimed that he had "never named anyone director," but had instead promised Saidazimbaev "the assistance of the authorities with his efforts to provide services and comforts to pilgrims during their travels." Since Saidazimbaev had made clear that his main goals were to "make money" he should be "denied in the future any special protection of the authorities."[113]

Saidazimbaev's removal marked the end of Russia's experiment with a hajj director. The government did not appoint another one to succeed him. Like the

British in India a decade or so earlier, the Russian government abandoned its efforts to organize the hajj under centralized leadership.

SAIDAZIMBAEV left behind a mixed legacy. His failed plan to organize the hajj had created a new set of problems around the pilgrimage, arguably worsening the situation the government faced, and making the task of organization even more difficult. His exclusive deal with the Volunteer Fleet had created a bitter rivalry between the fleet and ROPiT. In 1908 and early 1909 the Ministries of Internal Affairs and Trade would convene a series of emergency conferences to resolve tensions and repair relations between the two fleets, and get them to cooperate in organizing hajj transport moving forward. Saidazimbaev's heavy-handed attempts to force pilgrims to travel through Odessa and use the hajj complex had not streamlined the hajj traffic, as he had projected, but had produced the opposite effect. At these planning conferences, tsarist officials nervously reported that Muslim pilgrims were reverting to their old land routes through Afghanistan, and some worried that they had been scared away from the route through Odessa for good.[114]

Perhaps most worrisome for the regime, at a time of heightened fears of unrest and increased government rhetoric about equality to promote imperial unity and stability, Saidazimbaev's plan had helped expose the unequal treatment of Muslim and Orthodox pilgrims, and generated an empire-wide discussion in the press about the abusive, racialized treatment of hajj pilgrims in Russia's Black Sea ports. This, in turn, exacerbated concerns in the government about the hajj as a source of Muslim unrest in the empire, and reopened debates about how and to what extent the government ought to involve itself in the pilgrimage. And yet Saidazimbaev also left behind a clear blueprint for organizing the hajj, and a transimperial infrastructure, which was staffed in part by Muslim intermediaries he had identified and recruited from Turkestan and elsewhere. Apart from the hajj complex in Odessa, he had also built facilities for hajj pilgrims in Kharkov (a major transit point along pilgrims' railroad routes) and Tashkent, and had opened a network of ticket offices across Muslim regions of the empire.

Over the next several years, the tsarist government would co-opt and build upon Saidazimbaev's plan. Now more then ever before, officials agreed on the need and desirability for organizing the hajj, not only for sanitary concerns, but also for political, strategic, and economic reasons. This is clear from the flurry of articles at this time that reflected robust discussions and debates about the hajj.

Figure 4.6. Hajj pilgrims with Russian medical staff and officials, on the stairs of the khadzhikhane in Odessa. 1913. (*Odesskiia novosti*)

Liberals writing in the pages of the Kadet Party mouthpiece, *Russkoe slovo*, for instance, pushed for government organization of the hajj as a matter of justice and civil rights, directly related to Russia's promise of religious freedom and support for its Muslims.[115]

Conservatives, for their part, supported organization for other reasons. Writing in *Novoe vremia*, the leading paper of the conservative movement in the Duma, the politician M. O. Menshikov strongly supported the idea of government support for the hajj.[116] He claimed to have studied piles of documents about the hajj in Russia, given to him by "representatives of various sides of this issue," and he proclaimed that Saidazimbaev's attempted "monopoly" was a significant step in the right direction but "nowhere near final." There were obvious nationalist and anti-Semitic overtones to his view: he pushed organization of the hajj so that Muslims would "finally be wrested from the predatory claws of Jews, Greeks, and Armenians and other predators, including the Turkish police and others." And he seemed to have little sympathy or respect for Muslims or their sacred ritual of the pilgrimage. He described them as "dim," and those who followed strict dietary laws "fanatics."

Menshikov's support for hajj patronage was, above all, motivated by economic and strategic interests. He saw the hajj as enormously useful to Russia in both regards, and claimed that there had been a recent shift within the government, with more officials seeing the hajj as a useful network for Russia to tap into and control for these reasons. "Until recently," he wrote, "the Russian government was hostile towards the hajj . . . assumed that the hajj increased Muslim fanaticism and pan-Islamism . . . and actively discouraged [it]." However, since the pilgrimage "cannot be completely stopped," in recent years the idea had emerged to try a policy of "patronage of the pilgrimage" instead. Patronage, Menshikov noted, promised the government both political and material rewards. "The truth is that each trip to Mecca and back costs between 300 and 500 rubles: multiply that by 20,000 and you get tens of millions of rubles." Additionally, the hajj was a crucial issue in Anglo-Russian rivalries in Persia and the wider "Muslim East," as it provided Russia with an opportunity to win the trust and friendship of its Muslim neighbors. For a lasting peace with its neighboring "Muslim empires," Russia needed to "convince Islam" that "Russia bears no fundamental enmity toward it." By organizing the hajj, Russia could demonstrate to the "masses in the East" its "toleration" and good intentions toward Islam. No less importantly, Menshikov noted, Russia has its "very expensive Volunteer Fleet," which is "[perishing] due to insufficient cargo (especially passengers), and here we have passengers!"[117] This idea was echoed by other officials in the government, who lamented that Russia had missed out "on émigré transport and millions in revenues," and argued that it should "not make the same mistake" with the hajj.[118]

OVER the last years of the empire's existence, the tsarist government would embrace a more active, if also quiet, role as patron of the hajj. Through interministerial conferences held in 1908–9, ROPiT and the Volunteer Fleet were persuaded to join forces and cooperate in organizing the seasonal transport of hajj pilgrims. Together they created a new society, called the United Agency of the Volunteer Fleet and the Russian Society for Steam Navigation and Trade, which offered organized, subsidized transportation for Russia's hajj pilgrims. They split the traffic, each offering service along different routes, through three Black Sea ports (Sevastopol, Batumi, and Odessa), to Beirut and Jeddah. A July 1914 ad in *Terdzhuman* offered pilgrims a variety of options, and announced that the steamship companies were authorized to give out passports.[119]

Figure 4.7. Joint Volunteer Fleet-ROPiT advertisement, offering steamship service for the upcoming pilgrimage to Mecca. 1912. (*Turkistan wilayatining gazeti*)

By 1910, ROPiT and the Volunteer Fleet were both running ads for their "Hejaz Steamships" in Muslim newspapers across the empire. "Esteemed hajjis" were offered extensive services on board, discounts for buying round-trip tickets, and a variety of choices: ROPiT offered ships from Sevastopol or Feodosiia to Beirut, while the Volunteer Fleet ran service between Odessa and Beirut, Yanbu, or Jeddah.[120] But clearly the fleet continued to grapple with its past association with Saidazimbaev, and to search for ways to entice Muslims back to its ships. In fine print, at the bottom of a 1910 Volunteer Fleet ad, ran the following disclaimer: "Said Gani Saidazimbaev has nothing to do with the services of the Volunteer Fleet."[121]

The Russian government preserved the Odessa hajj complex, with its state-of-the-art "disinfection" facility, but did not make it mandatory for pilgrims to stay there, allowing various private companies to compete for the business of hajj pilgrims. Petr Gurzhi regained control of his company, renaming it in 1909 the Society for the Transport of Muslim Pilgrims. The society advertised its services in Muslim newspapers—they included passage on special

"Hejaz steamships," ticket sales in Odessa and places across the empire, and lodging in designated Odessa hotels at set prices. Gurzhi also had plans to open a Tashkent office. But he, too, was tainted from working with Saidazimbaev: in 1909 a group of Tashkent Muslims complained about his society to the Tashkent military governor and the Odessa city-governor, describing him and his associates as "famously shady," and having "exploited hajj crowds in the past."[122]

Russian officials also preserved and developed Saidazimbaev's model for coordinating round-trip, railroad-to-steamship travel on Russian modes of transport. During the next several hajj seasons, the Ministry of Transport coordinated with Russia's various railroads to arrange for extra rolling stock and direct service during hajj season, and special "hajj cars," which had plaques with the word "Hejaz" written in large, green letters fastened to their exterior, and inside a list of station stops where pilgrims could find free hot water.[123]

This development of Saidazimabev's plan would not be easy, not least of all because it was decentralized. And pilgrims complained that they continued to be subjected to force and coercion along their routes. To keep pilgrims taking routes through the Black Sea, and to its waiting ships, the Volunteer Fleet's agents employed a number of shady tricks. The fleet closed down rival companies, many of them opened by Muslim entrepreneurs along Russian hajj routes, when they seemed to threaten the fleet's business.[124] And its agents continued to pressure pilgrims to buy its tickets. One Turkestani hajj pilgrim, traveling in 1908–9, complained of the awful harassment he experienced at the hands of Volunteer Fleet agents, both inside and outside the empire—he described predatory agents swarming crowds of pilgrims in Odessa, Constantinople, and even Damascus.[125] It is unclear whether agents engaged in these activities on orders from the fleet, or whether they did so on their own initiative, for their own enrichment.

Whatever the case, it is clear that Russia's efforts to organize the hajj continued in a decentralized manner, and had many unintended effects. It is also clear that not all Russian officials thought it was the best idea to organize the hajj traffic through the empire. At least one official, M. E. Nikol'skii, a former Russian consul in Jeddah, raised the important question of what it meant for Russian and foreign Muslims to be rerouted through Russian lands, and to make their sacred pilgrimage through this officially non-Muslim empire. In a report written in 1911, Nikol'skii made clear his concerns about the long-term effects of Russia's hajj organization on the empire, and Muslims' perceptions of their place within it. What did they see along the way, what impressions did they gain of Russia, and how did they compare Russia in their mind to what they saw in Ottoman lands? He worried that the state-supported and state-promoted itinerary through Russian and Ottoman lands gave Muslim pilgrims a bad impression of Russia. They did not see Russia's "great cities," he noted, only drab train stations, where they encountered thieves and bandits. He imagined the hajj journey through Russia as one of hardship and abuse that would only reinforce their positive impressions of Constantinople when they arrived in the Ottoman capital.[126]

Nikol'skii's concerns made a great deal of sense, and they illustrate another dimension of the hajj. In addition to being a religious ritual, an economic event, a network that opened other parts of the world to Russia, and a conduit of infectious disease and dangerous Pan-Islamic teachings, it was also a long-distance journey taken by growing numbers of Russia's Muslims by the early twentieth century, largely with the help and support of the government. They were taking this journey at a crucial moment, when Russia was trying to integrate its vast regions and populations and encourage a sense of belonging in the empire. What did they experience on this journey, what did they see from the window of their trains, how did this momentous journey reshape their

Figure 4.8. Zlatoust station, view of mountains and railroad tracks. This station lay along the main rail route that hajj pilgrims from Central Asia followed to reach Odessa. Early 1900s. (Library of Congress, Prints and Photographs Division, Prokudin-Gorskii Collection, LC-DIG-prokc-20533)

Figure 4.9. A Bashkir switch operator poses alongside the tracks of the trans-Siberian railroad, near the town of Ust Katav, just east of Ufa. Early 1900s. (Library of Congress, Prints and Photographs Division, Prokudin-Gorskii Collection, LC-DIG-prokc-20617)

ideas not only about Islam, but also about Russia, the empire to which they belonged? These were open and critical questions, and increasingly of concern to Russian officials seeking to make Muslims Russians in the early twentieth century.

Despite decades of trying various strategies, by 1910 Russia still had not managed to bring the empire's hajj traffic under state control. Much to the frustration of tsarist officials inside and outside the empire, Russia's Muslims used the services of the state selectively and sporadically. Many continued to rely on informal Muslim networks to make the long journey. And as of the early twentieth century, many were still making the pilgrimage illegally, slipping abroad without a foreign passport, and only showing up at Russian consulates when they were in trouble or needed money.

State officials noted that, not surprisingly, elite Muslims were able to evade the state-sponsored Black Sea routes with greater ease than the far more numerous poor. A 1910 report by the ministry of internal affairs noted that Muslims of means sometimes returned to Russia by train through Central Europe— taking trains from Constantinople through Vienna and Warsaw and on to Moscow or St. Petersburg—bypassing registration and quarantine in Black Sea ports. Officials had no idea how numerous these pilgrims were; but they were frustrated, nonetheless, to know that some pilgrims continued to travel alternate routes and avoid the detection of the imperial authorities.[127]

Hajj memoirs confirm the growing popularity of this route. In one account from 1899, a Tatar from the Volga region named Khamidullah Al'mushev described his hajj journey by railroad from St. Petersburg (where he met with a wealthy patron, a Muslim Duma deputy, who was generously covering the costs of his pilgrimage) through Warsaw and Vienna and on to Constantinople, where he boarded a steamship to Jeddah. Al'mushev's account does not explain his choice of this indirect route. But in 1899 the Russian government had banned the hajj due to cholera, so it seems likely that Al'mushev chose this route to avoid the appearance of making the Muslim pilgrimage, and to evade strict border controls in the Black Sea during the hajj ban.[128] In another account of the hajj from 1911, Tatar merchant Hasan Akchura (a member of the wealthy industrialist family from Simbirsk, and a relative of the famous Muslim political leader, Yusuf Akchura) took a similar route by railroad through Central Europe and steamship via Trieste. In Akchura's case, this more circuitous route seems to have been determined by war and political upheaval in the Ottoman Empire: with the Balkan Wars raging, Constantinople was unsafe and he doubtless sought to avoid it.[129]

Still, most hajj pilgrims followed the Black Sea routes, which seemed to promise speed and safety over alternate land routes, but continued to disappoint pilgrims in many ways. The Russian press described the terrible conditions that the empire's hajj pilgrims continued to suffer abroad along the Black Sea–Red Sea route. In sharp contrast to ROPiT and Volunteer Fleet advertisements touting the ease, comfort, and speed of their "Hejaz steamships," many who took these ships went hungry on board for days, were abused along their routes and delayed in crowded quarantines, and found the journey altogether miserable.[130] In Constantinople, crowds of impoverished Russian and Bukharan pilgrims were fixtures in the city's landscape, begging and sleeping in the streets, most of them penniless and stranded on their way to or from Jeddah. In 1910 the mayor of Constantinople wrote the Ottoman interior minister about the "urgent need" to build a lodging house (misafirhane) to get them off the streets.[131]

Disagreements and miscommunications among tsarist officials involved in the functioning of Russia's hajj infrastructure were endemic and, apparently, unsolvable. As of 1913, tsarist officials were still convening interministerial conferences on how to organize the hajj "once and for all," and Muslim deputies in the Duma were angrily raising the issue in meetings of the parliament. The Russian press reported that the issue of government leadership of the hajj, first raised in the Duma by Stolypin, had "stalled" since then, to the detriment of the empire's Muslims.[132]

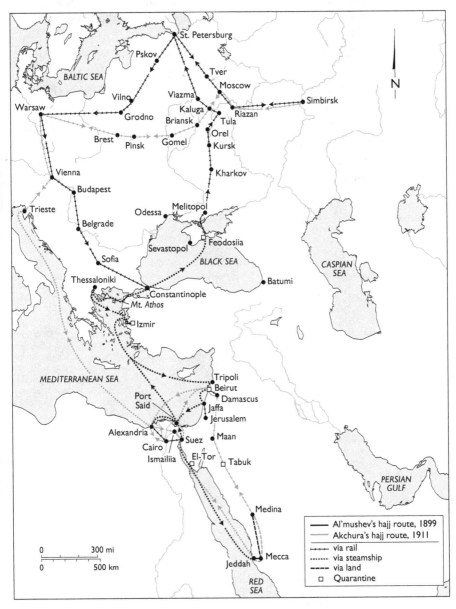

Map 6. Hajj routes through Central Europe followed by Al'mushev (1899) and Akchura (1911).

And yet, this does not mean that Russia's efforts to organize the hajj were a complete failure. Recall that the government had multifaceted goals for its involvement in the hajj, related to both internal and external processes. These were not limited to sanitary concerns, nor were they singularly focused on controlling the traffic, but were also related to strategic agendas. While Russia did not, in the end, achieve the hoped-for government "monopoly" of the hajj, the transimperial infrastructure that it built in pursuit of this goal was an achievement in its own right. And it served a crucial strategic purpose. In the context of global imperial rivalries, particularly between Russia and the British in Central Asia, Russia's hajj infrastructure extended Russia's presence and influence deeper into Ottoman, Persian, and Central Asian lands, and essentially functioned as a mechanism of Russian imperial expansion.

5

The Hajj and Socialist Revolution

THE outbreak of World War I in August 1914 ended the tsarist government's involvement in the hajj. The war disrupted global communication networks and patterns of human migration, including the flow of Muslim pilgrims to Mecca. Having peaked at 300,000 pilgrims annually in the early 1900s, global hajj traffic declined dramatically after 1914 and slowed to a trickle for the duration of the war.[1] War also contributed to the collapse of the tsarist regime in 1917 and the Bolshevik seizure of power in Russia, led by Vladimir Lenin. Over the next decade the Marxist Bolsheviks would consolidate their hold on power and reconquer most of the lands of the former Russian Empire to create the Union of Soviet Socialist Republics (USSR), the world's first socialist state.[2]

One might assume that the rise of Soviet power in Russia brought about the closure of hajj routes through former tsarist lands, and the end of Russian involvement in the hajj. After all, the USSR was governed by a communist regime with global ambitions for socialist revolution and was the first state in history ideologically committed to eliminating religion and imposing atheism. To disenfranchise religious institutions and remove religion from public life, the Soviets launched violent and destructive antireligion campaigns in the 1920s and 1930s. They confiscated and secularized religious property, harassed, exiled, and in some cases executed clergy, and taught atheism in Soviet schools.[3] But instead of prohibiting the hajj traffic, the Soviets reopened the old routes to Mecca through Russian lands in the late 1920s, and began to organize cross-border transport for hajj pilgrims on now-Soviet railroads and steamships. Soviet consuls in Persia, Afghanistan, and China issued passports to Muslims to make the pilgrimage through Soviet lands. Odessa reemerged as a hub of Eurasian hajj traffic as pilgrims again thronged the city to catch Soviet steamships bound for Jeddah. These steamships were former ROPiT and Volunteer Fleet vessels, now run by Sovtorgflot, the newly created Soviet merchant fleet—they now bore names such as *Il'ich* (Lenin's patronymic) and *Communist*, instead of *Tsarina* and *Jerusalem*. And in Jeddah, where the Soviets had opened a consulate in 1924, the consul began to offer support and services to hajj pilgrims moving through the port.

Soviet support for the hajj was patterned on the tsarist model and built upon the tsarist-era hajj infrastructure, but it was different in one crucial respect: it was designed for transit hajj pilgrims—that is, foreign Muslims who made the pilgrimage through Soviet lands, mainly from Persia, Afghanistan, and China. It did not to extend to Soviet Muslims, and in the late 1920s Soviet officials would struggle to block Soviet Muslims from making the hajj, and to isolate them from transit pilgrims moving through the country during hajj season.

As in the tsarist era, the Soviet hajj campaign grew out of pressure from below. In the late 1920s, foreign Muslims began to petition the Soviet state for access to their old routes via the Black Sea. But the Soviets also became involved in the hajj in support of pragmatic state agendas, as part of their broader efforts to spread the revolution globally, and build socialism in the USSR. Officials at Sovtorgflot, and in the Soviet ministries of trade and foreign policy, in particular, saw the hajj as a means to spread socialist revolution across Muslim Asia, and generate foreign currency to fund Stalin's ambitious project of industrialization, launched in 1927. (The Soviet ruble was not convertible on the international market.) In the late 1920s the Soviets would compete with foreign states, above all the British and Persians, to influence, control, and profit from the global hajj traffic.

Much has been written about the Soviet assault on Islam in Central Asia during the 1920s and 1930s, including the destruction of mosques and medreses, persecution of the ulama (religious elites), and the Soviet campaign to unveil women (*hujum*).[4] However, as this chapter will show, together with their domestic efforts to destroy Muslim social structures and remove Islam from public life, the Soviets also quietly supported Islam for foreign Muslims, encouraging and supporting the hajj along now-Soviet routes and in Arabia. This paradox is consistent with the more nuanced picture we now have of early Soviet religious policy. Recent studies have shown that Soviet antireligion campaigns were neither total nor indiscriminate. They were instead carried out selectively, and state interests shaped plans and policies toward particular religions.[5]

The Soviet hajj campaign would be brief. It began in 1926 and was over by 1930, when the Great Depression brought about a sharp decline once again in global hajj traffic. Yet however short lived, the hajj campaign is important in illuminating the global dimensions and ambitions of early Soviet policy toward Islam. The campaign was part of the broader project of Soviet cultural diplomacy in the late 1920s. Scholars have described how the Soviets welcomed foreign visitors to the USSR in the 1920s and early 1930s and organized tours for them around the new country to cultivate a positive image of the USSR in the world. This story has been told thus far with regard to Europe and the West, in terms of the nearly 100,000 foreigners who visited the USSR in the interwar years, among them tens of thousands of European and American writers, artists, and scientists, who wrote indelible works about their impressions of the Soviet experiment.[6] Less well known, however, are the Eastern dimensions of this story. By opening Soviet hajj routes to foreign Muslims, and organizing tours for them along set routes by Soviet transport, Soviet officials sought to expose them to the marvels of Soviet culture, industry, and society, and in this way plant the seeds of revolution across Asia. Hajj transport, then, was also part of the Soviet project to "showcase the great experiment."[7]

"LET us turn our faces towards Asia," Lenin famously proclaimed in the early 1920s, when the anticipated communist revolution in Europe did not happen. "The East will help us conquer the West." This call marked the start of Soviet efforts to "liberate" Muslims in India and other parts of Asia from imperial rule, and bring the Marxist revolution to them.[8] Having consolidated their hold over the central lands of the Russian Empire after a protracted civil war, the Bolsheviks next sought to recover and reclaim tsarist territories in Central Asia.

Home to millions of Turkic- and Persian-speaking Muslims, Central Asia was an important cultural and geographic point of entry into bordering Muslim societies under British colonial and Chinese rule. The Soviets hoped to make Central Asia a model of socialist transformation for Muslims across Eurasia, from Constantinople to China, at a time of great upheaval and political flux across the region. They sought not simply to reconquer Central Asia, but to bring the revolution to the people living there, a process that would involve violence and the destruction of existing hierarchies and social structures. In more conventionally colonial terms, the Soviets also saw Central Asia as an important source of agricultural products and raw materials they needed to "build socialism"—to collectivize agriculture, build cities and factories, and create a modern socialist state.

Predominantly Muslim and agricultural, Central Asia posed a unique challenge to Soviet efforts to spread the socialist revolution. Islamic elites held entrenched power in the region, and there was virtually no working class in Central Asia to excite to revolt. The Soviets sought to solve this problem by developing a strategy focused on women, as Gregory Massell has shown. Drawing on Western stereotypes about Islam, Soviet officials decided that Central Asia's women, as the oppressed class in society, were its weakest link and most ripe for revolt. Women were deemed a "surrogate proletariat," and Soviet officials launched a campaign that encouraged them to throw off their veils and demand an end to their oppression. Using socialist rhetoric of egalitarianism and emancipation to mobilize Central Asian women, the Soviets aimed to undermine traditional Islamic hierarchies and destroy the social structure in Turkestan. This destructive campaign caused violence against women and the breakdown of traditional hierarchies, and allowed the Soviets to establish power in the region by the late 1920s.[9]

But Soviet ambitions in Central Asia extended beyond the borders of the former Russian Empire. In the 1920s the Soviets engaged in a low-grade war across the region with the British, a kind of continuation of the Great Game, though with new political and ideological inflections. The outlines of this story are well known. Scholars have described how Anglo-Russian competition continued in this period across Central Asia, involving British spies, communist revolutionaries, White Russians, Muslim agents, and Chinese warlords.[10] Hajj pilgrims were part of this story as well. In their quest to penetrate the "unenlightened" masses of Muslims across Asia, and "liberate" them from colonial oppression, the Soviets would co-opt the hajj as an imperial mechanism of influence and control, as well as economic exploitation. They would do this largely by taking over and working through the consular system that the tsarist government had organized around the hajj traffic, including the constellation of networks across northern Persia and western China, and those in Constantinople and Jeddah.

Soviet interest in the hajj began in the Commissariat of Foreign Affairs (NKID), and was initially focused on Mecca. Interestingly, the Soviets valued in Mecca what the tsarist regime had feared about it: they imagined it as a site of conspiratorial political agitation and anticolonial scheming. "Getting to Mecca is of crucial importance to us," wrote Soviet commissar of foreign affairs Georgii Chicherin in 1924.[11] Chicherin and other Soviet officials had identified Mecca and Arabia as a crucial site in Soviet competition with the British across Asia.

They understood Mecca as a site where Muslim elites from around the world gathered once a year, and attached great political and strategic importance to it. They saw in the hajj an opportunity to cultivate broad Muslim loyalties and, they hoped, pave the way for Soviet-led socialist revolution across Asia.

In practical terms, the annual hajj was a precious opportunity for the Soviets to gather intelligence on Muslim politics across Eurasia, and the activities of their political rivals, above all the British. Since the fall of the USSR in the 1990s, scholars have engaged in lively discussions about how, notwithstanding its anti-imperial rhetoric and ideological antipathy to imperialism, the Soviet Union was by many measures an empire.[12] For their part, European colonial officials viewed Soviet involvement in Arabia this way, as essentially a continuation of nineteenth-century imperial rivalries, a new kind of Russian imperialism that had different ideological and political implications but encompassed much of the same geographic space. British and Dutch officials regarded the Soviet penetration of Arabia warily in the 1920s. They rightly feared it as the pivot of a Soviet strategy to undermine their empires in the Muslim East, by encouraging anticolonial movements among Muslims gathered in Mecca.[13]

To penetrate Mecca and establish Soviet influence over the hajj, Chicherin established a Soviet general consulate in Jeddah in 1924. He chose as Jeddah consul general Karim Abdraufovich Khakimov, a Muslim Tatar from Ufa and a trusted Bolshevik. Khakimov had joined the Bolshevik Party in 1918 and served in the Red Army during its invasion of Central Asia. Valued by the NKID for his linguistic abilities—he spoke Russian, Turkish, and Persian— Khakimov had been sent abroad to open consulates in key areas of Soviet-British competition. Before Arabia, the NKID sent him to Persia, where he served in Teheran, Mashhad, and Rasht. Khakimov's appointment to Jeddah made sense given Chicherin's goals: as a Muslim, Khakimov would have access to the Holy City of Mecca, and, presumably, serve as an emissary of Soviet influence among Muslims from around the world. In Jeddah Khakimov served alongside other Muslim Bolsheviks who would be instrumental to Soviet diplomacy with the Saudi state that emerged in Arabia.[14]

Soon after he opened the Jeddah consulate, Khakimov began to receive petitions from foreign hajj pilgrims, including many from China. Against the background of the protracted Husayn-Ibn Saud war in Arabia, which had broken out in 1921 in the wake of the collapse of the Ottoman Empire, lawlessness reigned, no state power existed to organize and protect pilgrims from historical predators, and pilgrims once again fell prey to thieves and Bedouin attacks. Harkening back to the pre-Soviet era, Kashgar pilgrims from Sinkiang began to approach Khakimov to ask for the diplomatic protection "they had enjoyed in the past."[15] Khakimov saw strategic and economic opportunities in these petitions. In 1925 he proposed to Chicherin that the Soviet government facilitate the hajj for Muslims from China, Afghanistan, and Persia. By simplifying the visa procedure through Soviet lands for hajj pilgrims, he argued, they could attract more Chinese, Persian, and Afghan Muslims to use Soviet railroads and steamships out of the Black Sea to get to Mecca. And the Soviet consulate could provide protection to them, given that they had no diplomatic representatives to help them in the Hejaz.[16]

Chicherin received Khakimov's proposal when the Soviet government was under growing pressure to reopen routes to Mecca through the USSR. In early 1926 the NKID received petitions from Persian Muslims who demanded access to their old routes by way of the Black Sea and Constantinople. They asked to be allowed to cross the border and take Soviet railroads and steamships to Mecca.[17] At the same time, Soviet consulates in Sinkiang reported similar requests from Chinese Muslims, who petitioned for permission to make the hajj through the USSR, instead of their usual way through India. The Soviet route appealed to Chinese Muslims because it allowed them to visit Constantinople, a site of important Muslim shrines and holy sites and a popular stop along pre–World War I hajj itineraries, as we have seen. The route through the USSR also offered Chinese hajj pilgrims a more comfortable climate for travel: in the late 1920s the hajj fell during the summer months, and many complained about the tropical heat in India.[18]

These demands from Persian and Chinese Muslims were not coincidental or isolated cases. They attest to the global revival of hajj traffic, largely due to political changes in Arabia. The war in Arabia had just ended, and the Saudis had declared their new state (in 1932 they would rename it the Saudi Kingdom).[19] This brought stability to Arabia and a revival of the pilgrimage. In 1926 the Saudi government organized and oversaw the hajj, bringing order to it for the first time in nearly a decade. The effects were immediate: the year 1927 saw the greatest hajj traffic since World War I, and Europe's imperial powers resumed responsibility for facilitating the traffic between their colonies and Arabia, built new facilities for pilgrims in and around Jeddah, and competed with one another for influence in Arabia and control over the hajj.[20]

Eager to bring the USSR into this imperial competition, Chicherin supported Khakimov's idea. In February 1926, he submitted an expanded proposal for Soviet involvement in the hajj to the Politburo (the highest policy-making body in the Communist Party), to ask for its approval. The proposal he submitted called for Soviet support and transport of foreign hajj pilgrims, as well as the dispatch of select Soviet Muslims on the hajj as political agents. It essentially called for a covert operation to use the pilgrimage as cover for political and revolutionary agitations. Specifically, Chicherin proposed that "persons of influence in Muslim quarters" in the USSR be sent to Mecca to "promote our policy there . . . under the guise of ordinary pilgrims." Beyond this, he proposed to "bring the Muslim masses' spontaneous drive for the hajj under our own control" and provide the pilgrims with direct passage to the Red Sea on Sovtorgflot ships.[21]

Many Soviet officials opposed Chicherin's proposal. Just when the Soviets were setting internal borders and struggling to create stable government, some local officials complained that the hajj traffic through their region posed a serious and as yet unmanageable sanitary problem. Some petitioned the state to close the old routes, or at least limit access to them. Other officials opposed hajj patronage on ideological grounds, asking an obvious question: How could a socialist state justify support for a major Islamic ritual? The strongest resistance came from the Soviet state security service (OGPU), which worried about spies and "saboteurs" slipping into Soviet territory amid the hajj traffic. The OGPU would frequently clash with the NKID over the Soviet hajj campaign.

Despite widespread resistance, the Soviet state embraced the proposal. In 1926 it launched a secret, never publicly announced "hajj campaign" that involved the collaboration of Soviet officials across vast regions and branches of government. The NKID and Sovtorgflot took the lead in the campaign. In 1926 the NKID opened the USSR to foreign hajj pilgrims, and authorized its consuls in Persia, Afghanistan, Jeddah, Constantinople, and Sinkiang to issue passports to hajj pilgrims. Over the next few years it would work closely with Sovtorgflot to encourage foreign Muslims to use Soviet routes, transport, and facilities to get to Mecca.

Sovtorgflot's Moscow headquarters contacted its branch offices across the Soviet Union to announce that it was "reviving" the project begun by tsarist steamship companies to "attract pilgrims" to Russian hajj routes. Given that the route was "relatively safe and comfortable," the announcement noted that there was every reason to think that restoring this route would be successful.[22] Sovtorgflot sent its announcement out to its agencies across the USSR, in Ufa, Semipalatinsk, Samara, Batumi, Tbilisi, Nizhnii Novgorod, Orenburg, Tashkent, Astrakhan, Baku, and Rostov. It instructed Sovtorgflot to sell tickets to Jeddah to foreign hajj pilgrims only. Soviet citizens were forbidden to buy them.

It established prices for foreign passports and round-trip fare, which included rail travel to and from Odessa, steamship travel with food, a five-day stay in the *khadzhikhane* (lodging house) in Odessa, and quarantine fees.[23]

Sovtorgflot officials spoke of a "revival" of the tsarist-era hajj infrastructure, but it was more of a reconstruction. The Soviets had inherited the foundations of this infrastructure—railroads, steamships, and a network of foreign consulates—as well as a blueprint for organizing the hajj traffic, but in many ways the Soviet hajj campaign had to start afresh. After more than a decade without access to the Russian routes, pilgrims from Persia and other neighboring lands had developed new itineraries and routes to Mecca. The Soviets would have to develop strategies to lure them in large numbers back to the routes. And the tsarist agents that had staffed the hajj infrastructure were now all gone, swept from their positions with the regime change in Russia. They had taken with them precious experience and knowledge about the pilgrimage and the disparate regions that now-Soviet routes encompassed. To staff their hajj infrastructure and organize pilgrims, the Soviets would need to find and recruit new agents on the ground from Odessa to Jeddah, Constantinople to Afghanistan, China to Persia.[24]

The world had also changed dramatically since 1914. The collapse of Europe's land empires during World War I—the Ottoman, Austro-Hungarian, Russian, and German empires all fell—disrupted frameworks that had undergirded global empires and facilitated long-distance migrations. New nation-states were created from the Balkans to China in the postwar period, and, with these, new political borders manned by modern border controls that interrupted global migration flows. Eurasia, a region that encompassed former Russian, Ottoman, Persian, and Chinese lands and had long been defined by human mobility, became fragmented after World War I, divided by new states that imposed controls over trade and migration.[25] Among other things, this new order in Eurasia put new obstacles in the way of pilgrims, and pushed many to seek alternate routes to Mecca.

The head of Sovtorgflot's Black Sea Division, a certain Comrade Lashanovetskii, surveyed the scene from Odessa and raised many of these issues.[26] He predicted that it would take several years for the Soviets to attract large crowds of foreign hajj pilgrims to the Black Sea routes. Optimistic officials had estimated that Sovtorgflot could expect 5,000 hajj pilgrims on its ships in 1927—but Lashanovetskii doubted this. Sovtorgflot would have to retrace the same path, with the same difficulties, of ROPiT and the Volunteer Fleet in their time: small groups of pilgrims, and deficits, early on; then building a reputation through word of mouth, slowly attracting hajj traffic, and turning deficits into profits over many years. Lashanovetskii noted how much the context, challenges, and political goals had changed in the late 1920s. ROPiT and the Volunteer Fleet in the early 1900s had only needed to overcome economic competition, but the Soviets were now engaged in that as well as a "nasty political struggle," in which their opponents tried all kinds of "dirty tricks."[27]

Luring pilgrims to Soviet routes would require thoughtful planning by Sovtorgflot. The state needed to develop a flexible apparatus staffed with experienced people, and organize the hajj in a serious, systematic way. The fleet had no idea how many pilgrims to expect, but it needed to be prepared to accommodate as many as possible, and it should plan to use its best ships—Lashanovetskii suggested the *Kursk* and the *Lakhta*, which together could accommodate 1,850 passengers. He strongly advised against chartering foreign ships to help with transport. This would defeat a key part of the Soviet campaign, to "treat very well" the first groups of pilgrims so that they would gain a positive impression of the USSR and Sovtorgflot, and would spread the word to other pilgrims, and in this way increase interest and inflow of pilgrims along Soviet routes. This could not be achieved using foreign ships and crews.[28]

A growing body of work explores the early Soviet state's development of domestic tourism as a form of cultural diplomacy. To showcase the socialist state and build international support for Soviet communism, the USSR in 1925 created the All-Union Society for Cultural Ties Abroad (VOKS). Tasked with promoting a positive image of the USSR in the world, VOKS engaged in, among other things, hosting and guiding foreign visitors to the Soviet Union, most of them from Western Europe and the United States.[29] There was economic motivation for Soviet tourism as well, as the historian Michael David-Fox has shown. Against the backdrop of the Stalinist campaign to rapidly industrialize the country and "build socialism," the Soviet government increasingly saw foreign tourists as a source of much-needed hard currency. The development of Soviet tourism—including the creation of Intourist, the iconic Soviet travel agency— accelerated in the late 1920s. This happened in the years of what Stalin called the Great Break (*velikii perelom*), 1928–31, a period distinguished by its accelerated, coercive, top-down, and utopian drive to industrialize. In this context, economic considerations became more central to Soviet state building, while cultural diplomacy became more radical in nature. This produced bitter tensions within the state between those more pragmatic and those more ideological, with the latter largely opposed to the development of "hard-currency tourism."[30]

Scholars of Soviet cultural diplomacy have so far focused on state efforts to court Western intellectuals and elites in the 1920s. There was an Eastern aspect to this diplomacy as well—and it targeted not just intellectuals and elites, as Lashanovetskii's report and relevant correspondence make clear. Before the Soviet state established Intourist in 1929—and with it an official tourist industry and infrastructure—Soviet officials would work to rebuild the infrastructure to support foreign hajj pilgrims in the USSR and along their global routes. Soviets officials facilitated the hajj through the country to pull large numbers of foreign Muslims into the USSR—ordinary people, most of them rural and illiterate—and expose them to Soviet industry, culture, and society. Just as tsarist officials had embraced hajj patronage to impress foreign Muslims favorably toward the Russian Empire, the foreign policy dimension was central for the Soviets, too. Sovtorgflot and the NKID were determined to influence foreign Muslims' hajj itineraries, and recruit them in large numbers to Soviet routes in order to profit from them, but they also sought to design a journey through Soviet lands that would instill in pilgrims a positive impression of the USSR.

THE Soviet hajj campaign began in earnest in 1927, coinciding with the start of Stalin's industrialization campaign and the first Five-Year Plan. "Building socialism" in the USSR was an enormously expensive undertaking, and one paradoxically dependent upon foreign capital and capitalist expertise. Involving itself in the potentially lucrative hajj transport was one strategy that the Soviet state tried among others—including tourism and the state's introduction of a hard-currency retail chain (*Torgsin*)—to raise foreign capital.[31] In a series of meetings starting in 1926, Sovtorgflot proposed ambitious measures to build new sanitary and lodging facilities across Soviet lands to support the foreign hajj traffic.[32] In the fall of 1926 Sovtorgflot and the NKID began to reconstruct the tsarist-era hajj infrastructure. The next hajj rituals were set to begin in Arabia in June 1927, and this gave them several months to prepare.

Sovtorgflot first tackled housing. In 1926 it opened a khadzhikhane for hajj pilgrims in Odessa, the port it had chosen through which to centralize hajj transport. As in the tsarist period, pilgrims could take Soviet railroads directly from Central Asia to Odessa, and there board Sovtorgflot steamships bound for Jeddah. With permission from the Water-Sanitation Division authorities in Odessa, Sovtorgflot took over an isolated building on the promenade above Odessa's port, No. 65 Primorskii Boulevard, and spent tens of thousands of rubles renovating it. Workers equipped the building with showers, added steam heat, repaired the roof, and built a disinfection room to process the anticipated masses of pilgrims.[33] It is unclear why Sovtorgflot did not use the khadzhikhane that Saidazimbaev had created for hajj pilgrims in 1908, in the outlying Perse-syp neighborhood. Perhaps the building had been repurposed in the intervening years. It is also true that the Primorskii Boulevard location was more convenient for pilgrims, just a five-minute walk down the famed Potemkin Staircase to board ships in the port below. This location made it easier for Soviet authorities to isolate pilgrims from the general population of the city.[34]

Outside the USSR's borders, Sovtorgflot hired foreign agents to advertise its new hajj service and recruit pilgrims to its ships. Over the fall of 1926 and winter of 1927, Sovtorgflot officials worked closely with Soviet consuls and Soviet Trade Agency representatives abroad to identify and hire potential agents: ideally wealthy Muslim merchants with a good reputation "among the religious masses," and connections to local hajj networks. In doing this, they followed a pattern established in the late nineteenth century by the European colonial powers, all of which built their hajj infrastructures by co-opting and building upon existing Muslim hajj networks, and hiring brokers and agents active in local hajj industries.[35]

Retracing prerevolutionary patterns of hajj traffic, Sovtorgflot officials focused on China, Persia, and Afghanistan, and Constantinople and Jeddah recruitment efforts. To find and hire Muslim agents, they relied on the support of Soviet diplomats and Trade Agency representatives, and the ground-level connections they had forged in these regions. In Persia, for example, the Soviet ambassador in Teheran put Sovtorgflot in touch with a certain Khalesi Zade, an experienced local hajj broker who knew all the Muslim agents involved in the local hajj industry. Khalesi Zade could help the fleet recruit brokers across Persia, and facilitate their "acquisition" (akvizatsiia) of pilgrims on a wide scale.[36]

In Sinkiang, Sovtorgflot worked through the Soviets' network of four consulates, which had been opened by the tsarist regime in the 1880s as part of Russo-British rivalries in Central Asia: in Kashgar, Urumchi, Kuldja, and Chuguchak. Chinese-ruled Sinkiang bordered on Soviet Central Asia and was now central to Soviet-British rivalries.[37] In January 1927, Sovtorgflot sent one of its directors, Comrade Suslin, to Kashgar to work with the Soviet consul to recruit agents. Suslin invited a group of wealthy local Muslim merchants to the Soviet consulate to ask them to work for the fleet. He offered them generous pay to participate in the "movement" of pilgrims through Soviet lands. He promised them the support of the Soviet consulate and asked them to "agitate" among local Muslims to get them to make the hajj through the USSR, instead of India.[38]

At the same time, a Sovtorgflot official approached two Turkish citizens in Constantinople, Muhammad Murat Remzi and Hasan Fahmi, to invite them to work for the fleet. They were hajj brokers and guides who worked in Sinkiang, organizing hajj pilgrims and escorting them to Mecca and back every year. That fall they were on their way back from Mecca, passing through the Turkish city; the Sovtorgflot official must have circled the crowd of arriving hajj pilgrims, and picked them out as pilgrim-guides and thus potential recruits. He offered them a fee to "agitate" among Muslims when they returned to Sinkiang to take Soviet routes and Sovtorgflot ships instead of routes through India and by British steamers. The two accepted the offer, with certain conditions. Upon their return to Sinkiang, they contacted the Soviet consul to ask him to improve conditions along the Soviet routes.[39]

In their negotiations with the Soviet consul, Remzi and Fahmi revealed a number of obstacles that deterred many Muslims from making the hajj through the USSR. These, in turn, revealed how dramatically conditions along the old routes had changed under Soviet rule. The first issue was related to currency. In 1926 the Soviet government had passed laws to limit the export of currency and valuables from the country as part of its efforts to build the state and economy.[40]

Figure 5.1. A postcard from 1930 shows hajj pilgrims from Central Asia strolling in Eminönü, Istanbul. They probably arrived in the city on Sovtorgflot ships. (*Hac, Kutsal Yolculuk* [Istanbul: Denizler Kitabevi, 2014])

Remzi and Fahmi reported that pilgrims were allowed to take only the equivalent of 300 rubles out of the USSR, not nearly enough to cover the costs of the hajj, estimated at 1,000 rubles for the round-trip voyage. Anything above that was heavily taxed. But many wealthy Muslims, planning extended stays abroad in and around Mecca, took as much as 50,000 rubles' worth of gold with them. The Soviet government forbade the export of gold and silver abroad, except in very small quantities—and yet in Arabia, nothing was accepted but silver and gold. To attract hajj pilgrims, the British government did not limit the amount of silver and gold pilgrims could take through India to Mecca. This had also been the case in tsarist Russia, and for that reason every year from Turkestan, Afghanistan, and India as many as 30,000 Muslims went to Mecca through Russia, and the tsarist government earned millions of rubles from these hajj pilgrims. Remzi and Fahmi urged the Soviet government to abolish the fee it charged hajj pilgrims for exporting valuables—after all, they were taking gold and silver out of China and not the USSR, and should therefore be given free passage.

Remzi and Fahmi also raised the issue of Soviet transit conditions, which were hard on hajj pilgrims. For example, when they got sick and were forced to stay in one place, they had to present themselves to the Foreign Department of the Secret Police (Inotdel). This required time and money, and was an inconvenience they did not face in British India. There were also questions about the cost of travel, as Sovtorgflot had not advertised its prices. Pilgrims often decided whether to go through the USSR or India based on a comparison of costs. All of these obstacles had to be removed for Sovtorgflot to "bring to fruition" its hajj transport plan, Remzi and Fahmi argued. They also urged Sovtorgflot to advertise, and offered their help. They proposed that it send them fifty or sixty copies of an announcement, printed in Turkish, about the comforts of traveling to Mecca through Russia to disseminate throughout Sinkiang.[41]

With the 1927 hajj season fast approaching, problems began to crop up inside and outside the USSR over the hajj transport plan. There was confusion about which Soviet institutions would pay for the preparations, which included the construction of new facilities for pilgrims across Soviet lands. In April, the Commissariat of Health in the Kazakh Soviet Socialist Republic (Kazakhstan) wrote to the Sovtorgflot office to complain about the costs it was incurring. It resented being asked to build "observation points" in Bakhty and Dzharkent, along pilgrims' land routes inside new Kazakh borders. No agreement had been signed between the commissariat and Sovtorgflot, and yet it was being asked to pay for this construction. Still worse, it had been given only two months' notice, and would not be able to complete construction in time. It accused Sovtorgflot of misleading it about the costs involved in serving pilgrims, and also raised the issue of disease. The commissariat's letter stressed that they had no way to protect themselves against epidemics brought into the country by pilgrims, so they "must strenuously protest the organization of transit pilgrims through Kazakhstan's borders this season."[42]

Sovtorgflot's agent in Afghanistan, Ali Akbar Kamalov, reported serious problems working with Soviet authorities. Although promised their help in organizing hajj transport, Kamalov found many uncooperative. Traveling to Ashkhabad (in today's Turkmenistan) in late spring 1927, he found that only the railroad authority had made preparations to receive pilgrims from Persia and Afghanistan. He learned that the Persians had no idea that the Soviets were planning transport for the hajj, and knew nothing about how to buy tickets or which routes to follow. He informed the OGPU of this, and was sent by them to the border town of Kushka to meet with Yahya Mamedov, Sovtorfglot's agent in Persia, and make arrangements. Kushka was a former Russian military outpost and the southernmost point of the USSR, on the border between the newly created Turkmen SSR (Turkmenistan) and Afghanistan. It was also the closest railway station for Afghans: the tsarist regime in 1901 had built a new branch that connected Kushka to the Merv and the Central Asian railroad, as part of its efforts to extend influence into Afghanistan. Kushka and its rail station lay along the main route used by Afghans to enter now-Soviet lands.[43] While in Kushka, Kamalov conducted talks with local officials from the Commissariat of Health and railroads, to organize services and facilities for pilgrims. He also found a local caravanserai that could be used as a khadzhikhane, where pilgrims could stay for as little as fifty kopecks a night. But in Kushka he also learned from local authorities that the hajj campaigns in Persia and Afghanistan had "collapsed." Kamalov blamed this on Seid Kerim, his fellow Sovtorgflot agent in Afghanistan, whom he accused of failing to advertise the fleet's services, and acting "indifferent" toward the hajj transport. Dejected, Kamalov returned to Tashkent to deliver the bad news to Sovtorgflot authorities there.[44]

The problems Kamalov reported had much to do with poor communication and planning among Soviet authorities, and between Moscow and its emerging internal republican governments. As of March, with the hajj traffic due to start in May, Turkmenistan's Commissariat of Health still had not set up planned border quarantine stations or medical stations for pilgrims in Kushka and Ashkhabad, because it had not received the 25,000 rubles that Gosplan (the State Planning Committee in Moscow, responsible for central economic planning) had allotted for it.[45] At the same time, Kamalov faced resistance from the Persian government to his efforts to organize the hajj across Soviet borders. In the spring of 1927 Kamalov had arranged a meeting at the border point of Gaudan—a Soviet town along the USSR-Persia border—of Soviet and foreign officials involved in the hajj campaign in Persia, Afghanistan, and the USSR. Mamedov never showed up, and Kamalov soon discovered why: the Persian government was refusing requests for travel to Soviet lands, in the hopes of defeating the Soviet hajj campaign.[46]

In April 1927 the OGPU wrote to Sovtorgflot to report that the recruitment of pilgrims was going poorly in Persia. The OGPU blamed Mamedov, the fleet's local agent there, for this. To encourage pilgrims to take only Soviet routes and transport, Sovtorgflot was selling exclusively round-trip tickets to pilgrims. Many pilgrims resented the set itinerary, and many liked to take alternate routes home, to visit different sites and countries. To show flexibility, Sovtorgflot offered pilgrims a thirty-percent reimbursement on their return fare, if they chose not to use the second half of the ticket. But Mamedov had erred and promised pilgrims a fifty-percent discount. The British seized upon this mistake, and stoked Persians' suspicions of Soviet motives to discourage them from taking Soviet routes.

But there was a larger issue: Mamedov had reported that the Persian government was refusing to issue any passports to Mecca in 1927. Scholars have argued that the Persian government blocked Muslims from making the hajj in 1927 for political and religious reasons—for fear of the Saudis' antipathy to heterodox Shi'ism, and to protect its predominantly Shi'i citizens from persecution.[47] But documents from the Soviet archives reveal other important factors. Busy with state-building projects of its own in the late 1920s, the Persian government saw the hajj as a drain on the domestic economy, and worried that Muslims were taking large sums of money out of the country. It could not formally prohibit the hajj, because of its obligatory nature for Muslims, so instead the Persian government spread lies about the Saudi government's destruction of sites in Mecca and Medina, and cholera and plague outbreaks. Whatever the motivations of the Persian government, Mamedov predicted few Persian pilgrims would take advantage of Soviet hajj transport in 1927.[48]

In Afghanistan, too, Sovtorgflot's agent Kamalov had been unsuccessful in recruiting large numbers of pilgrims. The OGPU blamed Sovtorgflot. It had not given Kamalov the resources he needed to build a planned khadzhikhane in Kushka, to support needy pilgrims and draw them to the Soviet routes. There had apparently been a misunderstanding between Kamalov and the Sovtorgflot agent in Tashkent: each thought it was the other's job to establish the khadzhikhane. Sovtorgflot also had not lowered the costs of transport, as the British had done, to make rates affordable to Afghans.[49] It had also become clear that Sovtorgflot's other agent in Afghanistan, Seid Kerim, had done nothing to recruit pilgrims. Caravan traders passing through Kushka told Soviet officials that most Afghan pilgrims were headed to Jeddah by way of India that year, not the USSR. It seemed that Seid Kerim had done a poor job advertising Sovtorgflot's services, as he had promised to do. He had received a stack of Sovtorgflot posters but had apparently not posted any beyond Herat.[50]

Based on this information, Kamalov predicted that few pilgrims from Persia or Afghanistan would use Soviet routes in 1927. The cost of travel by rail through Soviet lands and by steamships was much too high for Afghans. He noted that the Afghans were "not very cultured" and valued "inexpensive over comfort and quality."[51] It was certainly more dangerous for them to take the Indian route: they went on foot and horseback by way of Kandahar, where many died in the mountain passes, and then by steamship across the Indian Ocean, where more died from the tropical summer heat. But "Muslim teachings" told them that death while making the hajj was a "good death," and so few could easily be deterred from this route. Kamalov also noted the negative effects of the strict itinerary imposed along the Soviet routes. Afghans did not see the direct, rapid transport that Sovtorgflot offered from Kushka to Odessa as a positive thing, but rather as a hindrance on their movement. Many Afghans wanted to stop at holy shrines and sites in Soviet Central Asia on their hajj journey—not to be sped through the country by train, as the Soviets wanted. In India they enjoyed freedom of movement. Last minute planning by the Soviets had made recruitment all but impossible. Kamalov blamed Seid Kerim: not only had he not done his job, he had sabotaged the Soviet hajj campaign.[52]

In western China, too, Soviet officials had difficulties recruiting hajj pilgrims. In Kashgar the British had launched a "rabid campaign" to prevent Soviet hajj transport. The Soviet trade representative there, identified in documents as Comrade Klidzin, reported that the British consulate had Chinese authorities and leading merchants solidly under its influence, and through them it was urging pilgrims to take routes to Mecca through India. The British were spreading rumors about terrible things that would happen to Muslims if they went through Soviet territory. And they were "aggressively" issuing passports to India to all would-be pilgrims.[53]

To reverse this situation, Klidzin suggested that the fleet funnel money into the region. Soviet officials could use the money to bribe Chinese officials, and to tap into the "middle merchantry," getting them to organize a "broad, public campaign" to encourage hajj travel through the USSR. They had tried this already with a merchant named Akhub Abdulrasulev, paying him handsomely to agitate among Muslims and use his connections to Chinese merchants to pressure Chinese officials to side with the Soviets. Chinese officials were susceptible to bribes, and easily swayed, and this strategy had yielded some success already, enough to upset the British. Klidzin urged Sovtorgflot to take action immediately to help the Soviets in their "desperate struggle with the British over the pilgrimage." The time was right, and if the fleet acted quickly, it could expect several thousand Kashgar pilgrims to take Soviet routes. Klidzin took a long-range view—noting that "in the East personal trust plays a big role," he argued that the treatment of the first year's group of pilgrims would determine Sovtorgflot's success with hajj transport in the future. With this in mind, he urged Sovtorgflot to order Soviet officials across the country and aboard steamships to treat pilgrims "with care." He also urged it to resolve the issue of hard currency and valuables and announce the fleet's rates for return transport. Finally, he urged the fleet to assign an official to send its director, Suslin, back to China to escort the pilgrims on their round-trip journey, which was to begin in early May.[54] In spite of all this, the Soviet consul in Kashgar reported that, based on the lan (the local currency)-ruble exchange rate set by the Commissariat of Finance and the State Bank, Kashgar pilgrims could not afford Sovtorgflot tickets and were opting for the less expensive British steamers from India.[55]

At the same time, Sovtorgflot itself was struggling to manage the complex logistics and timing of the hajj as the season approached. Officials approached the NKID's Near Eastern Division to ask about travel logistics in the new age of British colonialism and Saudi rule along the old routes. They were unclear as to whether they needed entry visas to the Hejaz for pilgrims in Jeddah or in Port Said.[56] Sovtorgflot and NKID officials worked hard over the spring of 1927 to make the hajj transport campaign a success. The NKID found Soviet citizens who spoke the many languages pilgrims spoke, and sent them to Odessa to work as pilgrim guides. Sovtorgflot worked with the railroads to staff them with interpreter-guides on trains carrying pilgrims, to assist them on the weeklong train journey from Central Asia to the Black Sea.[57]

If Sovtorgflot's motives were mainly economic, NKID officials placed great stock in the political potential of Soviet hajj patronage. This is clear from a report by an NKID official named Nazarev, based in Kushka. In a report to the NKID in Moscow in March 1927, Nazarev offered a fascinating analysis of what the pilgrimage meant to Afghans, and how they felt compelled to describe to their compatriots what they saw and experienced on the long journey. He argued that the journey through the USSR was an opportunity to expose Afghans to Soviet government structure, cultural and industrial achievements, and "the rights of all of our nationalities." While helping them make the hajj through Soviet lands, "we should be careful not to propagandize," he warned, but instead let Afghan pilgrims discover and become interested in Soviet life on their own. He urged the government to subsidize facilities for pilgrims and give them "bountiful meals" during their time in Soviet lands, which they could compare to what they had back home.[58]

Nazarev also proposed that the Soviet state gently try to reshape foreign Muslims' itineraries through the USSR, using suasion rather than force. The idea was to accede to pilgrims' demands to visit holy sites in Central Asia, while also exposing them to Soviet life in all of its splendid dimensions. "If we could find some cultured, politically restrained Muslims who could . . . show pilgrims around the holy sites in Bukhara, Samarkand, and Tashkent, and then along the way squeeze in side trips to the electric station, factories, tractor tillage of fields, the Sovietized *kishlak* (rural settlement of seminomadic peoples in Central Asia), a model cooperative shop, a session of the Soviet court," he wrote, "this could help our Soviet propaganda in Afghanistan." Considering the "low cultural level of the Afghans," Soviet officials should not propagandize in written form, but should instead show them around, and influence them "in a subtle way." In sum, Nazarev argued that "the movement of Afghan pilgrims through Kushka has huge meaning for us, and we need to be sure they are comfortable, well treated, and experience no red tape."[59]

THE Soviet hajj campaign in 1927 went poorly, although it was not a complete failure: Sovtorgflot transported 1,200 hajj pilgrims from Odessa to Jeddah in 1927, most of them from western China.[60] But this was far less than the projected 5,000, and the fleet lost money on this transport because pilgrims could not afford its rates. The Chairman of Sovtorgflot, Comrade Ivanov, estimated that the fleet lost thirty-four rubles per pilgrim, and wrote to the Commissariat of Finance to ask it to cover the losses.[61]

Many Muslims complained to Sovtorgflot about their awful experience. Conditions along Soviet railroads had been terrible, even deadly. Promised second-class cars, pilgrims were forced instead to travel in freight cars that had no berths. They were overcrowded, and pilgrims had to sleep together in a heap on the floor. There was no water on the trains for pilgrims to drink and perform ablutions. The train cars lacked stepladders, which made it difficult for the many elderly pilgrims. Most had never ridden a train before, and climbed on and off while the was moving. In one awful case, an elderly man slipped under the train and the wheels amputated both of his legs.[62] Baggage was lost as well. Boxes and cases belonging to Kashgar pilgrims got held up in customs in Odessa. They arrived in Kashgar late and spoiled—there were split-open boxes of rotten dates, and the names were rubbed off the packages.[63]

Planning and communication among Soviet officials had been poor. This is not surprising. The hajj campaign was carried out against a backdrop of domestic chaos and upheaval caused by Stalin's First Five-Year Plan, which involved forced collectivization of agriculture and fast-paced construction of new cities and factories across the country. Preoccupied with these enormous tasks, at a time when Soviet internal borders and institutions were still under construction, Soviet officials were slow to coordinate and cooperate in organizing the movement of transit pilgrims through the country that summer.

Perhaps the greatest problem was foreign resistance to Soviet involvement in the hajj. Writing to the NKID in fall 1927, Ivanov lamented the "colossal difficulties" that Chinese pilgrims from Sinkiang had experienced making the hajj through Odessa. The Chinese authorities and British steamship companies had done all they could to discourage the pilgrimage through Soviet territory. The steamship companies had persuaded Chinese officials not to issue passports to the USSR; and to lure pilgrims to Indian routes and British ships, they had slashed their rates by fifty percent. To compete, Sovtorgflot had been forced to drop its rates, but British ships were still far superior to Sovtorgflot's in terms of comfort, service, and amenities.[64]

Additionally, officials in the Commissariat of Finance discovered that pilgrims had illegally taken valuables out of the country. In August officials at the Commissariat's Hard Currency Division wrote to Sovtorgflot to complain. While Kashgar pilgrims were registering and depositing their rubles with the authorities in Odessa, the authorities had discovered on them large amounts of precious metals and stones, which they had bought with rubles during their travels through the USSR. The division ordered Sovtorgflot to remind its agents in China of Soviet laws regarding currency and valuables, so that they could inform hajj pilgrims: it was illegal to take Soviet rubles out of the country, and to export gold or other "hard-currency valuables" that had been bought in the country with rubles. And those with transit visas through the USSR were not allowed to exchange rubles for hard currency or precious metals. The division suggested that pilgrims be told to bring no more Soviet currency than they could spend while in the USSR.[65] Some Soviet officials began to express concerns that the hajj transport was a drain on the country's hard-currency holdings, rather than a source of enrichment.

The 1927 hajj season had revealed the complexities involved in hajj transport, and the enormity of the task of organizing pilgrim transport from three foreign countries through Soviet lands. It had also revealed the potential risks—economic, ideological, sanitary, and otherwise—of Soviet involvement in the hajj. The Soviet state could have abandoned the plan for hajj transport at this point. Instead, it committed greater resources to it.

Political concerns doubtless were central to this decision. Despite all of the problems reported from the 1927 hajj season, there was also evidence that the Soviet strategy was working, that Muslims returned home with positive impressions of the USSR. In Sinkiang, for instance, the Chinese governor-general, Yan Tsen Sin, increased efforts to block Muslims from the Soviet routes after the 1927 hajj season. Soviet consular reports from the region cited political and ideological concerns on the part of the Chinese. Pilgrims had returned in 1927 with "favorable" impressions of their transit through the USSR. The governor-general feared that their exposure to "new trends" in the USSR would lead to the destruction of the old order in Sinkiang. His concerns extended beyond the USSR: he also feared Muslims' exposure to political ideas in republican Turkey. He tried to discourage the hajj altogether, enlisting local Muslim clergy to warn Muslims against making the pilgrimage, and warning them that they, too, stood to lose if Muslims moved away from the "true faith" in Sinkiang.[66]

In a sign of its endorsement of the plan for Soviet involvement in the hajj, in April 1928 the Soviet state passed a new law, "On the Sea Transport of Hajj Pilgrims from the Soviet Union to the Hejaz and Back." Approved by the Council of People's Commissars (Sovnarkom, the highest authority of executive power in the USSR), this law stipulated that the transport of hajj pilgrims from Soviet ports be carried out by Sovtorgflot on its own ships and on foreign ships that it chartered, as well as on other ships flying under the flag of other countries that had concluded agreements with the Soviet government.[67] This law suggests both rising demand among foreign hajj pilgrims for access to Soviet routes, ports, and transport, and the Soviet government's desire to monopolize the transport of hajj pilgrims from its ports. Apparently Sovnarkom hoped the state could profit from hajj transport: the state stipulated that all hard currency that Sovtorgflot made from hajj transport must go into Sovnarkom's treasury.

It committed precious ruble resources to building Sovtorgflot's service, allotting a subsidy of up to 330,000 rubles from Sovnarkom's reserve fund to cover losses from the transport.[68]

In 1928 the NKID expanded support for hajj pilgrims in Arabia. That year the newly arrived Soviet consul general in Jeddah, a Kazakh from Kokand named N. T. Tiuriakulov, set up a Soviet medical aid station for pilgrims. He assured the Soviet government that it would be strategically and politically useful. "It will be tremendously significant in the struggle for the USSR," he wrote to the NKID in Moscow, "as tens of thousands of Muslims come to the Hejaz from all over the Muslim world."[69]

With the support of the NKID and the Commissariat of Transport, Sovtorgflot in 1928 created regular service for hajj pilgrims between Odessa and Jeddah. The fleet instructed Soviet embassies and consuls to advertise its new service, and to provide estimates of expected volume of hajj traffic, so that it could plan accordingly.[70] That year it drafted "Instructions on Procedure for Transporting Pilgrims to Jeddah and Back." This document appears to have been modeled on plans developed by ROPiT and the Volunteer Fleet, and it gives a clear sense of how Sovtorgflot envisioned hajj transport would work.

The instructions had eight sections that covered timing; steamship schedules; cost of travel; transport of valuables; transport of religious objects; transport of baggage; lodging in Odessa; and passports. The hajj was scheduled to begin on May 23, 1928. All pilgrims taking Sovtorgflot ships were to follow the same route, from Odessa to Jeddah, and for the convenience of pilgrims steamships were to leave Odessa on four separate dates in March, April, and May for Jeddah. They would return from Jeddah to Odessa also on four separate dates in June and July, allowing enough time for pilgrims to complete the rituals in Mecca and visit Medina (this usually took three to four weeks), and, for some, to spend extra time in the holy cities to study or visit with relatives. The trip from Jeddah to Odessa would take ten days, and pilgrims would be given a choice of first-, second-, or third-class tickets, with payment in US dollars or local hard currency. Pilgrims were allowed to carry valuables and money in unlimited amounts: they would receive papers to document their valuables and money, and show these at customs. Returning pilgrims were allowed to bring into the USSR from Mecca religious objects and souvenirs in the following quantities per person: twenty-five jars of holy water; thirty pounds of dates; two hundred strings of prayer beads; two belt-scarves; two turbans; and two small rugs. Pilgrims were allowed unlimited luggage in transit through the USSR; on the steamship they were allowed free transport of up to 180 pounds of luggage. During their stay in Odessa they would stay free of charge in the khadzhikhane. Each pilgrim was required to carry a passport.[71]

To attract pilgrims to its ships in larger numbers in 1928, Sovtorgflot placed advertisements in newspapers across Persia and China, and sent thousands of pamphlets to its agents there and in Afghanistan to hand out to local Muslims. The advertisements, printed in local languages, depicted Muslims praying at the Kaaba in Mecca, underneath which was a schedule for Sovtorgflot's service from Odessa to Jeddah. Sovtorgflot's advertising campaign was a great success. In 1928 and 1929 many thousands of hajj pilgrims took Soviet routes and Sovtorgflot ships to Mecca and back. Pleased by the results of the 1928 hajj season, Sovnarkom gave Sovtorgflot a subsidy for the 1929 season, too, to help it expand its "pilgrim operation." Officials involved cited the economic benefits, noting that the hajj transport brought "a substantial flow of foreign currency into the USSR," and was consistent with the USSR's "hard-currency politics."[72]

But as the hajj traffic through Soviet lands grew, logistical problems multiplied, and Soviet officials grew increasingly concerned about the political and ideological implications of the project. They had embraced hajj transport hoping to impress foreign Muslims and pique their interest in socialism, but by 1928 many worried that it was having the opposite effect. There were numerous reports of Soviet officials' poor treatment of pilgrims along their journey through the USSR. The NKID complained that Soviet border guards were mocking and mistreating pilgrims as they entered Soviet territory. In Irkeshtam, a border-crossing point between the USSR and China, for instance, there were no customs buildings, and Soviet border guards forced Chinese hajj pilgrims to undress in the snow, to search their belongings.[73] And by all accounts, the transport of hajj pilgrims was worse in these years than before. Sovtorgflot's meticulous organization of transport outlined in its instructions existed on paper only. Disorganization, miscommunication, and poor planning were endemic in both the 1928 and the 1929 hajj seasons, and made conditions along the Soviet routes awful for many pilgrims.

Surveying the scene in 1928 in Baku and Batumi—Caspian and Black Sea ports, respectively—an NKID official was appalled. Both of these ports lay along Persian routes to the Black Sea. And yet until the last minute, Sovtorgflot officials posted there had no idea how many pilgrims to expect. In mid-April the Batumi official learned that as many as 3,000 pilgrims were on their way, leaving him inadequate time to prepare. The results were disastrous. Expecting superior comfort based on Sovtorgflot's "flashy" newspaper advertisements, Persian pilgrims instead found chaos and primitive conditions. Some Sovtorg-flot officials refused to help hajj pilgrims, either because they had never been informed of the plan, or out of subversion. When more than two hundred Persian hajj pilgrims showed up at the Sovtorgflot office in Baku, the official in charge, Comrade Slutskii, told them he was not interested in "profiting from pilgrims," and refused to let them in the door, for fear that they carried "infectious diseases."[74]

Sovtorgflot officials had no plan to receive Persian pilgrims in Baku or Batumi, and lacked the local knowledge and connections needed to quickly put one in place. In Baku, local officials bundled pilgrims onto freight cars, instead of the promised passenger cars. There was no specially outfitted khadzhikhane in Baku: pilgrims were ushered into an empty customs warehouse instead. Rail transport from Baku to Batumi was not free, as advertised. In Batumi, where they expected a prompt departure by steamship to Odessa, they were delayed for two weeks. Next came a mix-up about the port of departure. The fleet sent pilgrims on a pointless trip from Batumi to Odessa, and then back to Batumi, the actual departure point for the fleet's steamships to Jeddah. Pilgrims were exhausted and angry and worried that they would miss the scheduled hajj rituals in Mecca. The NKID official was beside himself with anger: he warned Sovtorgflot about the potential "scandals" that could come from this disaster, especially given that several "distinguished people" were aboard one of the ships.[75] Poor conditions created an ugly scene at the Baku train station between Sovtorgflot officials and the city's Persian consul. Witnessing Persian pilgrims boarding freight cars intended for horses, the consul berated the fleet's officials, who vainly tried to explain that pilgrims had chosen these third-class cars over more expensive options. There was a shortage of cars, and the local OGPU had to intervene to bring in more rolling stock.[76]

Sovtorgflot had also failed to monopolize the flow of Persian hajj pilgrims through the USSR by ensuring that all bought round-trip tickets on its ships. This created problems for many Soviet officials, especially those in the OGPU, which opposed unescorted foreigners moving through Soviet lands. The NKID official noted that many "wild" pilgrims—more than 1,000—showed up in Batumi with just transit visas from the Soviet consulate in Tabriz. They spoke no Russian, had no steamship tickets, no plan for travel, and little money. This was not supposed to happen. Sovtorgflot and the NKID had agreed that foreign consuls and ambassadors would issue transit visas only to those Muslims holding Sovtorgflot tickets. But miscommunication bungled this well-laid plan: a later investigation revealed that the Soviet consul in Tabriz had not received this order, and had issued hundreds of transit visas to Muslims.[77] Sovtorgflot was unable to care for them all: they needed housing, help with visas and quarantine procedures, and interpreters to guide them. To the embarrassment of the NKID, the local branch of the Red Crescent (the Muslim version of the Red Cross) stepped in to help, housing and feeding pilgrims. Their staff was more experienced and adept than Sovtorgflot's in managing pilgrims' needs.[78]

Service aboard Sovtorgflot's ships was terrible. Concerned about onboard conditions that pilgrims experienced, the fleet sent the head of its passenger division in Batumi, Comrade Taraian, aboard the *Il'ich* in 1929. Taraian wrote a damning report that described poor communication among Sovtorgflot officials and rough treatment of pilgrims, and stressed a "lack of discipline" among the crew. He was taken aghast by the crew's surly treatment of two international quarantine representatives, who boarded in Samsun to observe sanitary procedures. There were no sheets or blankets and when they asked for some, an irritated captain's assistant descended to their cabin and angrily jabbed his fingers in the air, pointing to the steam pipes. He told them the heat was coming up and that they did not need blankets; the two resorted to sleeping with their coats on.[79]

Then came the "glass scandal." The leadership of Sovtorgflot had invited a delegation of dignitaries and pilgrims from Yemen to board the *Il'ich*, as part of Soviet efforts to build diplomatic and trade ties with the Yemeni ruler. Despite orders to give them the royal treatment, the crew of the *Il'ich* treated the delegation shabbily. The delegation had boarded at 11:00 a.m. but received nothing to eat or drink until 8:00 p.m. They asked for glasses of water, and were made to wait a long time. Finally, a worker from the mess hall arrived in their cabin and slammed a single glass on the table, angrily telling them he was not "obliged to work after 9:00 p.m!" The next day, one of the ship's mechanics came to their cabin to extort money, and screamed insults at them when they refused. Mercifully, a fellow passenger intervened—a Soviet writer who reproached the crew and befriended the delegation. Taraian was sorry to report that the crew members in question were Communist Party members.[80] This episode was one of many that worried Soviet officials, and made them fear a backlash from their hajj campaign.

By 1929 tensions had deepened among Soviet officials over the ideological and political implications of Soviet involvement in hajj transport. The OGPU had long resisted the project, but now the NKID, too, began to question some of the strategies being used, and worry about their long-term implications. NKID officials opposed Sovtorgflot's recruitment and hiring of foreign mullahs and imams to work as hajj brokers. It was one thing to work with merchants; another to work directly with religious leaders. The NKID asked Sovtorgflot to stop the practice, but the fleet was loath to do this—religious elites offered invaluable connections to foreign Muslim communities, and they often served as excellent brokers for the fleet.[81]

Sovtorgflot's advertising of its hajj transport service also created conflict with the NKID. In 1928 the NKID refused to help Sovtorgflot get permission to print posters because of the religious imagery the fleet used. Officials were uncomfortable with the image depicting religious rituals at the Kaaba, and wanted it changed. The NKID wanted the fleet to avoid religious depictions in general. It acknowledged that the USSR was trying to attract pilgrims to Soviet routes, but nevertheless should avoid "agitating" for the expansion of the pilgrimage, especially agitation of a religious nature. It also noted that the Persian government in no way wanted to see an expansion of the pilgrimage and might object to advertisements with a religious character.[82] It encouraged the fleet to change its advertisements to appeal to Muslims traveling to many destinations, including Constantinople, Egypt, and Arabia. "It should appear that we seek all kinds of passengers, not just pilgrims."[83] By 1929 resistance to Sovtorgflot's advertisements was widespread. For the first time, Glavlit (the central Soviet censorship office, which had authority over all printed materials) refused to print Sovtorgflot's posters. Fleet officials were upset. They rightly pointed out that this opposition frustrated preparations for that year's hajj campaign. And the sudden opposition confused them. The previous year Glavlit had printed 5,000 copies of their brochures to distribute to "all the foreign Eastern countries."[84]

These tensions reveal the dilemma the Soviets faced with regard to hajj transport. Encouraging tourism to the USSR was one thing, but support for the hajj was different. By facilitating and supporting a central Islamic ritual, the Soviets were effectively helping Muslims practice their faith. As the hajj traffic through Soviet lands grew, this support became more visible to Soviet populations. Soviet officials worried about the domestic repercussions, especially for its Muslim citizens. In 1928 OGPU officials noted with dismay a rise in domestic demand for access to Mecca. That year it received applications for hajj passports from Muslims across the USSR, in Central Asia, the Volga region, Altai, and the Far East. It issued passports to sixty people, and Sovtorgflot sold them tickets. At the same time, the fleet quietly raised its rates for "internal" hajj pilgrims, hoping to discourage them and ensure "minimal" pilgrimages by Soviet citizens in the future.[85]

Isolating Soviet citizens from transit hajj pilgrims was difficult, given the variety of routes they took, and their large numbers. From Afghanistan crowds of pilgrims crossed the border on foot or horseback. Locals greeted them at border railroad stations such as Kushka. They offered to sell the pilgrims food, and to buy goods and objects from them, including their horses. The hajj traffic had thus generated illegal economic activity, beyond the purview of the state.[86] To address this problem, the OGPU in 1928 proposed streamlining pilgrims' movement from Afghanistan and China into Central Asia along a set route, by building an infrastructure along that route, complete with teahouses and lodging houses. Sovtorgflot made an agreement with the Commissariat of Transport to have passenger cars waiting at all the necessary stations: Karasu, Bishkek, Semipalatinsk, Ashkhabad, Baku, and Julfa. It also tried to organize a state "buying up" (*skupka*) of pilgrims' horses. Guides would be assigned to escort pilgrims from border regions to Odessa, where they would go straight to the khadzhikhane and from there to a waiting Sovtorgflot ship. The idea was to keep hajj pilgrims moving along, so that "undesirable elements" would stop gathering in these border areas to engage in illegal economic activity.[87]

THE Soviet hajj campaign ended abruptly in 1930, in line with global trends. Soviet involvement in the hajj appears to have ended with the Great Depression and the dramatic decline of hajj traffic worldwide that it caused. There is no evidence that the Soviets ever again attempted a hajj campaign on a global scale. This jibes as well with the xenophobia and isolationism of the 1930s under Stalin. And some of the key architects of the Soviet hajj campaign perished in the Stalinist purges of the 1930s, including Khakimov and Tiuriakulov.

This chapter has described the Soviet Union's involvement in an interwar colonial story from which it is largely missing in the historiography: the global competition for influence over the hajj as part of the larger struggle among twentieth-century ideologies of communism, imperialism, and nationalism.[88] No less strikingly, it shows that the foundations of Soviet global power—a story often construed as having begun in 1945, when decolonization and accelerated forms of globalization opened up new connections and possibilities for the spread of Soviet socialism worldwide—were laid in part during the interwar period, and upon inherited human mobility networks and the global structures the tsarist government had built around them.[89]

Conclusion: Russian Hajj in the Twenty-First Century

In the twenty-first century, the hajj has once again become a European and a Russian phenomenon, as a result of global events and processes. Since the 1980s, large-scale Muslim immigration to western Europe and the collapse of communism in eastern Europe have made Islam the fastest-growing religion on the Continent, and brought a revival of the old colonial powers' involvement in the Muslim pilgrimage. Nearly 100,000 European and Russian citizens make the pilgrimage to Mecca annually, and their numbers rise every year, apace with the steady growth of Muslim communities in Europe, most recently fueled by refugees fleeing war in Syria. To support their citizens making the hajj, European governments have created new institutions and services, including medical stations in and around Mecca, and discount rates for pilgrims on national airlines during hajj season. Major European airports are now hubs in global hajj networks: in the days leading up to the scheduled hajj rituals in Arabia, at airports in London and Berlin, Paris and Moscow, crowds of robed and veiled Muslim pilgrims pray at the gates before boarding flights to Jeddah.

In 2007, citing Soviet-era prohibitions on the hajj and high demand, Russian president Vladimir Putin persuaded the Saudi government to increase Russia's annual hajj quota, from 20,000 to 26,000.[1] This was a major diplomatic achievement. The hajj today involves as many as three million Muslims a year, a number kept artificially low by the quota system the Saudis introduced in the 1980s to control the crushing crowds. Demand today far exceeds the number of spots allowed, and the hajj is a major issue in Saudi diplomatic relations: the Saudis regularly receive requests from Muslim-majority countries to increase their quotas, and almost never grant them. Many countries have long waiting lists, and Muslims often wait years for the chance to make the pilgrimage.[2]

In addition to making the hajj a diplomatic issue with the Saudis, the Russian government under Putin in the 2000s introduced new subsidies and state agencies to support the hajj. Today Russia's Muslims enjoy discounted flights to Jeddah during hajj season on Aeroflot, the state airline. They also have at their disposal a government-created liaison office that helps them arrange visas and transportation for the pilgrimage. Observers of this policy have argued that Putin's motives are mainly about security and economics—to monitor and appease Russia's Muslims, and to improve ties with Saudi Arabia, where Russia has budding economic interests.[3]

Putin's very public cooperation with the Saudi government around the hajj seems at odds with his close ties to the leadership of the Russian Orthodox Church, and the image of Russia he often seeks to promote—as a country deeply rooted in Eastern Orthodox traditions. But Putin's political use of the Russian Orthodox Church and his simultaneous involvement with the hajj is actually quite consistent with Russia's colonial past. Russia today, as in the late nineteenth century, is a multiethnic and multiconfessional state. Even after the disintegration of the Soviet Union in 1991 into fifteen separate states, six with Muslim majorities, Russia remains home to large Muslim populations. Two million Muslims live in the Russian capital of Moscow alone, making it the city with the largest Muslim population in all of Europe. In terms of numbers, the place of Islam in Russia today essentially mirrors its place in late imperial Russia—it is the largest minority religion, second only to Orthodox Christianity, with some twenty million Russian citizens identifying as Muslim, about fifteen percent of Russia's overall population.

Putin's efforts to expand Russian citizens' access to Mecca attest to the revival of Islam in post-Soviet Russia, and, with it, state strategies for managing Islam and integrating Muslims. Knowingly or not, Putin is building upon traditions and policies toward the hajj that were forged more than a century ago under tsarist rule, including the tsarist-era infrastructure upon which the Soviets built global influence in the twentieth century, and which today undergirds Russian political power in the Middle East.

Russia co-opted the hajj in the nineteenth century, using it as a mechanism of imperial integration and expansion. I have argued, in contrast to scholarly orthodoxies about Russia and other European powers in the late nineteenth century, that Russia did not entirely fear Islam's global dimensions as a threat to its empire, nor did it solely attempt to contain and control Islam in its colonies. To the contrary, tsarist Russia forged its empire in part through global Islamic networks, building new imperial pathways upon the hajj routes that connected the tsarist empire to Arabia.

This story has particular resonance today. As in the early twentieth century, governments today perceive migration and immigration as double-edged. Migration is both a threat—based on fears and high anxiety about terrorism, extremism, and contagion—and an opportunity, based on the economic fluorescence of globalization. Globally, fears of migration are perhaps especially tied to Islam, which many in the West see as violent, fanatical, and essentially incompatible with Western democracy and progressive social values.

In today's era of globalization the term "Muslim world" does not mean much: accelerated patterns of migration and immigration over the past century have uprooted Muslims from their historical homes to a degree never before seen in history. Muslims today live everywhere in the world, perhaps most precariously in Europe, where anti-Islamic sentiment has been mounting for decades, a reflection of Europe's economic troubles and a general unease with Europe's newfound status as an immigrant destination, after centuries of being a source of immigrants.

In the late nineteenth century, Russia, too, struggled to reconcile its historic identity as an Orthodox empire with the reality of its internal diversity and its large and increasingly mobile Muslim populations, whose loyalties, it feared, may have belonged to the neighboring Ottoman sultan, a rival of the tsar. This struggle converged around the important issue of the hajj, and debates among officials on how to deal with it. Many Russian officials wanted to restrict the hajj for many reasons. But how could they do this without appearing to intervene in Muslim practice, and to violate Muslims' religious freedom? Russia's attempts to sponsor the hajj promised to give it greater access to Muslim communities and control over the pilgrimage—but this approach, too, had its problems. Patronage was not supposed to encourage the hajj and increase the numbers going, but it had just that effect. And patronage raised broader questions related to Russia's identity and legitimacy, and the institutions that helped to build imperial stability. How could Russia, an Orthodox state, justify supporting a major Islamic ritual? And how could it extend patronage without upsetting the Russian Orthodox Church and losing its crucial institutional support for the regime?

Many of these same questions confront European and Russian officials today as they struggle to manage the hajj and accept it as part of their evolving national cultures. These are not so much new questions as old ones, rooted in

Europe's colonial past and made urgent for the European powers during the first wave of globalization in the late nineteenth century.

By revealing Russia's long overlooked, ambivalent, and multivalent role in the history of the colonial-era hajj, and adding new complexity to that story by including the specific Russian case, this book contributes more broadly to our understanding of the history of Islam and Europe. It reminds us that present-day discussions of Islam in Europe have a much deeper history, and that our perceptions today are in many ways colored by stereotypes and prejudices refined in the late nineteenth century. For example, Russia and other European powers in the late 1800s and early 1900s feared that Mecca was a center of clandestine, conspiratorial, anticolonial plotting. But no great anticolonial revolt was ever plotted in Mecca. And firsthand accounts by several Pan-Islamic thinkers reveal how disappointed they were by hajj pilgrims' indifference to politics while in Mecca. Abdürreşid Ibrahim, for one, a leading Pan-Islamic intellectual from Russia, complained about the simple, pious Muslims he met in Mecca, and his inability to engage them in political discussion.[4]

It remains to be seen how Russia and Europe will adapt to their new role as centers of the global hajj. This book has reconstructed a story previously hidden, which reveals much greater ambivalence in Russian officials' attitudes about Islam. It restores to history the optimism shared among many tsarist officials, that Russia's Islamic inheritance of the hajj offered opportunities, not just dangers, and could be remade, not just suppressed, into a Russian tradition.

ACKNOWLEDGMENTS

AFTER a long time working on this book, it is a pleasure to acknowledge the many people who helped make it happen. I thank first Laura Engelstein and Stephen Kotkin at Princeton for their extraordinary support over the years. Both Laura and Steve impressed on me the need for clarity and precision, and forbade jargon, incoherence, and pretentiousness. I thank them for that. Their insistence on seeing Russia in relation to other parts of the world made Russian history so much more interesting, and has left a deep imprint on my thinking. Laura's devotion to her students is legendary, and I must thank her for the time she has given me, reading drafts and helping me to release my arguments, in person, by phone, and over e-mail. I am grateful to Suzanne Marchand and Christine Stansell, whom I also studied with and met at Princeton. They were both crucial sources of support and encouragement in graduate school and beyond. I got my start in Russian history as an undergraduate at Brown, where I had the great fortune to study with Pat Herlihy and Tom Gleason. I thank them both for their support and inspiration.

I am grateful to the many institutions that supported this book. At Princeton, I received generous funding from the Department of History, the Center for the Study of Religion, the Center for Trans-Regional Study, and the University Committee on Research in the Humanities and Social Sciences. A fellowship from the American Council of Teachers of Russian (ACTR) helped fund my dissertation research in Russia. The Harriman Institute at Columbia University supported this project with a postdoctoral fellowship, which allowed me to write the first chapters. Grants from the American Historical Association, the National Council for Eurasian and East European Research, and the International Research and Exchange Board funded overseas research trips to Russia, Ukraine, and Georgia. A fellowship from the National Endowment for the Humanities supported a year of research and writing, and a grant from the American Association of University Women paid for child care and camp one summer so that I could focus full-time on writing.

I have benefited from the extraordinary generosity of colleagues who invited me to their institutions to present my work, read drafts of book chapters, and shared precious sources and data from the archives. Doug Northrop was an enthusiastic and crucial supporter of this project early on. I thank him for inviting me to share my ideas as part of a migration series at Michigan. John Randolph and Eugene Avrutin included me in their marvelous conference on mobility in Russia, and this experience helped me to see the hajj as part of that history. John generously read a draft of chapter 2, and his thoughtful comments helped me refine my ideas. Allen Frank took time to answer my questions about Old Tatar and helped with transliteration. Bob Crews offered intellectual support and good advice throughout the writing of this book. Paul Werth deserves special mention: he alerted me to the Tbilisi archives as a rich source on the hajj, and shared his hard-won list of relevant documents from that archive to help me get started. Pat Herlihy shared her unrivaled knowledge of Odessa and her contacts there, and read multiple drafts of chapter 4. Mustafa Tuna sent me copies of hajj memoirs he had collected for his own work, and Benjamin Schenk gave me precious lists of documents on hajj pilgrims and railroads in RGIA. Norihiro Naganawa kindly let me cite his marvelous unpublished work on early Soviet involvement in the hajj. Peter Holquist also shared sources, and showed great interest in this project. The fantastically talented Halit Dündar Akarca helped me read through Turkic-language manuscripts and newspapers; I could never have included these crucial sources without his help. Pamela Haag's superb editing helped me get this book into the shape I wanted. In Russia, the Islamicist Efim Rezvan helped me locate photographs at the Kunstkamera, and shared his knowledge of the hajj. In Odessa, Oleg Gubar, one of the city's best *kraeveds*, helped me track down sources I would never have found on my own. I must also thank my superb research assistants in Odessa, St. Petersburg, and Istanbul: Victoria Mudraya, Evgenii Grishin, and Ceyda Yüksel.

Bill Nelson made the excellent maps for this book. And my colleague at Connecticut College, Beverly Chomiak, generously spent hours helping me create map templates using GIS software. I thank them both. I am deeply grateful to

Roger Haydon at Cornell University Press for acquiring this book, and for guiding me through the process with patience, excellent editorial advice, and humor. I could not have asked for a better editor. At Cornell I also sincerely thank Marian Rogers, who did a superb job copyediting the manuscript; Susan Barnett, for helping prepare the copy; and Sara Ferguson, for cleaning up the final manuscript.

Friendships have sustained me for the past decade as I wrote this book. I thank especially Deborah Cole, Jasmin Darznik, Pat Herlihy, Caroleen Sayej, Kip Schubert, Chris Stansell, Duncan Watson, and Hannah Wilentz. I lucked out when Shira Robinson moved in next door to me in Princeton in summer 2006. I've never had a better friend. She more than anyone else helped me finish this book, and I am forever grateful to her. Luck also brought about the reunion of my old writers group last spring by Skype. I thank Denver Brunsman, Brendan Kane, and Thierry Rigogne for reading drafts of my chapters, for great advice on how to finish a book, and for bringing a healthy sense of the absurd to the process.

At Connecticut College, I thank Abby van Slyck, Joan Chrisler, Julie Rivkin, and Sarah Queen for their crucial support, encouragement, and good advice. I thank David Canton for being a supportive department chair, and Nancy Lewandowski for her help putting together my tenure file. I also thank my colleague Sheetal Chhabria; this book is better for our extended discussions about migrations and global history. Special thanks to Emily Aylward, goddess of ILL at the college, whose help in getting sources was crucial to this project.

During the past decade that I was researching and writing this book, I was also busy bearing, birthing, breastfeeding, and caring for my two daughters, Beatrice (age eight), and Mary (age three). I am so grateful to be their mother. They make my life wonderful. There is no way I could have written this book without the help my husband and I received in caring for Bea and Mary. I am grateful to the team of professionals in Princeton, Syracuse, and New London who cared for our daughters while we worked and studied. I thank Laura Hill, Mamie Rock, Bette Ziemba, Fahreta Alic, Amy Hernandez, Annette Fitch, Katie O'Connor, Beatrice DeMitte, Lisa Aldrich, Deborah Golub, Brenda Couture, Lindsay Lilly, Leny McGarry, Jeffrey Stone, Tiffany Hubbard, Michelle Williams, Liz Thompson, Lori Hebert, Julie Pryke, Pam Chaplin, Mary Gernhard, Chelsea Denham, Patricia McIlveen, Hilary Golembeski, Suzanne Matteson, Amanda Padua, Karen Littell, April Jacques, Lisa Gray, Wendi Packham, and Amy Bevan. My mother traveled with me across the United States and took care of Bea while I gave talks and attended conferences, and helped care for her during my long research trips abroad. My in-laws, Vivian and Peter Barnett, took care of Bea for a week so that I could attend a conference in Japan, and pitched in countless other times. My sister Maggie looked after five-month-old Mary in my hotel room in Cambridge so that I could attend a splendid two-day workshop, and helped me care for my children many other times. I thank them all.

I thank JC for the light and the love. I thank my sister Maggie and brother Tut and their wonderful families. I miss my brother Matthew so much and wish he were here to celebrate this book with me. I thank Alex Barnett for marrying me, loving me, and supporting me in so many ways. My mother and father, Regina S. Kane and William F. X. Kane, have loved and supported me always. This book is for them.

ABBREVIATIONS

AKAK	*Akty, sobrannye Kavkazskoiu arkheograficheskoiu kommissieiu*
AVPRI	Arkhiv vneshnei politiki Rossiiskoi imperii (Moscow, Russia)
BOA	Başbakanlık Osmanlı Arşivi (Istanbul, Turkey)
DAOO	Derzhavnyi arkhiv Odeskoi oblasti (Odessa, Ukraine)
IV RAN	Institut Vostokovedeniia, Rossiiskaia Akademiia Nauk (St. Petersburg, Russia)
MDBPU	*Materialy dlia biografii Porfiriia Uspenskogo*
RGAE	Rossiiskii gosudarstvennyi arkhiv ekonomiki (Moscow, Russia)
RGAVMF	Rossiiskii gosudarstvennyi arkhiv voenno-morskogo flota (St. Petersburg, Russia)
RGIA	Rossiiskii gosudarstvennyi istoricheskii arkhiv (St. Petersburg, Russia)
SSSA	Sakartvelos Sakhelmtsipo Saistorio Arkivi (Tbilisi, Georgia)
UNT RAN	Otdel Rukopisei, Ufinskii Nauchnyi Tsentr, Rossiiskaia Akademiia Nauk (Ufa, Russia)

NOTES

Introduction

1. D. Iu. Arapov, comp., *Imperatorskaia Rossiia i musul'manskii mir: sbornik statei* (Moscow: Natalis, 2006), 359–360. Charykov was a key player in setting up this system from the start, first as the founding agent of the Russian Political Agency in Bukhara in the 1880s, where he was in charge of issuing Russian passports to Bukharan hajj pilgrims, and later as Russian ambassador in Constantinople in the early 1900s.

2. Robert Crews, *For Prophet and Tsar: Islam and Empire in Russia and Central Asia* (Cambridge, MA: Harvard University Press, 2006), 1–14; Adrienne Lynn Edgar, *Tribal Nation: The Making of Soviet Turkmenistan* (Princeton, NJ: Princeton University Press, 2004), 18.

3. D. Iu. Arapov, "Pervyi Rossiiskii ukaz o palmonichestve v Mekku," *Rossiia v srednie veka i novoe vremia: sbornik statei k 70-letiiu chl. korr. RAN L. V. Milova* (Moscow: ROSSPEN, 1999), 299.

4. Sunil S. Amrith, *Migration and Diaspora in Modern Asia* (New York: Cambridge University Press, 2011), 65–66.

5. RGIA, f. 821, op. 8, d. 1196, ll. 74–75.

6. In the United States this neglect had much to do with government-funded area studies, introduced in American universities after World War II, which ahistorically divided Russia/USSR and the Middle East into two discrete and separate regions of study. It was at this time that scholars in the American academy came to associate Islam narrowly with the Arabic-speaking world. See Zachary Lockman, *Contending Visions of the Middle East: The History and Politics of Orientalism* (Cambridge: Cambridge University Press, 2004), 121–147. In post-war France, by contrast, several prominent historians studied the Muslim "nationalities" under Soviet rule, in some cases drawing comparisons between Soviet Muslims and other Muslim populations under colonial rule. See for example Alexandre Bennigsen, "Colonization and Decolonization in the Soviet Union," *Journal of Contemporary History* 4, no. 1 (1969): 141–152; and Alexandre A. Bennigsen and S. Enders Wimbush, *Muslim National Communism in the Soviet Union: A Revolutionary Strategy for the Colonial World* (Chicago: University of Chicago Press, 1980).

7. Adeeb Khalid, *Islam after Communism: Religion and Politics in Central Asia* (Berkeley, CA: University of California Press, 2007), 2–4. Islamic studies existed as a field of study under the Soviet regime and even expanded between the 1960s and 1980s when new scholarly centers were established in Moscow. But most Soviet Islamicists were specialists on Islam outside the USSR. See

Dimitri Mikoulski, "The Study of Islam in Russia and the former Soviet Union: An Overview," in Azim Nanji (ed.) *Mapping Islamic Studies: Geneaology, Continuity and Change* (Berlin: Walter de Gruyter, 1997), 95–107; and S.D. Miliband, *Vostokovedy Rossii, XX-nachalo XXI veka: bibliografich-eskii slovar' v dvukh knigakh* (Moscow: Vostochnaia literatura RAN, 2008).

8. Andreas Kappeler et al. (eds.), *Muslim Communities Reemerge: Historical Perspectives on Nationality, Politics, and Opposition in the Former Soviet Union and Yugoslavia* (Durham, NC: Duke University Press, 1994).

9. Two leading historians of Islam in Russia, Adeeb Khalid and Robert Crews, take very different approaches in their work. Khalid's first book challenges standard depictions of Central Asia as a colonial backwater of the Russian Empire, and seeks to reframe its history as part of the dynamic, global story of Islam and modernity. See Adeeb Khalid, *The Politics of Muslim Cultural Reform: Jadidism in Central Asia* (Berkeley: University of California Press, 1998), xiv–xv. Crews, by contrast, emphasizes Russia's effective "domestication" of Islam in the modern era, and puts Islam and Muslims at the center of the story of Russian empire-building. See Crews, *For Prophet and Tsar*. On Muslims in Soviet and post-Soviet Central Asia, see Khalid, *Islam after Communism*.

10. This institution, created in the late eighteenth century, was first called the Ufa Ecclesiastical Assembly of the Muhammadan Creed, and was later renamed the Orenburg Muhammadan Ecclesiastical Assembly. Crews, *For Prophet and Tsar*: 55.

11. Crews, *For Prophet and Tsar*, 2–3.

12. For a critique of Crews's argument, see Mustafa Tuna, *Imperial Russia's Muslims: Islam, Empire, and European Modernity, 1788–1914* (Cambridge: Cambridge University Press, 2015), 9; and Paul W. Werth, *The Tsar's Foreign Faiths: Toleration and the Fate of Religious Freedom in Imperial Russia* (Oxford: Oxford University Press, 2014), 9.

13. David Motadel, ed., *Islam and the European Empires* (Oxford: Oxford University Press, 2014), 1.

14. Michael Wolfe, ed., *One Thousand Roads to Mecca: Ten Centuries of Travelers Writing about the Muslim Pilgrimage* (New York: Grove Press, 1997), 191–195; Jürgen Osterhammel, *The Transformation of the World: A Global History of the Nineteenth Century* (Princeton, NJ: Princeton University Press, 2014), 164.

15. On Conrad's novel and the real-life events that inspired it, see Michael Gilsenan, "And You, What Are You Doing Here?" *London Review of Books*, Vol. 28, No. 20, 19 October 2006.

16. Daniel Brower, "Russian Roads to Mecca: Religious Tolerance and Muslim Pilgrimage in the Russian Empire," *Slavic Review* 55, no. 3 (1996): 567. On state officials' deep suspicions about the hajj, and their desire to control and limit it, see Crews, *For Prophet and Tsar*, 71–74; Khalid, *The Politics of Muslim Cultural Reform*, 52–54; and A.S. Morrison, *Russian Rule in Samarkand, 1868–1910: A Comparison with British India* (Oxford: Oxford University Press, 2008): 63–64.

17. Suraiya Faroqhi, *Pilgrims and Sultans: The Hajj under the Ottomans* (London: I.B. Tauris, 1994).

18. Osterhammel, *The Transformation of the World*, 164.

19. On late nineteenth-century peasant migration in Russia as part of the processes of urbanization, the growth of the working class, and internal colonization in Russia, see Barbara A. Anderson, *Internal Migration during Modernization in Late Nineteenth-Century Russia* (Princeton, NJ: Princeton University Press, 1980); Barbara Alpern Engel, *Between the Fields and the City* (Cambridge: Cambridge University Press, 1996); Robert Johnson, *Peasant and Proletarian: The Working Class of Moscow in the Late Nineteenth Century* (New Brunswick, NJ: Rutgers University Press, 1979); and Willard Sunderland, *Taming the Wild Field: Colonization and Empire on the Russian Steppe* (Ithaca, NY: Cornell University Press, 2004). See also selected essays in Nicholas Breyfogle, Abby Schrader, and Willard Sunderland, eds., *Peopling the Russian Periphery: Borderland Colonization in Eurasian History* (London: Routledge, 2007); and David Moon, "Peasant Migration, the Abolition of Serfdom, and the Internal Passport System in the Russian Empire, c. 1800–1914," in *Coerced and Free Migration: Global Perspectives*, ed. David Eltis (Stanford, CA: Stanford University Press, 2002), 349.

20. Work on Muslim migrations in Russia and the USSR from other fields and disciplines is vast, multilingual, and by a multinational group of scholars primarily from Europe, the former Soviet Union, Japan, and Turkey. See, for example, see Allen J. Frank, *Islamic Historiography and "Bulghar" Identity among the Tatars and Bashkirs of Russia* (Leiden: Brill, 1998); Michael Kemper, "Khalidiyya Networks in Daghestan and the Question of Jihad," in *Die Welt des Islams* vol. 42, 1 (2002): 41–71; and H. Komatsu, C. Obiya and J. Schoeberlein, eds. *Migration in Central Asia: Its History and Current Problems* (Osaka: Japan Center for Area Studies, National Museum of Ethnology, 2000).

21. For a brilliant attempt to narrate history in a way that overcomes (and undermines) the false clarity of formal state borders, see Paul Carter, *The Road to Botany Bay: An Exploration of Landscape and History* (Minneapolis: University of Minnesota Press, 1987). See also Martin W. Lewis and Kären E. Wigen, *The Myth of Continents: A Critique of Metageography* (Berkeley: University of California Press, 1997).

22. For a fascinating recent study that extends the Russian Empire to encompass nonterritorial spaces on the ocean, see Ryan Tucker Jones, *Empire of Extinction: Russians and the North Pacific's Strange Beasts of the Sea* (New York: Oxford University Press, 2014). For a marvelously innovative narrative of Russian history through the biography of one man, and one that ventures somewhat beyond Russia's formal borders, see Willard Sunderland, *The Baron's Cloak: A History of the Russian Empire in War and Revolution* (Ithaca, NY: Cornell University Press, 2014). See also Martin and Wigen, *The Myth of Continents*, 1–19.

23. David Harvey, "Space as a Keyword," in *David Harvey: A Critical Reader*, ed. Noel Castree and Derek Gregory (Malden, MA: Wiley-Blackwell, 2006).

24. Khadzhi Salim-Girei Sultanov, "Sviashchennaia oblast' musul'man v Aravii (iz vospominanii palomnika)," *Zemlevedenie* kniga 1–2 (1901): 85–144.

25. *Sayahatnama, Astarkhan ghubernasi Krasni Yar uyezi Sayyid qaryasining al-hajj al-haramayn Er 'Ali Rahimberdiyef al-Qaraghachining hajj safarinda kurganlari* (Astrakhan: Tipografiia Torgovogo Doma "Umerov i Ko." 1911), 6.

26. On the Dutch "Hajj Bureau" in Jeddah, see Robert R. Bianchi, *Guests of God: Pilgrimage and Politics in the Islamic World* (Oxford: Oxford University Press, 2004). On European medical facilities and personnel, see David Edwin Long, *The Hajj Today: A Survey of the Contemporary Pilgrimage to Makkah* (Albany: State University of New York Press, 1979). On British vice-consul in Jeddah, Dr. Abdurrezak, a British Muslim subject from India, see BOA, Y.A.HUS., Dosya: 252, Gömlek: 40, Vesika 1, (Oct. 13, 1891).

27. Alexandre Papas, "Following Abdurresid Ibrahim: A Tatar Globetrotter on the Way to Mecca," in *Central Asian Pilgrims: Hajj Routes and Pious Visits between Central Asia and the Hijaz*, eds. Alexandre Papas et al. (Berlin: Klaus Schwarz, 2012).

28. See, for example, Andrew Petersen, *The Medieval and Ottoman Hajj Route in Jordan: An Archaeological and Historical Study* (Oxford: Oxbow Books, 2012).

29. Viktor Golovan', *Nekropol' Odessy: pervoe Odesskoe Kladbishche* (Odessa: RIF "Fotosintetika," 1999).

30. Nick Baron and Peter Gatrell, "Population Displacement, State-Building, and Social Identity in the Lands of the Former Russian Empire," *Kritika: Explorations in Russian and Eurasian History* 4, no. 1 (Winter 2003): 52–53.

31. David Ludden, "Presidential Address: Maps in the Minds and Mobility of Asia," *Journal of Asian Studies* 62, no. 4 (November 2003): 1062.

1. Imperialism through Islamic Networks

1. On the imperial hajj caravans sponsored by the Ottomans in the nineteenth century, see Suraiya Faroqhi, *Pilgrims and Sultans: The Hajj under the Ottomans* (London: I.B. Tauris, 1994);

F. E. Peters, *The Hajj: Pilgrimage to Mecca* (Princeton, NJ: Princeton University Press, 1995), 147–162; and Abdul-Karim Rafeq, "Damascus and the Pilgrim Caravan," in *Modernity and Culture: From the Mediterranean to the Indian Ocean*, ed. Leila Tarazi Fawaz and C. A. Bayly (New York: Columbia University Press, 2002), 130–143.

2. SSSA, f. 11, op. 1, d. 1957. Russian subjects, like those of other European empires, were entitled to extraterritorial rights and diplomatic protection in Ottoman lands in line with Russo-Ottoman treaties dating back to the late eighteenth century.

3. Faroqhi, *Pilgrims and Sultans*, 45. For a firsthand description of how estate cases of deceased pilgrims were handled (and mishandled) by Ottoman officials in Damascus in the mid-eighteenth century, see the hajj memoir by Russian subject Ismail Bekmukhamedov, *Ismail sayahati*, ed. Rizaeddin Fahreddin (Kazan: Lito-tipografiia I.N. Kharitonova, 1903), 28–29.

4. SSSA, f. 11, op. 1, d. 1957.

5. For a comparative look at Russian and Portuguese expansion onto hajj routes starting in the sixteenth century, see Naim R. Farooqi, "Moguls, Ottomans, and Pilgrims: Protecting the Routes to Mecca in the Sixteenth and Seventeenth Centuries," *International History Review* 10, no. 2 (May 1988): 198–220. See also Michael N. Pearson, *Pilgrimage to Mecca: The Indian Experience, 1500–1800* (Princeton, NJ: Markus Wiener Publishers, 1996).

6. Michael Khodarkovsky, *Russia's Steppe Frontier: The Making of a Colonial Empire, 1500–1800* (Bloomington: Indiana University Press, 2002), 115–117.

7. On the historical geography of Eurasian hajj routes, see S. E. Grigor'ev, "Rossiiskie palomniki v sviatykh gorodakh Aravii v kontse XIX-nachale XX v.," in *Istoriografiia i istochnikovedenie istorii stran Azii i Afriki*, ed. N. N. D'iakov (St. Petersburg: Izd. S.-Peterburgskogo universiteta, 1999), 88–110; R. D. McChesney, "The Central Asian Hajj-Pilgrimage in the Time of the Early Modern Empires," in *Safavid Iran and Her Neighbors*, ed. Michel Mazzaoui (Salt Lake City: University of Utah Press, 2003), 129–156; and Alexandre Papas, Thomas Welsford, and Thierry Zarcone. eds., *Central Asian Pilgrims: Hajj Routes and Pious Visits between Central Asia and the Hijaz* (Berlin: Klaus Schwarz, 2012). See also "Note of a Pilgrimage Undertaken by an Usbek and His Two Sons from Khokend or Kokan, in Tartary, through Russia &c. to Mecca," *Journal of the Asiatic Society of Bengal* 3 (1834): 379–382.

8. On state bans on the hajj and efforts to "discourage" Muslims from making the hajj, see, for example, SSSA, f. 4, op. 8, d. 61; f. 8, op. 1, d. 256.

9. On this process in Russia see Robert D. Crews, *For Prophet and Tsar: Islam and Empire in Russia and Central Asia* (Cambridge, MA: Harvard University Press, 2006).

10. On Russian support for Orthodox pilgrimage to Jerusalem, see Derek Hopwood, *The Russian Presence in Syria and Palestine, 1843–1914: Church and Politics in the Near East* (Oxford: Clarendon Press, 1969); N. N. Lisovoi, *Russkoe dukhovnoe i politicheskoe prisutstvie v Sviatoi Zemle i na Blizhnem Vostoke v XIX-nachale XX v.* (Moscow: Indrik, 2006); and Theofanis George Stavrou, *Russian Interests in Palestine, 1882–1914: A Study of Religious and Educational Enterprise* (Thessaloniki: Institute for Balkan Studies, 1963).

11. Austin Jersild, *Orientalism and Empire: North Caucasus Mountain People and the Georgian Frontier, 1845–1917* (Montreal: McGill-Queen's University Press, 2002); Michael Khodarkovsky, *Bitter Choices: Loyalty and Betrayal in the Russian Conquest of the North Caucasus* (Ithaca, NY: Cornell University Press, 2011); and Nicholas B. Breyfogle, *Heretics and Colonizers: Forging Russia's Empire in the South Caucasus* (Ithaca, NY: Cornell University Press, 2005).

12. D. Iu. Arapov, "Pervyi rossiiskii ukaz o palomnichestve v Mekku," in *Rossiia v srednie veka i novoe vremia: sbornik statei k 70-letiiu chl. korr. RAN L.V. Milova* (Moscow: ROSSPEN, 1999), 298. For cases of the Foreign Ministry arranging and subsidizing travel to Mecca through Russian lands for foreign Muslim elites, see, for example, AVPRI, f. 161, II–15, op. 58, d. 4; and SSSA, f. 11, op. 1, d. 41.

13. AVPRI, f. 161/4, op. 729 (1/2), d. 35. *AKAK*, vol. IV, pt. 1, 713–714. Khodarkovsky, *Bitter Choices*, 19, 70–73.

14. AVPRI, f. 161/4, op. 729 (1/2), d. 35; *AKAK*, vol. VI, pt. 1, 712–714.

15. *AKAK*, vol. VI, pt. 1, 714.

16. AVPRI, f. 161, II-15, op. 58, d. 4; *AKAK*, vol. VI, pt. 1, 717.

17. *AKAK*, vol. VI, pt. 1, 715–716, 779.

18. *AKAK*, vol. VI, pt. 2, 83.

19. In Indonesia Dutch colonial officials tried to restrict the hajj by passing a resolution in 1825 that required passports and charging an exorbitant tax for pilgrims. Muslims responded to the measure by shifting their routes to avoid Dutch officials and travel to Mecca without passports. In 1852 colonial officials reversed the measure: they abolished the hajj tax and issued free passports, hoping to coax pilgrims back to state-monitored routes and in order to count their numbers and regulate the hajj. See Jacob Vredenbregt, "The Haddj: Some of Its Features and Functions in Indonesia," *Bildragan voor Taal-, Land-, en Volkenkunde* 118, 1 (1962): 98–100. Similarly, in West Africa in the early 1850s French colonial officials subsidized hajj trips for select "friends of the colonial regime" as part of a broader effort to co-opt Muslim elites and put a "tolerant face on imperialism." See David Robinson, *Paths of Accommodation: Muslim Societies and French Colonial Authorities in Senegal and Mauritania, 1880–1920* (Athens: Ohio University Press, 2000), 75, 77.

20. *AKAK*, vol. VI, pt. 1, 715–716.

21. Ibid.

22. Khodarkosvky, *Bitter Choices*, 70; and Charles King, *The Ghost of Freedom: A History of the Caucasus* (Oxford: Oxford University Press, 2008), 45–46, 49.

23. Ulrike Freitag, "The City and the Stranger: Jeddah in the Nineteenth Century," in *The City in the Ottoman Empire: Migration and the Making of Urban Modernity*, ed. Ulrike Freitag, Malte Fuhrmann, Nora Lafi, and Florian Riedler (London: Routledge, 2011), 220.

24. Bruce Masters, "Aleppo: The Ottoman Empire's Caravan City," in *The Ottoman City between East and West: Aleppo, Izmir, and Istanbul*, ed. Edhem Eldem, Daniel Goffman, and Bruce Masters (Cambridge, Cambridge University Press, 1999), 17–78; Roger Owen, *The Middle East in the World Economy, 1800–1914* (London: I.B. Tauris, 2005), 85–87.

25. For a standard account of the Eastern Question, see M. S. Anderson, *The Eastern Question, 1774–1923: A Study in International Relations* (London: Macmillan, 1966).

26. Dominic Lieven, *Empire: The Russian Empire and Its Rivals* (New Haven, CT: Yale University Press, 2000), 152; Moshe Ma'oz, *Ottoman Reform in Syria and Palestine, 1840–1861: The Impact of the Tanzimat on Politics and Society* (Oxford: Clarendon Press, 1968), 216; and I. M. Smilianskaia, "K.M. Bazili—rossiiskii diplomat i istorik Sirii," in *Ocherki po istorii russkogo vostokovedeniia*, sb. IV (Moscow: Izdatel'stvo vostochnoi literatury Akademiia nauk SSSR, 1959), 63.

27. AVPRI, f. 313, op. 823, d. 3; Eileen M. Kane, "Pilgrims, Holy Places, and the Multi-Confessional Empire: Russian Policy toward the Ottoman Empire under Tsar Nicholas I, 1825–1855," (PhD diss., Princeton University, 2005), 63.

28. In recent years, the Russian government has started to emphasize its "historic" Orthodox ties to the Middle East, in part to lay claim to valuable tsarist-era land and property in Israel. In line with this, there has been a resurgence of scholarly work on Russian Orthodox pilgrimage to the Holy Land. See, for example, N. N. Lisovoi, comp., *Rossiia v Sviatoi Zemle: dokumenty i materialy*, 2 vols. (Moscow: Mezhdunarodnye otnosheniia, 2000); K. A. Vakh et al., comps., *Rossiia v Sviatoi Zemle: k 130-letiiu sotrudnichestva Imperatorskogo Pravoslavnogo Palestinskogo Obshchestva s narodami Blizhnego Vostoka: katalog mezhdunarodnoi iubileinoi vystavki* (Moscow: Indrik, 2012); and I. A. Vorob'eva, *Russkie missii v Sviatoi Zemle v 1847–1917 godakh* (Moscow: Institut vostokovedeniia RAN, 2001). On the Russian Compound in Jerusalem, see Ely Schiller, ed., *The Heritage of the Holy Land: A Rare Collection of Photographs from the Russian Compound, 1905–1910* (Jerusalem: Arie

Publishing House, 1982); and (in Hebrew) David Kroyanker, ed., *The Russian Compound: Toward the Year 2000; From Russian Pilgrimage Center to a Focus of Urban Activity* (Jerusalem: The Jerusalem Municipality, 1997).

29. AVPRI, f. 313, op. 87, d. 57; *MDBPU*, t. 2, 451; Kane, "Pilgrims, Holy Places, and the Multi-Confessional Empire," 175. See also Shalom Ginat, "The Jewish Settlement in Palestine in the 19th Century," in *The Jewish Settlement in Palestine, 634–1881*, ed. Alex Carmel, Peter Schafer, and Yossi Ben-Artzi (Wiesbaden: L. Reichert, 1990), 166–167; and Albert M. Hyamson, ed., *The British Consulate in Jerusalem in Relation to the Jews of Palestine, 1883–1914*, pt. 1 (New York: AMS Press, 1975).

30. Andrew Petersen, *The Medieval and Ottoman Hajj Route in Jordan: An Archaeological and Historical Study* (Oxford: Oxbow Books, 2012), 10, 20; see also works cited in note 1 above.

31. Faroqhi, *Pilgrims and Sultans*, 9.

32. The *surre* was an ancient hajj tradition, introduced by the Abbasids in the eighth century. On the history of this institution, see Münir Atalar, *Osmanlı Devletinde Surre-i Hümayûn ve Surre Alayları* (Ankara: Diyanet İşleri Başkanlığı, 1991); Faroqhi, *Pilgrims and Sultans*, 54–58; Peters, *The Hajj*, 267–269; and Syed Tanvir Wasti, "The Ottoman Ceremony of the Royal Purse," *Middle Eastern Studies* 41, no. 2 (March 2005): 193–200.

33. Petersen, *The Medieval and Ottoman Hajj Route in Jordan*, 52–54.

34. Karl Barbir, *Ottoman Rule in Damascus, 1708–1758* (Princeton, NJ: Princeton University Press, 1980), 133–142; Faroqhi, *Pilgrims and Sultans*, 6–9; Peters, *The Hajj*, 160–161, 269; Petersen, *The Medieval and Ottoman Hajj Route in Jordan*, 52–54; and Abdul-Karim Rafeq, "New Light on the Transportation of the Damascene Pilgrimage during the Ottoman Period," in *Islamic and Middle Eastern Societies: A Festschrift in Honor of Professor Wadie Jwaideh* (Brattleboro, VT: Amana Books, 1987), 129, 131.

35. P. de Ségur Dupeyron, "La Syrie et les Bedouins sous l'administration turque," *Revue des deux mondes* (March 15, 1855): 348.

36. Rafeq, "Damascus and the Pilgrim Caravan," 134–135; Peters, *The Hajj*, 147–149.

37. Rafeq, "Damascus and the Pilgrim Caravan," 132.

38. Faroqhi, *Pilgrims and Sultans*, 54–73; and R. Tresse, *Le pèlerinage syrien aux villes saintes de l'Islam* (Paris: Imprimerie Chaumette, 1937), 49–50, 82.

39. Rafeq, "Damascus and the Pilgrim Caravan," 132, 138; *Records of the Hajj: A Documentary History of the Pilgrimage to Mecca* (Cambridge: Archive Editions, 1993), 4, 503, 512.

40. Rafeq, "Damascus and the Pilgrim Caravan."

41. Thousands of Muslims fled the French conquest of Algeria in 1830 and resettled in Ottoman lands, including Damascus, where they worked as merchants and became Ottoman subjects. By the 1840s, with the expansion of France's consular system into Damascus, some started claiming French subjecthood to take advantage of the extraterritorial privileges it brought, including consular protection in making the pilgrimage to Mecca. See Pierre Bardin, *Algériens et tunisiens dans l'empire ottoman de 1848 à 1914* (Paris: Éditions du Centre National de la Recherche Scientifique, 1979). See also A. Popoff, *La question des lieux saints de Jérusalem dans la correspondance diplomatique russe du XIXme siècle*, pt. 1 (St. Petersburg: Impr. Russo-Franç., 1910), 350, 354–355.

42. AVPRI, f. 208, op. 819, d. 413.

43. See, for example, SSSA, f. 11, op. 1, d. 888.

44. A.K. "Kazikumukhskie i Kiurinskie khany," in *Sbornik svedenii o kavkazskikh gortsakh* issue 2 (Tiflis, 1869), 1–39. On the Kazikumukh khanate, see also Khodarkovsky, *Bitter Choices*, 40, 54, 93.

45. AVPRI, f. 208, op. 819, d. 413.

46. Ibid; AVPRI, f. 180, op. 517/I, d. 734, ll. 38–40.

47. AVPRI, f. 180, op. 517/I, d. 734, ll. 206–206ob.

48. Ibid., l. 202.

49. AVPRI, f. 208, op. 819, d. 413.

50. On the Capitulations, see A. H. de Groot, "The Historical Development of the Capitulatory Regime in the Ottoman Middle East from the Fifteenth to the Nineteenth Centuries," *Oriente moderno* 83, no. 3 (2003): 575–604; and H. İnalcık, "Imtiyazat," in *Encyclopedia of Islam*, new ed. (Leiden: Brill, 1971), 3:1179a–1189b. See also Lisovoi, *Rossiia v Sviatoi Zemle: dokumenty i materialy* t. 1, 7.

51. Bruce Masters, "The Treaties of Erzurum (1823 and 1848) and the Changing Status of Iranians in the Ottoman Empire," *Iranian Studies* 24 (1): 6.

52. AVPRI, f. 208, op. 819, d. 413.

53. AVPRI, f. 180, op. 517/I, d. 734, ll. 38–40.

54. Smilianskaia, "K.M. Bazili," 58.

55. SSSA, f. 11, op. 1, d. 888; "Raport komanduiushchego voiskami na Kavkazskoi linii i v Chernomorii Gen-Ad" iut. Neidgardtu o deistviiakh Gadzhi-Magomeda na Severo-zapadnom Kavkaze," in *Dvizhenie gortsev severo-vostochnogo Kavkaza v 20–50 gg. XIX veka: sbornik dokumentov* (Makhachkala: Dagestanskoe knizhnoe izdatel'stvo, 1959), 448.

56. AVPRI, f. 180, op. 517/I, d. 739.

57. Ibid.

58. SSSA, f. 5, op. 1, d. 424, ll. 50ob–51.

59. AVPRI, f. 180, op. 517/I, d. 739.

60. SSSA, f. 11, op. 1, d. 1351.

61. Ibid.

62. Anthony L. H. Rhinelander, *Prince Michael Vorontsov: Viceroy to the Tsar* (Montreal: McGill-Queen's University Press, 1990); AVPRI, f. 161, op. 12/3, d. 14; SSSA, f. 4, op. 8, d. 61; SSSA, f. 5, op. 1, d. 424.

63. SSSA, f. 5, op. 1, d. 424.

64. AVPRI, f. 161, op. 12/3, d. 14.

65. SSSA, f. 4, op. 8, d. 61.

66. Andreas Kappeler, *The Russian Empire: A Multiethnic History* (London: Routledge, 2001), 177, 183–185; SSSA, f. 4, op. 8, d. 61.

67. AVPRI, f. 180, op. 517/I, d. 739. On the disastrous 1846 hajj caravan, see also *Records of the Hajj*, 4, 482. In 1846 there was also a deadly cholera outbreak in Mecca that killed 15,000. See http://www.ph.ucla.edu/epi/Snow/pandemic1846-63.html.

68. AVPRI, f. 180, op. 517/I, d. 739.

69. AVPRI, f. 208, op. 819, d. 421, ll. 62–64, 68–69; SSSA, f. 11, op. 1, d. 2792; SSSA, f. 11, op. 1, d. 1586, ll. 1–24.

70. AVPRI, f. 180, op. 517/I, d. 739, ll. 217–218ob.

71. Faroqhi, *Pilgrims and Sultans*, 45.

72. SSSA, f. 11, op. 1, d. 1957, ll. 7–7ob.

73. Ibid., ll. 19–21ob.

74. Ibid., ll. 7–7ob, 25–26.

75. SSSA, f. 11, op. 1, d. 2369, ll. 3–3ob.

76. Ibid., ll. 3–5.

77. Ibid., ll. 8–11.

78. Popoff, *La question des lieux saints*, 350, 354–355.

79. "Dokaladnaia zapiska general-maiora general'nogo shtaba E.I. Chirikova o vozmozhnosti nastupleniia anglichan iz Indii na Sredniuiu Aziiu i merakh protivodeistviia etomu so storony Rossii," in *Russko-Indiiskie otnosheniia v XIX v.: sbornik arkhivnykh dokumentov i materialov* (Moscow: Vostochnaia literatura RAN, 1997), 93.

80. E. I. Chirikov, "Obzor deistvii Mezhdunarodnoi Demarkatsionnoi Komissii na Turetsko-Persidskoi granitse," in *Putevoi zhurnal E. I. Chirikova russkago komissara-posrednika po turetsko-*

persidskomu-razgranicheniiu, 1849–1852, ed. M. A. Gamazov (St. Petersburg, 1875), LV–LVII; and *Russko-Indiiskie otnosheniia v XIX v.*, 93.

81. SSSA, f. 11, op. 1, d. 2369, ll. 1–2.

82. SSSA, f. 4, op. 8, d. 61, ll. 1–14ob.

83. Ibid., ll. 4–5; SSSA, f. 8, op. 1, d. 256.

84. SSSA, f. 11, op. 1, d. 2369; SSSA, f. 4, op. 8, d. 61, l. 15ob.

85. SSSA, f. 11, op. 1, d. 2369, ll. 8–11.

86. Alison Games, *Migration and the Origins of the English Atlantic World* (Cambridge, MA: Harvard University Press, 2001); Games, *The Web of Empire: English Cosmopolitanism in an Age of Expansion, 1560–1660* (Oxford: Oxford University Press, 2008); Thomas R. Metcalf, *Imperial Connections: India in the Indian Ocean Arena, 1860–1920* (Berkeley: University of California Press, 2007). On migrations and nation-states, see also Annemarie H. Sammartino, *The Impossible Border: Germany and the East, 1918–1922* (Ithaca, NY: Cornell University Press, 2010).

2. Mapping the Hajj, Integrating Muslims

1. Robert D. Crews, *For Prophet and Tsar: Islam and Empire in Russia and Central Asia* (Cambridge, MA: Harvard University Press, 2006), 13.

2. Frithjof Benjamin Schenk, "'This New Means of Transportation Will Make Unstable People Even More Unstable': Railways and Geographic Mobility in Tsarist Russia," in *Russia in Motion: Cultures of Human Mobility since 1850*, ed. John Randolph and Eugene M. Avrutin (Urbana: University of Illinois Press, 2012), 218–234; Derek W. Spring, "Railways and Economic Development in Turkestan before 1917," in *Russian Transport: An Historical and Geographical Survey*, ed. Leslie J. Symons and Colin White (London: G. Bell, 1975), 46–74; W. E. Wheeler, "The Control of Land Routes: Railways in Central Asia," *Journal of the Royal Central Asian Society* 21 (1934): 585–608. On how modern transport "reinvigorated" older patterns of pilgrimage in Asia in the early twentieth century, see Sunil S. Amrith, *Migration and Diaspora in Modern Asia* (Cambridge: Cambridge University Press, 2011), 57–58.

3. Hafez Farmayan and Elton L. Daniel, eds. and trans., *A Shiʿite Pilgrimage to Mecca, 1885–1886: The Safar-nameh of Mirza Mohammad Hosayn Farahani* (Austin: University of Texas Press, 1990), 184.

4. For numbers of Russian Orthodox pilgrims to Jerusalem, see Simon Dixon, "Nationalism versus Internationalism: Russian Orthodoxy in Nineteenth-Century Palestine," in *Religious Internationals in the Modern World: Globalization and Faith Communities since 1750*, ed. Abigail Greene and Vincent Viaene (New York: Palgrave Macmillan, 2012), 139–162.

5. John Randolph's work on early modern Russia's roads and the *iam* system yields marvelous insights into how the tsarist state conceptualized Russia's vast spaces in terms of itineraries. See John W. Randolph, "The Singing Coachman Or, The Road and Russia's Ethnographic Invention in Early Modern Time," *Journal of Early Modern History* 11, 1–2 (2007): 32–61. On the eighteenth-century tsarist state's practice of viewing Russia's roads as a set of stations, see I. K. Kirilov, *Tsvetushchee sostoianie vserossiiskogo gosudarstva* (Moscow: Nauka, 1977); and A. N. Vigilev, *Istoriia otechestvennoi pochty*, vol. 1 (Moscow: Sviaz', 1977).

6. Russia opened a Baghdad consulate in 1880, and a vice-consulate in nearby Karbala, a Shiʿi pilgrimage site, soon after. In 1889 it opened a consulate in Mashhad, also a center of Shiʿi pilgrimage, followed by the Jeddah consulate in 1891, and the Bombay consulate in 1900. All were involved in tracking Russia's hajj traffic, providing services to pilgrims, and reporting on the traffic to the Foreign Ministry. On the founding of the Bombay consulate in connection with organizing the hajj, see *Russko-indiiskie otnosheniia v 1900–1917 gg.: sbornik arkhivnykh materialov* (Moscow: Vostochnaia literatura RAN, 1999), 30; and "Ob obrazovanii general'nogo konsul'stva Rossii v Bombee," *Diplomaticheskii vestnik* (March 1, 2000): 81–85.

7. Home to the shrine of the martyred seventh-century imam Husayn, Karbala (located today in Iraq) is among the holiest cities for Shiʿi Muslims, alongside Mecca and Medina. Karbala drew increasing numbers of Muslim pilgrims from the South Caucasus by the late nineteenth century, as did Mashhad and Najaf, important Shiʿi shrines located today in Iran and Iraq, respectively. On the tsarist state's interest in and documentation of Shiʿi pilgrimages abroad in the early twentieth century, see Aleksandr Dmitrievich Vasil'ev, "Palomniki iz Rossii u shiitskikh sviatyn' Iraka. Konets XIX veka," *Vostochnyi arkhiv*, 1, 27 (2013): 9–17.

8. See, for instance, Nick Baron, "New Spatial Histories of Twentieth-Century Russia and the Soviet Union: Surveying the Landscape," *Jahrbücher für Geshchichte Osteuropas* 55, no. 3 (2007): 374–401; Nick Baron and Peter Gatrell, "Population Displacement, State-Building, and Social Identity in the Lands of the Former Russian Empire, 1917–1923," *Kritika: Explorations in Russian and Eurasian History* 4, no. 1 (Winter 2003): 51–100; Mark Bassin, *Imperial Visions: Nationalist Imagination and Geographical Expansion in the Russian Far East, 1840–1865* (Cambridge: Cambridge University Press, 1999); and Mark Bassin, Christopher Ely, and Melissa K. Stockdale, eds., *Space, Place, and Power in Modern Russia: Essays in the New Spatial History* (DeKalb: Northern Illinois University Press, 2010). See also the groundbreaking GIS project "Imperiia: Mapping the Russian Empire," by the historian Kelly O'Neill, http://worldmap.harvard.edu/maps/886.

9. Michael Laffan's excellent study is an exception to this trend. See his *Islamic Nationhood and Colonial Indonesia: The Umma below the Winds* (London: Routledge, 2003). Anthropologists of pilgrimage have noted the stubborn trend in studies across pilgrimage traditions of scholars focusing on the holy-site destination, while overlooking important questions about "movement." See the introduction to *Reframing Pilgrimage: Cultures in Motion*, ed. Simon Coleman and John Eade (London and New York: Routledge, 2004), 8.

10. For a detailed account of bureaucratic procedures and practical dimensions of the twenty-first-century hajj, see Abdellah Hammoudi, *A Season in Mecca: Narrative of a Pilgrimage* (New York: Hill and Wang, 2006).

11. See, for example, *Sayahatnama, Astarkhan ghubernasi Krasni Yar uyezi Sayyid qaryasining al-hajj al-haramayn Er ʿAli Rahimberdiyef al-Qaraghachining hajj safarinda kurganlari* (Astrakhan: Tipografiia Torgovogo Doma "Umerov i Ko.," 1911); and IV RAN, A1522, "Awwali hajj al-haramayn. Al-hajj sighri sabil katib hajji al-haramayn Ayyub Bikan thalith al-hajji Ghubaydullah bin Arali katib thani Abu'l-Ghazi bin Baynaki."

12. Barbara D. Metcalf, "The Pilgrimage Remembered: South Asian Accounts of the Hajj," in *Muslim Travellers: Pilgrimage, Migration, and the Religious Imagination*, ed. Dale F. Eickelman and James Piscatori (Berkeley: University of California Press, 1990), 86–87. On Ibn Battuta, see Ross E. Dunn, *The Adventures of Ibn Battuta: A Muslim Traveller of the 14th Century* (Berkeley: University of California Press, 2005).

13. Several hajj accounts from imperial Russia have been published since the collapse of communism, as part of the revival of Islam and the hajj in former Soviet lands. See, for example, Khamidullah Al'mushev, *Khadzhname: Kniga o khadzhe* (Nizhnii Novgorod: Izd. NIM "Makhinur," 2006).

14. *Ismail sayahati*, ed. Rizaeddin Fahreddin (Kazan: Lito-tipografiia I.N. Kharitonova, 1903). On this text, see also Michael Kemper, "Von Orenburg nach Indien und Mekka: Ismails Reisebuch als Genremischung," in *Istochniki i issledovaniia po istorii tatarskogo naroda: Materialy k uchebnym kursam. V chest' iubileia akademika AN RT M.A. Usmanova*, ed. Diliara Usmanova i Iskander Giliazov (Kazan: Kazanskii gosudarstvennyi universitet, 2006): 318–330; and M. A. Usmanov, "Zapiski Isma'ila Bekmukhamedova o ego puteshestvii v Indiiu," in *Blizhnii i Srednii vostok: Istoriia, ekonomika: sbornik statei*, ed. L. M. Kulagina (Moscow: Nauka, 1967), 88–103.

15. Kemper, "Von Orenburg nach Indien und Mekka," 323.

16. *Ismail sayahati*, 11.

17. Ibid., 7–12.

18. Ibid., 12.

19. Ibid., 8, 27–29.

20. Khadzhi Salim-Girei Sultanov, "Sviashchennaia oblast' musul'man v Aravii (iz vospominanii palomnika)," *Zemlevedenie* kniga 1–2 (1901): 85–144; IV RAN, A1522, "Evveli hac el-harameyn," 1–2.

21. "Rixlätel-Märcäni," in *Bolğar wä Qazan Töreklärе*, ed. Rizaeddin Fakhreddinev (Kazan: Tatarstan kitap näşriyatı, 1997), 130–150.

22. F. E. Peters, *The Hajj: Pilgrimage to Mecca* (Princeton, NJ: Princeton University Press, 1995), 266–315.

23. The literature on colonial knowledge and imperial conquest is vast. See, for example, Bernard S. Cohn, *Colonialism and Its Forms of Knowledge: The British in India* (Princeton, NJ: Princeton University Press, 1996), ix; Nicholas B. Dirks, ed., *Colonialism and Culture* (Ann Arbor: University of Michigan Press, 1992); and Francine Hirsch, *Empire of Nations: Ethnographic Knowledge and The Making of the Soviet Union* (Ithaca, NY: Cornell University Press), 146. On map-making as a technology of empire, see Matthew H. Edney, *Mapping an Empire: The Geographical Construction of British India, 1765–1843* (Chicago: University of Chicago Press, 1990); and Barbara Mundy, *Mapping New Spain: Indigenous Cartography and the Maps of the Relaciones Geograficas* (Chicago: University of Chicago Press, 1996).

24. In seeing, and making, this distinction, I have drawn inspiration from the geographer David Harvey's theorizing of space, in particular his division of space into three categories (absolute, relative, and relational). See David Harvey, "Space as a Keyword," in *David Harvey: A Critical Reader*, ed. Noel Castree and Derek Gregory (Malden, MA: Blackwell Publishing, 2006), 70–93.

25. V. G. Chernukha, *Pasport v Rossii, 1719–1917* (St. Petersburg: Liki Rossii, 2007), 257.

26. On the 1865 order, see DAOO, f. 1, op. 174, d. 7, ll. 1–3.

27. David Edwin Long, *The Hajj Today: A Survey of the Contemporary Pilgrimage to Makkah* (Albany: State University of New York Press, 1979), 69.

28. Ibid., 72–73; Peters, *The Hajj*, 301–305.

29. DAOO, f. 1, op. 174, d. 7, ll. 54–55.

30. In 1859, based on information that the Crimean Tatars had collaborated with the Ottomans in the Crimean War, the Russian government had encouraged and to some extent forced their migration, causing a mass exodus of some 100,000 Crimean Tatars into Ottoman lands. Within a year the tsar-ist government would change its mind, worried about the negative effects of emigration on the economic and agricultural development of the region. In 1860 it reversed the order, ordering tsarist officials to stop issuing passports to Tatars, and to instead encourage them to stay. But the damage had been done. Tatars had become wary of the government, and the region had lost much of its productive population. Alan W. Fisher, *The Crimean Tatars* (Stanford, CA: Hoover Institution Press, 1978), 89, 93. See also James H. Meyer, "Immigration, Return, and the Politics of Citizenship: Russian Muslims in the Ottoman Empire, 1860–1914," *International Journal of Middle East Studies* 39, no. 1 (Feb. 2007): 15–32.

31. On the ease with which Jewish migrants in Russia got fake passports, see Eugene M. Avrutin, *Jews and the Imperial State: Identification Politics in Tsarist Russia* (Ithaca, NY: Cornell University Press, 2010), 127–130. On the problem of venal officials easily bribed to issue illegal passports, see DAOO, f. 1, op. 249, d. 468.

32. DAOO, f. 1, op. 174, d. 7, ll. 17–20ob, 21–22ob; f. 1, op. 249, d. 468.

33. Suraiya Faroqhi, *Pilgrims and Sultans: The Hajj under the Ottomans* (London: I.B. Tauris, 1994), 139–142. Robert McChesney, while acknowledging that some Central Asians got to Mecca by way of Constantinople, questions claims by Faroqhi and others that this "northern" route was preferred by Central Asians in the sixteenth and seventeenth centuries. See R. D. McChesney, "The

Central Asian Hajj-Pilgrimage in the Time of the Early Modern Empires," in *Safavid Iran and Her Neighbors*, ed. Michel Mazzaoui (Salt Lake City: University of Utah Press, 2003), 132–135.

34. Hamid Algar, "Tariqat and Tariq: Central Asian Naqshbandis on the Roads to the Haramayn," in *Central Asian Pilgrims: Hajj Routes and Pious Visits between Central Asia and the Hijaz*, ed. Alexandre Papas, Thomas Welsford, and Thierry Zarcone (Berlin: Klaus Schwarz, 2012), 76–95. See also Lâle Can, "Connecting People: A Central Asian Sufi Network in Turn-of-the-Century Istanbul," *Modern Asian Studies* 46, no. 2 (2012): 373–401; Grace Martin Smith, "The Özbek Tekkes of Istanbul," *Der Islam* 57, no. 1 (1980): 130–139; and Al'fina Sibgatullina, *Kontakty tiurok-musul'man Rossiiskoi i Osmanskoi imperii na rubezhe XIX–XX vv.* (Moscow: Istok, 2010), 89–99.

35. See, for example, these three hajj memoirs, from 1899, 1909, and 1911, respectively. Kh. Al'mushev, *Khadzh-name: Kniga o khadzhe* (Nizhnii Novgorod: Izd. NIM "Makhinur," 2006); *Sayahatnama, Astarkhan ghubernasi Krasni Yar uyezi Sayyid qaryasining al-hajj al-haramayn Er 'Ali Rahimberdiyef al-Qaraghachining hajj safarinda kurganlari* (Astrakhan: Tipografiia Torgovogo Doma "Umerov i Ko." 1911); and UNT RAN, f. 7, "Makhammed Khasan Akchura tarzhemaikhale."

36. SSSA, f. 5, op. 1, d. 3305.

37. *Records of the Hajj: A Documentary History of the Pilgrimage to Mecca* (Cambridge: Archive Editions, 1993), 4, 331.

38. Pierre Boyer, "L'administration française et la règlementation du pèlerinage à la Mècque (1830–1894)," *Revue d'histoire maghrébine* 9 (July 1977): 277.

39. *Records of the Hajj*, 4, 185.

40. Boyer, "L'administration française," 277.

41. On efforts by European empires to accommodate Islam, see, for example, David Robinson, *Paths of Accommodation: Muslim Societies and French Colonial Authorities in Senegal and Mauritania, 1880–1920* (Athens, OH: Ohio University Press, 2000). See also various essays in *Islam and the European Empires*, ed. David Motadel (Oxford: Oxford University Press, 2014).

42. William R. Roff, "Sanitation and Security: The Imperial Powers and the Nineteenth-Century Hajj," *Arabian Studies* 6 (1982): 146.

43. According to records from Russian officials in charge of the North Caucasus, large numbers of Muslims from Dagestan made the pilgrimage to Mecca, and most of them were poor, and traveled on foot along land routes through eastern Anatolia to Damascus. As Russia's consular network in eastern Anatolia expanded, indigent hajj pilgrims increasingly were showing up at consulates to beg for money. The loans they received were small, 5 to 10 rubles per person, but they added up. SSSA, f. 5, op. 1, d. 424, ll. 50ob–51.

44. SSSA, f. 5, op. 1, d. 424, ll. 50ob–51. On the 1857 law, see st. 477 "Ustav o pasportakh," in *Polnoe sobranie zakonov Rossiiskoi imperii* XIV-tom (St. Petersburg, 1857). On this point Loris-Melikov seems to have been mistaken. No such law favoring Muslim pilgrims exists on the books. His confusion illustrates the mess of laws regarding passports, and the general incoherence of imperial passport policy, which Tsar Alexander II had been trying, with little success, to clarify and codify. See Chernukha, *Pasport v Rossii, 1719–1917*, 98–99.

45. SSSA, f. 8, op. 1, d. 256; f. 5, op. 1, d. 424.

46. Hans Rogger, *Jewish Policies and Right-Wing Politics in Russia* (Berkeley: University of California Press, 1986), 58. For a recent study of Ignat'ev's diplomatic career see V. M. Khevrolina, *Rossiiskii diplomat graf Nikolai Pavlovich Ignat'ev* (Moscow: Institut Rossiiskoi istorii RAN, 2004).

47. DAOO, f. 1, op. 174, d. 7.

48. SSSA, f. 5, op. 1, d. 1396, l. 1.

49. SSSA, f. 5, op. 1, d. 1396, l. 1.

50. DAOO, f. 1, op. 174, d. 7.

51. Ibid.

52. Ibid.

53. Daniel Brower, "Russian Roads to Mecca: Religious Tolerance and Muslim Pilgrimage in the Russian Empire," *Slavic Review* 55, no. 3 (1996): 570.

54. Ibid., 569–570.

55. DAOO, f. 1, op. 174, d. 7.

56. Ibid.

57. Ibid.

58. Ibid.

59. John D. Klier, "The Pogrom Paradigm in Russian History," in *Pogroms: Anti-Jewish Violence in Modern Russian History*, ed. John Doyle Klier and Shlomo Lambroza (Cambridge: Cambridge University Press, 2004), 20–26.

60. RGIA, f. 821, op. 8, d. 1174.

61. Ibid.

62. Ibid. This increase was a direct result of the expansion of Russia's railroad network into the Caucasus and Central Asia. Russia's opening of the trans-Caucasian and trans-Caspian lines during the 1880s—the first railroads ever in these regions, built mainly for Russia's military and economic purposes—opened up access to the hajj even wider, and drew greater numbers of Muslim pilgrims out of these regions, through Russian lands, and onto the Black Sea-Constantinople-Jeddah sea route. On the building of the trans-Caspian railroad in the 1880s to "strengthen Russia's position in Central Asia" and as part of its involvement in the "Great Game," see Frithjof Benjamin Schenk, "Imperial Inter-Rail: Vliianie mezhnatsional'nogo i mezhimperskogo vospriiatiia i sopernichestva na politiku zheleznodorozhnogo stroitel'stva v tsarskoi Rossii," in *Imperium inter pares: Rol' transferov v istorii Rossiiskoi imperii (1700–1917)*, ed. Martin Aust, Ricarda Vulpius, and A. I. Miller (Moscow: Novoe literaturnoe obozrenie, 2010), 366.

63. RGIA, f. 821, op. 8, d. 1174.

64. Eickelman and Piscatori, *Muslim Travellers*, xii–xv. See also Laffan, *Islamic Nationhood and Colonial Indonesia*.

65. RGIA, f. 821, op. 8, d. 1174.

66. Ibid.

67. BOA, Fon: Y.A.HUS, Dosya: 252, Gömlek: 40, Vesika: 1; Fon: I.MMS, Dosya: 116, Gömlek: 4980, Vesika: 1–4.

68. Ibid.

69. Selim Deringil, *The Well-Protected Domains: Ideology and the Legitimation of Power in the Ottoman Empire, 1876–1909* (London: I.B. Tauris, 1999), 56.

70. A Turkic-language insert called *Turkistaning gazeti* was published as part of the Russian-language *Turkestanskie vedomosti*, the region's first newspaper, published under the auspices of the viceroy's office starting in 1870. In 1883 an independent Turkic-language twice-weekly paper was launched, *Turkistan wilayatining gazeti*, with a print run of five hundred to six hundred copies. See E. A. Masonov, "Sh.M. Ibragimov—drug Ch.Ch. Valikhanova," *Vestnik akademii nauk Kazakhskoi SSR* 9 (1964): 53–60; and N. P. Ostroumov, *Sarty: etnograficheskie materialy* (Tashkent: Tip. "Sredneaziatskaia zhizn'," 1908), 156.

71. Crews, *For Prophet and Tsar*, 224, 227–229, 231; Masonov, "Sh.M. Ibragimov," 53–54.

72. BOA, Fon: Y.A.HUS, Dosya: 252, Gömlek: 41, Vesika 1–3.

73. Sh. Ishaev, "Mekka—sviashchennyi gorod musul'man," *Sredneaziatskii vestnik* pt. 1 (Nov. 1896): 62.

74. RGIA, f. 821, op. 8, d. 1202. It is not clear why Russia never again put a Muslim in charge of the Jeddah consulate. It was probably due in part to the Ottoman outcry over Russia's appointment of Ibragimov, and a desire on the Foreign Ministry's part to ensure the cooperation of local Ottoman

officials and smooth functioning of the consulate. But it may have also been because of the resistance of Russian officials to the idea; many doubted the loyalty of Russia's Muslims, and resisted putting them into important positions in Russian consulates abroad, especially in Ottoman lands.

75. Adeeb Khalid, *The Politics of Muslim Cultural Reform: Jadidism in Central Asia* (Berkeley: University of California Press, 1998), 86–88. See also Alexandre Bennigsen and Chantal Lemercier-Quelquejay, *La presse et le mouvement national chez les musulmans de Russie avant 1920* (Paris: Mouton, 1964).

76. Crews, *For Prophet and Tsar*, 241–292.

77. "Rukovodstvo dlia rossiiskikh konsul'stv v Turtsii, otnositel'no russkikh poddannykh, otpravliaiushchikh na poklonenie v Mekku," *Turkestanksaia Tuzemnaia Gazeta*, no. 11, March 21, 1892, cited in V. P. Litvinov, *Vneregional'noe palomnichestvo musul'man Turkestana (epokha novogo vremeni)* (Elets: EGU im. I.A. Bunina, 2006), 163; "Izvlechenie iz spetsial'nogo Ustava o palomnichestve v Khedzhaz v techenie 1892 goda," *Turkestanksaia Tuzemnaia Gazeta*, no. 12, March 30, 1892, cited in Litvinov, *Vneregional'noe palomnichestvo musul'man Turkestana*, 163.

78. "O musulmanskikh palomnikakh, sovershavshikh khadzh v 1894 godu," *Turkistan wilayatining gazeti*, May 12, 1895, 3.

79. Ibid.

80. David Ludden, "The Process of Empire: Frontiers and Borderlands," in *Tributary Empires in Global History*, ed. Peter Fibiger Bang and C. A. Bayly (London: Palgrave Macmillan, 2011), 146–147.

81. On Turkestani tekkes in Ottoman lands, see Hamid Algar, "Tariqat and Tariq," in Papas, Welsford, and Zarcone, *Central Asian Pilgrims*, 76–95; Can, "Connecting People," 373–401; Smith, "The Özbek Tekkes of Istanbul," 130–139; and Sibgatullina, *Kontakty tiurok-musul'man Rossiiskoi i Osmanskoi imperii na rubezhe XIX–XX vv.*, 89–99.

82. AVPRI, f. 180, op. 517/2, d. 5301, ll. 2–3.

83. Ibid. Gülden Sarıyıldız, "II. Abdülhamid'in Fakir Hacılar için Mekke'de İnşa Ettirdiği Misafirhane," *Tarih Enstitüsü Dergisi* 14 (1994): 134, 141.

84. Peters, *The Hajj*, 301–302. On the 1892 cholera epidemic in Russia, see Nancy A. Frieden, "The Russian Cholera Epidemic, 1892–93 and Medical Professionalization," *Journal of Social History* 10 (1977): 538–599, 546; and Charlotte E. Henze, *Disease, Health Care, and Government in Late Imperial Russia: Life and Death on the Volga, 1823–1914* (New York: Routledge, 2011), 51.

85. Peters, *The Hajj*, 303.

86. Long, *The Hajj Today*, 72–73.

87. Sarıyıldız, "II. Abdülhamid'in Fakir Hacılar için Mekke'de İnşa Ettirdiği Misafirhane," 134, 141.

88. AVPRI, f. 180, op. 517/2, d. 5301, ll. 2–3.

89. Ibid.

90. An Algerian émigré community also developed in Damascus after the 1830 French conquest. As the French consular presence in Syria grew from the 1830s onward, some émigrés began to claim French subjecthood, for the legal and economic advantages diplomatic protection brought them. See Pierre Bardin, *Algériens et tunisiens dans l'empire ottoman de 1848 à 1914* (Paris: Éditions du Centre National de la Recherche Scientifique, 1979).

91. BOA, Fon: HR.HM.IŞO, Dosya: 177, Gömlek: 34; Fon: DH.MKT, Dosya: 2287, Gömlek: 65.

92. Mehmed Sakır, Ayşe Kavak, and Gülden Sariyildiz, eds., *Halife II. Abdülhamid'in hac siyaseti: Dr. M. Sakir Bey'in hatıraları* (Istanbul: Timaş yayınları, 2009), 11–12.

93. BOA, Fon: HR.HMŞ.IŞO, Dosya: 177, Gömlek: 34.

94. Faroqhi, *Pilgrims and Sultans*, 45.

95. Peters, *The Hajj*, 272–273.

96. See Article 8 of the "Convention de commerce et de navigation avec la Russie, 1783" in *Recueil d'actes internationaux de l'empire ottoman: traités, conventions, arrangements, déclarations, protocoles, procés-verbaux, firmans, bérats, lettres patentes et autres documents rélatifs au droit public extérieur de la Turquie, recueillis et publiés par Gabriel Effendi Noradounghian*, ed. Gabriel Noradounghian vol. 1 (Paris: Librairie Cotillon, 1897), 354.

97. BOA, Fon: BEO, Dosya: 1643, Gömlek: 123165, Vesika 1–23; Fon: DH.MKT, Dosya: 694, Gomlek: 11, Vesika: 1–4; Fon: I. HR, Dosya: 383, Gomlek: 1321/M–10.

98. In 1902 at least one of the guards at Russia's Jeddah consulate was a Muslim from Tashkent. See AVPRI, f. 180, op. 517/2, d. 5303, l. 51.

99. AVPRI, f. 180, op. 517/2, d. 5303, l. 51.

100. On Ishaev, see Z. V. Togan, *Bugünkü Türkili Türkistan ve Yakın Tarihi* (Istanbul: Enderun Kitabevi, 1983), 269, 274.

101. AVPRI, f. 180, op. 517/2, d. 5303, l. 51.

102. Sh. Ishaev, "Mekka—sviashchennyi gorod musul'man," *Sredneaziatskii vestnik* pt. 2 (Dec. 1896): 69.

103. C. Snouck Hurgronje, *Mekka in the Latter Part of the 19th Century* (Leiden: Brill, 2007).

104. Sh. Ishaev, "Mekka—sviashchennyi gorod musul'man," *Sredneaziatskii vestnik* pt. 1 (Nov. 1896): 74–75; pt. 2 (Dec. 1896), 69–71.

105. Ishaev, "Mekka" (Nov. 1896), 61; (Dec. 1896), 50.

106. Ishaev, "Mekka" (Nov. 1896), 82–83.

107. Ishaev, "Mekka" (Dec. 1896), 68.

108. Ibid., 66–69.

109. Ishaev, "Mekka" (Nov. 1896), 73.

110. Ibid., 79.

111. Ibid., 74.

112. AVPRI, f. 180, op. 517/2, d. 5301, ll. 4–5.

113. Ibid.

114. AVPRI, f. 180, op. 517/2, d. 5301, ll. 12–13.

115. *Otchet o komandirovke v Dzheddu vracha D. Zabolotnago* (St. Petersburg: Tip. V. Kirshbauma, 1897); D. F. Sokolov, *O palomnichestve musul'man v Dzheddu* (St. Petersburg: Tip. Stasiulevich, 1901).

116. The result was this book: *Otchet Kapitana Davletshina po komandirovke v Turkestanskii krai i stepnyia oblasti, dlia oznakomleniia s dieiatel'nost'iu narodnykh sudov* (St. Petersburg: Tip. M.M. Stasiulevicha, 1901). See also Alex Marshall, *The Russian General Staff and Asia, 1860-1917* (New York: Routledge, 2006), 65.

117. *Otchet shtabs-kapitana Davletshina o komandirovke v Khidzhaz* (St. Petersburg: Voennaia tipografiia [v zdanii Glavnago Shtaba], 1899).

118. RGIA, f. 821, op. 8, d. 1174, ll. 127–142ob.

119. Ibid., ll. 129ob–130.

120. Ibid., l. 129ob.

121. Ibid., ll. 134ob–135ob.

122. Bassin, *Imperial Visions*; Baron, "New Spatial Histories," 379–380, 382.

3. Forging a Russian Hajj Route

1. RGIA, f. 821, op. 8, d. 1202.

2. Charles Steinwedel, "Resettling People, Unsettling the Empire: Migration and the Challenge of Governance, 1861–1917," in *Peopling the Russian Periphery: Borderland Colonization in Eurasian History*, ed. Nicholas B. Breyfogle, Abby Schrader, and Willard Sunderland (New York: Routledge,

2007), 130; Donald W. Treadgold, *The Great Siberian Migration: Government and Peasant in Resettlement from Emancipation to the First World War* (Princeton, NJ: Princeton University Press, 1957).

3. See, for example, SSSA, f. 11, op. 1, d. 2369, ll. 3–5.

4. RGIA, f. 821, op. 8, d. 1174, ll. 143–143ob.

5. Ibid.

6. Russian consulates in Constantinople, Jaffa, Izmir, Beirut, and elsewhere along Orthodox pilgrims' routes through Ottoman lands provided them with crucial legal, logistical, and financial services and support in getting to Jerusalem and back. On the infrastructure the IOPS built to encourage and organize Orthodox pilgrimage to Jerusalem, see Theofanis George Stavrou, *Russian Interests in Palestine, 1882-1914: A Study of Religious and Educational Enterprise.* (Thessaloniki: Institute for Balkan Studies, 1963).

7. RGIA, f. 821, op. 8, d. 1202.

8. Russia's consuls estimated that between 12,000 and 15,000 Muslims (mostly Shi'is) took the land route through the Caucasus; another 4,000 to 7,000 the land route from Central Asia through Afghanistan and Indian lands; and about 2,000 to 3,000 took the Black Sea route. RGIA, f. 821, op. 8, d. 1174, ll. 127–133ob.

9. Ibid., ll. 138ob–140ob.

10. RGIA, f. 821, op. 8, d. 1202, ll. 123ob–124ob. On KOMOCHUM, see K. M. Tokarevich and T. I. Grekova, *Po sledam minuvshikh epidemii* (Leningrad: Lenizdat, 1986). On the quarantine cordon, see John Tchalenko, *Images from the Endgame: Persia through a Russian Lens, 1901-1914* (London: SAQI, 2006), 36–37.

11. RGIA, f. 821, op. 8, d. 1174, l. 134.

12. Ne-Moriak, *Za chto russkoe obshchestvo parakhodtsva i torgovli zhelaet poluchit' 22 milliona rublei?* (Odessa: Tip. Odesskiia Novosti, 1910).

13. ROPiT was founded with an imperial charter in 1856, on the initiative of Grand Duke Konstantin Nikolaevich. It would become Russia's largest shipping company. The Volunteer Fleet was not a company but instead a state-sponsored steamship line. It had been started in 1879 with six million rubles in donations raised by a group of Russian patriots that included the Slavophile writer Ivan Aksakov, and Timofei Morozov, a philanthropist and member of one of Russia's leading industrialist families. In 1883 the government nationalized the Volunteer Fleet and transferred it to the Naval Ministry. See Thomas C. Owen, *Dilemmas of Russian Capitalism: Fedor Chizhov and Corporate Enterprise in the Railroad Age* (Cambridge, MA: Harvard University Press, 2005), 136, 155. See also Werner E. Mosse, "Russia and the Levant, 1856–1862: Grand Duke Constantine and the Russian Steam Navigation Company," *Journal of Modern History* 24 (1954): 39–48. On the Volunteer Fleet charter see 2–58585 in *Polnoe sobranie zakonov Rossiiskoi imperii* n. 22767, t. XXIII (1903). See also S. I. Ilovaiskii, *Istoricheskii ocherk piatidesiatiletiia Russkogo obshchestva parokhodstva i torgovli* (Odessa: Tip. Iuzhno-Russkago o-va pechatnago diela, 1907); M. Poggenpol', *Ocherk vozniknoveniia i deiatel'nosti Dobrovol'nago Flota za vremia XXV-ti letniago ego sushchestvovaniia* (St. Petersburg: Tip. A. Benke, 1903), 113; and Thomas C. Sorenson, "The End of the Volunteer Fleet: Some Evidence on the Scope of Pobedonostsev's Power in Russia," *Slavic Review* 34, no. 1 (March 1975): 131–137.

14. RGIA, f. 821, op. 8, d. 1174.

15. Ibid., ll. 138ob–140ob.

16. Ibid., l. 140ob.

17. Theodore H. von Laue, *Sergei Witte and the Industrialization of Russia* (New York: Columbia University Press, 1963), 5–7.

18. Witte was Russia's minister of finance from 1892 to 1903. He introduced a new law on December 1, 1894, making long-distance rail travel (more than 160 versts) much less expensive. The effects would prove dramatic. Long-distance passenger traffic soared; the number of third-class tickets sold between 1894 and 1912 quadrupled, from 42.5 million to 163.1 million. See Frithjof

Benjamin Schenk, "'This New Means of Transportation Will Make Unstable People Even More Unstable': Railways and Geographical Mobility in Tsarist Russia," in *Russia in Motion: Cultures of Human Mobility since 1850*, ed. John Randolph and Eugene M. Avrutin (Urbana: University of Illinois Press, 2012), 224–225.

19. On the creation of ROPiT's "Persian Line," see Aleksandr Adamov, *Irak arabskii: Bassorskoi vilaiet v ego proshlom i nastoiaschem* (St. Petersburg: Tip. Glav. Upr. Udielov, 1912), 475; *Polnoe sobranie zakonov Rossiiskoi imperii* n. 22767, t. XXIII (1903), 360; and Efim Rezvan, *Russian Ships in the Gulf, 1899–1903* (London: Garnet Publishing & Ithaca Press, 1993).

20. Rezvan, *Russian Ships in the Gulf.*

21. Geoffrey Hosking, *Russia: People and Empire* (Cambridge, MA: Harvard University Press, 1997), 392–393; and Paul W. Werth, *The Tsar's Foreign Faiths: Toleration and the Fate of Religious Freedom in Imperial Russia* (Oxford: Oxford University Press, 2014), 203.

22. RGIA, f. 821, op. 8, d. 1174.

23. Donald W. Treadgold, *The Great Siberian Migration: Government and Peasant in Resettlement from Emancipation to the First World War* (Princeton, NJ: Princeton University Press, 1957), 67–81.

24. RGIA, f. 821, op. 8, d. 1174.

25. This was not ROPiT's first attempt to get involved in hajj transport. In the 1880s it had started advertising steamship service especially for hajj pilgrims in *Terdzhuman* (*Perevodchik* in Russian), the empire's first Turkic-language newspaper for Muslims, published in Bahchesarai in the Crimea. But these advertisements appeared sporadically, and ROPiT got only limited help from Russia's railroads to coordinate rail and steamship schedules to ease travel. Most Muslims continued to take foreign steamships from Russia's Black Sea ports, which charged lower rates. On this, see Mustafa Tuna, *Imperial Russia's Muslims: Islam, Empire, and European Modernity, 1788–1914* (Cambridge: Cambridge University Press, 2015), 182.

26. RGIA, f. 98, op. 2, d. 285.

27. See, for example, C. A. Bayly, *The Birth of the Modern World, 1780–1914: Global Connections and Comparisons* (Oxford: Blackwell Publishing, 2004), 354–355.

28. Shovosil Ziyodov, "The Hajjnamas of the Manuscript Collection of the Oriental Institute of Uzbekistan (mid-19th to early 20th centuries)," in *Central Asian Pilgrims: Hajj Routes and Pious Visits between Central Asia and the Hijaz*, ed. Alexandre Papas, Thomas Welsford, and Thierry Zarcone (Berlin: Klaus Schwarz, 2012), 228–229; and Sharifa Tosheva, "The Pilgrimage Books of Central Asia: Routes and Impressions (19th and early 20th Centuries)," ibid., 242.

29. Hafez Farmayan and Elton T. Daniel, eds. and trans., *A Shi'ite Pilgrimage to Mecca, 1885–1886: The Safarnameh of Mirza Mohammad Hosayn Farahani* (Austin: University of Texas Press, 1990), 74.

30. George Dobson, *Russia's Railway Advance into Central Asia* (London: W.H. Allen & Co., 1890), 150–152.

31. Ibid., 112, 121–123.

32. Ibid., 180–181.

33. "S palomnikami do Dzheddy i obratno," *Turkistan wilayatining gazeti*, February 2, 1914, 1–2.

34. Alexandre Papas, "Following Abdurreşid Ibrahim: A Tatar Globetrotter on the Way to Mecca," in Papas et al., *Central Asian Pilgrims*, 207; Abdürrechid Ibrahim, *Un Tatar au Japon: Voyage en Asie (1908–1910)* (Paris: Sindbad-Actes Sud, 2004), 233.

35. "S palomnikami do Dzheddy i obratno," 1–2.

36. RGIA, f. 821, op. 8, d. 1202.

37. AVPRI, f. 180, op. 517/2, d. 5301, l. 15.

38. "Pis'mo ministra inostrannykh del Rossii M. N. Murav'eva poslu Rossii v Londone E. E. Staalo," in *Diplomaticheskii vestnik* (March 1, 2000): 82.

39. *Russko-Indiiskie otnosheniia v 1900–1917 gg.: sbornik arkhivnykh materialov* (Moscow: Vostochnaia literatura RAN, 1999), 30.

40. Ibid.

41. Ibid., 192–193.

42. Stuart Thompstone, "Tsarist Russia's Investment in Transport," *Journal of Transport History* 3, no. 19/1 (March 1998): 61–62.

43. Ibid.

44. RGIA, f. 98, op. 2, d. 285.

45. Ibid.

46. RGIA, f. 98, op. 2, d. 285, ll. 118, 28.

47. RGAVMF, f. 417, op. 1, d. 2757.

48. Patricia Herlihy, *Odessa: A History, 1794–1914* (Cambridge, MA.: Harvard Ukrainian Research Institute, 1986), 107, 203; Thompstone, "Tsarist Russia's Investment in Transport," 63; RGAVMF, f. 417, op. 1, d. 2757, l. 3ob.

49. RGIA, f. 98, op. 2, d. 285, ll. 307–309.

50. On the difficulties European steamship companies faced in profiting from the transport of hajj pilgrims in the modern era, see Michael B. Miller, "Pilgrims' Progress: The Business of the Hajj," *Past & Present* 191 (May 2006): 189–228. See also Michael B. Miller, *Europe and the Maritime World: A Twentieth-Century History* (Cambridge: Cambridge University Press, 2012), 123–124.

51. RGIA, f. 98, op. 2, d. 285.

52. *Records of the Hajj: A Documentary History of the Pilgrimage to Mecca* (Cambridge: Archive Editions, 1993), 4, 340–342.

53. RGIA, f. 98, op. 2, d. 285; RGAVMF, f. 417, op. 1, d. 2757.

54. Before 1906, when Russia became a constitutional monarchy with a parliament (Duma), the State Council was a legislative advisory body to the tsar, made up of his trusted officials. The council's job was to consider proposed laws.

55. In 1881, for example, then minister of internal affairs N. P. Ignat'ev had introduced "Temporary Rules" regarding peasant migration, which shared many features with these new proposed rules regarding Muslim pilgrimage. Treadgold, *The Great Siberian Migration*, 76.

56. D. S. Sipiagin was minister of internal affairs briefly, from 1900 to 1902. He was preceded by I. L. Goremykin (1895–99). Von Laue, *Sergei Witte and the Industrialization of Russia*, 202–203.

57. Edward H. Judge, *Plehve: Repression and Reform in Imperial Russia, 1902–1904* (Syracuse, NY: Syracuse University Press, 1983); Hans Rogger, *Jewish Policies and Right-Wing Politics in Imperial Russia* (Berkeley: University of California Press, 1986).

58. RGIA, f. 821, op. 8, d. 1174.

59. V. G. Chernukha, *Pasport v Rossii, 1719–1917* (St. Petersburg: Liki Rossii, 2007). See also Eugene Avrutin, *Jews and the Imperial State: Identification Politics in Tsarist Russia* (Ithaca, NY: Cornell University Press, 2010); and Eric Lohr, *Russian Citizenship: From Empire to Soviet Union* (Cambridge, MA: Harvard University Press, 2012).

60. RGIA, f. 821, op. 8, d. 1202, ll. 133–136ob.

61. Robert D. Crews, "The Russian Worlds of Islam," in *Islam and the European Empires*, ed. David Motadel (Oxford: Oxford University Press, 2014), 40.

62. RGIA, f. 821, op. 8, d. 1202, ll. 133–136ob.

63. Ibid., l. 136ob.

64. Ibid., l. 137ob.

65. Ibid., ll. 137ob–138ob.

66. Ibid., ll. 23ob–24.

67. Ibid., l. 53.

68. This project was handed off by the Committee of Ministers to the State Council, which made its decision in June 1903.

69. "Vremennye pravila dlia palomnikov-musul'man," in *Sobranie zakonodatel'stva Rossiiskoi imperii*, t. XIV (Ustav o pasportakh; prilozhenie k stat'e 187) (1903), http://russky.com/history/library/vol.14/vol.14.1.htm.

70. RGIA, f. 821, op. 8, d. 1196, ll. 1–1ob.

71. RGIA, f. 821, op. 8, d. 1202, l. 144–144ob.

72. Ibid., ll. 145ob–146.

73. Ibid., ll. 149–149ob.

74. Ibid., ll. 146–147.

75. *Krymskii vestnik*, no. 208, Sept. 19, 1907. For a description of ROPiT's khadzhilar-sarai in Sevastopol, see RGIA, f. 273, op. 10, ch. 1, d. 253, ll. 1–2.

76. DAOO, f. 2, op. 3, d. 3391, l. 128–128ob.

77. RGIA, f. 98, op. 2, d. 285, l. 382.

78. BOA, Fon: Y.PRK.AZJ, Dosya: 51, Gömlek: 71.

79. An *akhund* (also *akhun*) had somewhat ambiguous status in Muslim communities in late imperial Russia. Allen Frank has argued that in the Russian context this title referred in the seventeenth century to a high-ranking legal expert, but this title gradually lost its prestige and authority by the late nineteenth century. See Frank's discussion of the changing meaning of this title in Allen J. Frank, *Muslim Religious Institutions in Imperial Russia: The Islamic World of Novouzensk District and the Kazakh Inner Horde, 1780–1910* (Leiden: Brill, 2001), 109–111.

80. *Krymskii vestnik*, no. 208, Sept. 19, 1907.

81. DAOO, f. 2, op. 3, d. 3391, ll. 92–94ob.

82. RGIA, f. 98, op. 2, d. 287, l. 44.

83. RGIA, f. 821, op. 8, d. 1202, ll. 197–200.

84. Ibid., ll. 180–180ob.

85. DAOO, f. 2, op. 3, d. 3391, l. 42.

86. Ibid., ll. 1–2, 222ob.

87. Ibid., ll. 56–61.

88. Ibid., l. 40.

89. Ibid., ll. 40, 46.

90. Ibid., ll. 51–52.

91. Ibid., l. 44.

92. Ibid., ll. 40ob–42, 51–52.

93. DAOO, f. 2, op. 3, d. 3391.

94. DAOO, f. 2, op. 3, d. 3391, l. 100.

95. Ibid. See, for example, "Musul'mane-palomniki," *Russkoe slovo*, March 7, 1908. RGIA, f. 821, op. 8, d. 1196, l. 8.

96. *Pravila perevozki na sudakh palomnikov-musul'man iz Chernomorskikh portov v Gedzhasa i obratno* (St. Petersburg: Pervaia tsentral'naia vostochnaia elektropechatnia, 1908).

97. DAOO, f. 2, op. 3, d. 3391, ll. 128–129ob.

98. Ibid., ll. 187–188.

4. The Hajj and Religious Politics after 1905

1. DAOO, f. 2, op. 3, d. 3391, l. 64.

2. Peter Waldron, "Religious Toleration in Late Imperial Russia," in *Civil Rights in Imperial Russia*, ed. Olga Crisp and Linda Edmondson (Oxford: Clarendon Press, 1989), 112–113.

3. Leonard Schapiro, "Stolypin," in *Major Problems in the History of Imperial Russia*, ed. James Cracraft (Lexington, MA: D.C. Heath, 1994), 615; Waldron, "Religious Toleration in Late Imperial

Russia," 107–108, 112. See also Abraham Ascher, *P. A. Stolypin: The Search for Stability in Late Imperial Russia* (Stanford, CA: Stanford University Press, 2001).

4. Paul W. Werth, *The Tsar's Foreign Faiths: Toleration and the Fate of Religious Freedom in Imperial Russia* (Oxford: Oxford University Press, 2014), 253. See also Elena Campbell, "The Muslim Question in Late Imperial Russia," in *Russian Empire: Space, People, Power, 1700–1930*, ed. Jane Burbank, Mark von Hagen, and Anatolyi Remnev (Bloomington: Indiana University Press, 2007), 320–347.

5. Muslims constituted a small and gradually decreasing minority in the Duma, a ratio deliberately engineered by the regime, which sought to block certain candidates for election and decreased their overall numbers over time. There were twenty-five Muslim representatives (out of 496 total) in the First Duma of 1906; thirty-six (out of 517) in the Second Duma of 1907; ten (out of 487) in the Third Duma of 1907–12; and just seven (out of 444) in the Fourth Duma of 1912–17. See Werth, *The Tsar's Foreign Faiths*, 225.

6. DAOO, f. 2, op. 3, d. 3391, ll. 78–81.

7. Ibid., l. 78ob.

8. RGIA, f. 821, op. 8, d. 1196, ll. 55–62ob.

9. RGIA, f. 821, op. 8, d. 1202, l. 50b.

10. M. O. Menshikov, "Uvazhenie k Islamu," *Novoe vremia*, November 25, 1908.

11. Daniel Brower, *Turkestan and the Fate of the Russian Empire* (London: RoutledgeCurzon, 2003), 74–75; Adeeb Khalid, *The Politics of Muslim Cultural Reform: Jadidism in Central Asia* (Berkeley: University of California Press, 1998), 67–68; A. Zeki Veilidi Togan, *Bugünkü Türkili Türkistan ve Yakın Tarihi* (Istanbul: Enderun Kitabevi, 1981), 272–273.

12. Eugene Schuyler, *Turkistan: Notes of a Journey in Russian Turkistan, Khokand, Bukhara, and Kuldja* (New York: Scribner, Armstrong, 1876), 1, 97–98, 157–158.

13. Elise Kimerling Wirtschafter, *Social Identity in Imperial Russia* (DeKalb: Northern Illinois University Press, 1997).

14. Khalid, *The Politics of Muslim Cultural Reform*, 67–68.

15. DAOO, f. 2, op. 3, d. 3391, ll. 40ob–42, 257–258.

16. Ibid., ll. 78ob–79ob.

17. William R. Roff, "Sanitation and Security: The Imperial Powers and the Nineteenth-Century Hajj," *Arabian Studies* 6 (1982): 143–160; see also F. E. Peters, *The Hajj: Pilgrimage to Mecca* (Princeton, NJ: Princeton University Press, 1995), 266–315.

18. DAOO, f. 2, op. 3, d. 3391, l. 77. For Russian press coverage, see the March 1908 article in *Russkoe slovo*, in RGIA, f. 821, op. 8, d. 1196, l. 8; and "Staryi Turkestanets. Palomnichestvo v Mekku," *Golos pravdy*, no. 708 (Jan. 24, 1908), cited in Al'fina Sibgatullina, *Kontakty tiurok-musul'man Rossiiskoi i Osmanskoi imperii na rubezhe XIX–XX vv.* (Moscow: Istok, 2010), 30.

19. DAOO, f. 2, op. 3, d. 3391, l. 77.

20. Ibid., l. 76ob.

21. Ibid., l. 77.

22. Ibid., ll. 79–79ob.

23. Ibid., ll. 79ob–80.

24. Piers Brendon, *Thomas Cook: 150 Years of Popular Tourism* (London: Martin Secker and Warburg, 1991), 110; Edmund Swinglehurst, *Cook's Tours: The Story of Popular Travel* (Poole, Dorset, UK: Blandford Press, 1982).

25. Louise McReynolds, "The Prerevolutionary Russian Tourist: Commercialization in the Nineteenth Century," in *Turizm: The Russian and East European Tourist under Capitalism and Socialism*, ed. Anne E. Gorsuch and Diane P. Koenker (Ithaca, NY: Cornell University Press, 2006), 26.

26. In 1885 the British colonial government in India hired Thomas Cook to organize the hajj out of a central office in Bombay; by 1893, unhappy with the results, the government fired Cook. See

Roff, "Sanitation and Security," 152; *The Mecca Pilgrimage: Appointment by the Government of India of Thos. Cook and Son as Agents for the Control of the Movements of Mahomedan Pilgrims from All Parts of India to Jeddah for Mecca, Medina, etc., and Back* (London: Printed for Private Circulation, 1886); Swinglehurst, *Cook's Tours*, 80–82; and Brendon, *Thomas Cook*, 205–210.

27. David Edwin Long, *The Hajj Today: A Survey of the Contemporary Pilgrimage to Makkah* (Albany: State University of New York Press, 1979).

28. Suraiya Faroqhi et al., eds., *An Economic and Social History of the Ottoman Empire: 1600–1914* (Cambridge: Cambridge University Press, 1997), 2, 612.

29. DAOO, f. 2, op. 3, d. 3391, ll. 273–284.

30. Ibid., l. 276.

31. Ibid., ll. 273–284.

32. Victor and Edith Turner made this point in their 1978 seminal essay on pilgrimage as a subject of scholarly study, "Pilgrimage as a Liminoid Phenomenon." And yet scholars have been slow to explore the economic aspects of pilgrimage. See Victor Turner and Edith Turner, eds. *Image and Pilgrimage in Christian Culture: Anthropological Perspectives* (New York: Columbia University Press, 1978), 25.

33. For centuries the economy of Damascus, a major hub of land routes to Mecca, was based almost entirely on the hajj traffic. See Abdul-Karim Rafeq, "Damascus and the Pilgrim Caravan," in *Modernity and Culture: From the Mediterranean to the Indian Ocean*, ed. Leila Tarazi Fawaz and C. A. Bayly (New York: Columbia University Press, 2002), 130–143.

34. See note 5 above on the Dumas between 1906 and 1917. See Dilyara M. Usmanova, "The Activity of the Muslim Faction of the State Duma and Its Significance in the Formation of a Political Culture among the Muslim Peoples of Russia (1906–1917)," in *Muslim Culture in Russia and Central Asia from the 18th to the Early 20th Centuries*, ed. Michael Kemper et al. vol. 2 (Berlin: Schwarz, 1996), 2, 429.

35. RGIA, f. 821, op. 8, d. 1196, ll. 17–17ob.

36. S. I. Ilovaiskii, *Istoricheskii ocherk piatidesiatiletiia Russkago obshchestva parokhodstva i torgovli* (Odessa: Tip. Iuzhno-russkago obshchestva pechatnago diela, 1907); M. Poggenpol', *Ocherk vozniknoveniia i deitel'nosti Dobrovol'nago Flota za vremia XXV-ti letnago ego sushchestvovaniia* (St. Petersburg: Tip. A. Benke, 1903).

37. DAOO, f. 2, op. 3, d. 3391, ll. 83–85, 95ob.

38. Patricia Herlihy, *Odessa: A History, 1794–1914* (Cambridge, MA.: Harvard Ukrainian Research Institute, 1986), 107, 203; Stuart Thompstone, "Tsarist Russia's Investment in Transport," *Journal of Transport History* 3, no. 19/1 (March 1998): 63; RGAVMF, f. 417, op. 1, d. 2757, l. 3ob.

39. DAOO, f. 2, op. 3, d. 3391. ll. 40ob–42.

40. Ibid., l. 95ob.

41. Ibid., ll. 83–85.

42. Ibid.

43. Ibid., l. 76.

44. *Pravila perevozki na sudakh palomnikov-musul'man iz Chernomorskikh portov v Gedzhasa i obratno* (St. Petersburg: Pervaia tsentral'naia vostochnaia elektropechatnia, 1908); DAOO, f. 2, op. 3, d. 3391, ll. 128–129ob.

45. DAOO, f. 2, op. 3, d. 3391, l. 78.

46. Ibid., ll. 78–81.

47. Ibid., ll. 76–82.

48. RGIA, f. 821, op. 8, d. 1196.

49. "Zapiski P. A. Stolypina po 'musul'manskomu voprosu,' 1911 g.," in *Imperatorskaia Rossiia i musul'manskii mir (konets XVIII–nachalo XX v.): sbornik materialov*, comp. D. Iu. Arapov (Moscow: Natalis, 2006), 315.

50. Schapiro, "Stolypin," 615.

51. Waldron, "Religious Toleration in Late Imperial Russia," 117.

52. See, for example, Robert D. Crews, *For Prophet and Tsar: Islam and Empire in Russia and Central Asia* (Cambridge, MA: Harvard University Press, 2006), 10–11.

53. DAOO, f. 2, op. 3, d. 3391, l. 64.

54. Ibid., ll. 204–205.

55. Ibid., ll. 92–92ob.

56. Ibid., ll. 64, 82; 79–79ob, 274ob; 80ob, 276.

57. Ibid., ll. 62, 71.

58. Sibgatullina, *Kontakty tiurok-musul'man Rossiiskoi i Osmanskoi imperii na rubezhe XIX–XX vv.*, 30; DAOO, f. 2, op. 3, d. 3471, ll. 5, 7, 12; f. 2, op. 3, d. 3391, ll. 40ob–42.

59. DAOO, f. 2, op. 3, d. 3391, ll. 56–61.

60. Ibid., l. 81ob.

61. Ibid., l. 87ob.

62. Ibid., l. 88ob.

63. Ibid., l. 74.

64. Ibid., ll. 95–96.

65. Ibid., ll. 91–91ob.

66. Ibid., ll. 125–125ob.

67. Ibid., l. 78ob.

68. Ibid., ll. 76–85.

69. Ibid., ll. 79ob–80ob.

70. Ibid., ll. 62, 71.

71. Robert Weinberg, *The Revolution of 1905 in Odessa: Blood on the Steps* (Bloomington: Indiana University Press, 1993); Stephen Zipperstein, *The Jews of Odessa: A Cultural History* (Stanford, CA: Stanford University Press, 1987).

72. DAOO, f. 2, op. 3, d. 3391, ll. 270ob–272.

73. Ibid., ll. 104–106.

74. Ibid.

75. These institutions were built in cities across the empire starting in the 1890s to address the growing problems of unemployed workers in cities and labor unrest. See Adele Lindenmeyr, *Poverty Is Not a Vice: Charity, Society, and the State in Imperial Russia* (Princeton, NJ: Princeton University Press, 1996), 168–195.

76. DAOO, f. 2, op. 3, d. 3391, l. 276ob. He originally proposed 4,000 rubles, but later reported that he spent 7,500. See l. 110.

77. DAOO, f. 2, op. 3, d. 3391, ll. 110, 270ob.

78. *Odesskii listok*, no. 270, Nov. 21, 1908. On newspapers in early twentieth-century Odessa, see Roshanna P. Sylvester, *Tales of Old Odessa: Crime and Civility in a City of Thieves* (DeKalb: Northern Illinois University Press, 2005), 5–8.

79. DAOO, f. 2, op. 3, d. 3391, ll. 204–204ob.

80. For the full text of the rules, see A. T. Sibgatullina, " 'Delo' Saidazimbaeva—Rukovoditelia musul'manskogo palomnicheskogo dvizheniia iz Rossii," *Nauchnyi Tatarstan* 1 (2009): 86–87.

81. Peters, *The Hajj*, 267–315.

82. DAOO, f. 2, op. 3, d. 3391, l. 100.

83. Stephen J. Zipperstein, "Urban Legend," *New Republic*, Feb. 1, 2011.

84. Sylvester, *Tales of Old Odessa*, 22; Robert Weinberg, "Workers, Pogroms, and the 1905 Revolution in Odessa," *Russian Review* 46, no. 1 (Jan. 1987): 53–75.

85. DAOO, f. 2, op. 3, d. 3391, ll. 148–149ob.

86. DAOO, f. 2, op. 3, d. 3391, ll. 121–122.

87. Ilovaiskii, *Istoricheskii ocherk piatidesiatiletiia Russkago obshchestva parokhodstva i torgovli*.

88. RGIA, f. 821, op. 8, d. 1202, l. 172ob.

89. DAOO, f. 2, op. 3, d. 3391, l. 148ob.

90. RGIA, f. 821, op. 8, d. 1202, l. 171ob.

91. "Khadzhi-khane. Pis'mo iz Odessy," *Rech'*, no. 244, Oct. 12, 1908, cited in Sibgatullina "'Delo' Saidazimbaeva," 82.

92. DAOO, f. 2, op. 3, d. 3391.

93. See, for example, James H. Meyer, *Turks across Empires: Marketing Muslim Identity in the Russo-Ottoman Borderlands, 1856–1914* (New York: Oxford University Press, 2014).

94. Robert D. Crews, "Islam and the European Empires," 38.

95. RGIA, f. 821, op. 8, d. 1196, ll. 21ob–22.

96. Ibid., ll. 24–24ob.

97. Ibid.

98. On Odessa as a hub of Russian Orthodox pilgrimage to Jerusalem, see Nikolaos Chrissidis, "The Athonization of Pious Travel: Shielded Shrines, Shady Deals, and Pilgrimage Logistics in Late Nineteenth-Century Odessa," *Modern Greek Studies Yearbook* 28/29 (2012/2013): 169–191. See also Patricia Herlihy, *Odessa Memories* (Seattle: University of Washington Press, 2003), 3–37.

99. RGIA, f. 821, op. 8, d. 1196.

100. Alexandre Papas, "Following Abdurreşid Ibrahim: A Tatar Globetrotter on the Way to Mecca," in *Central Asian Pilgrims: Hajj Routes and Pious Visits between Central Asia and the Hijaz*, ed. Alexandre Papas et al. (Berlin, 2012), 207; Abdürrechid Ibrahim, *Un Tatar au Japon: Voyage en Asie, 1908–1910* (Paris: Sindbad-Actes Sud, 2004).

101. RGIA, f. 821, op. 8, d. 1196, l. 25.

102. Ibid., ll. 21ob–22.

103. Ibid., ll. 18–18ob; 24–24ob.

104. Ibid., ll. 24–24ob.

105. DAOO, f. 2, op. 3, d. 3391, ll. 204–204ob.

106. Ibid., ll. 204–205.

107. Ibid., ll. 176–176ob.

108. Ibid., ll. 176ob, 206.

109. Sibgatullina, "'Delo' Saidazimbaeva," 83.

110. Ibid., 80.

111. DAOO, f. 2, op. 3, d. 3391, ll. 204–205, 202ob.

112. RGIA, f. 821, op. 8, d. 1202, l. 175.

113. Ibid., l. 173ob.

114. Ibid., l. 10.

115. *Russkoe slovo*, March 1908. RGIA, f. 821, op. 8, d. 1196, l. 8.

116. M. O. Menshikov, "Uvazhenie k Islamu," *Novoe vremia*, November 25, 1908.

117. Ibid.

118. RGIA, f. 821, op. 8, d. 1202, l. 38ob.

119. *Terdzhuman*, July 18, 1914.

120. *Turkistan wilayatining gazeti*, September 22, 1911.

121. Ibid., August 19, 1910.

122. RGIA, f. 821, op. 8, d. 1196, ll. 55–62ob.

123. RGIA, f. 273, op. 10, d. 330, ll. 30–31.

124. "K svedeniiu nashikh musul'manskikh palomnikov," *Turkistan wilayatining gazeti*, April 10, 1911.

125. See the hajj memoir by Mullah Alim published in *Turkistan wilayatining gazeti*, March 7, 1910, 1–2.

126. M. E. Nikol'skii, "Palomnichestvo v Mekku," *Istoricheskii vestnik* 124 (April 1911): 621–622.

127. RGIA, f. 821, op. 8, d. 1202, l. 118ob.

128. Kh. Al'mushev, *Khadzhname: kniga o khadzhe* (N. Novgorod: Izd. NIM "Makhinur," 2006).

129. Ufinskii Nauchnyi Tsentr RAN, f. 7, op. 1, d. 14 "Makhammed Khasan Akchura tarzhe-maikhale." In the context of the Balkan Wars, in November 1912 Bulgarian forces had reached the outskirts of Constantinople. See Michael A. Reynolds, *Shattering Empires: The Clash and Collapse of the Ottoman and Russian Empires, 1908–1918* (Cambridge: Cambridge University Press, 2011), 35.

130. "S palomniki do Dzheddy i obratno," *Turkistan wilayatining gazeti*, February 2, 1914, 1–2.

131. BOA, Fon: DH.ID, Dosya: 77, Gömlek: 9.

132. "Palomniki musul'mane," *Odesskiia novosti*, no. 9082, July 24/Aug. 6, 1913, 2.

5. The Hajj and Socialist Revolution

1. Sugata Bose, *A Hundred Horizons: The Indian Ocean in the Age of Global Empire* (Cambridge, MA: Harvard University Press, 2006), 202–204; F. E. Peters, *The Hajj: Pilgrimage to Mecca* (Princeton, NJ: Princeton University Press, 1995), 316–352.

2. At its greatest territorial extent after World War II, the Soviet Union consisted of all of the lands of the former Russian Empire ca. 1914, except for Poland and Finland.

3. On Soviet antireligion campaigns, see William B. Husband, *"Godless Communists": Atheism and Society in Soviet Russia, 1917–1932* (DeKalb: University of Illinois Press, 2000); and Daniel Peris, *Storming the Heavens: The Soviet League of the Militant Godless* (Ithaca, NY: Cornell University Press, 1998). See also Victoria Smolkin-Rothrock, "'The Confession of an Atheist Who Became a Scholar of Religion': Nikolai Semenovich Gordienko's Last Interview," *Kritika: Explorations in Russian and Eurasian History* 15, no. 3 (Summer 2014): 597–620.

4. See Gregory J. Massell, *The Surrogate Proletariat: Moslem Women and Revolutionary Strategies in Soviet Central Asia, 1919–1929* (Princeton, NJ: Princeton University Press, 1974); and Douglas Northrop, *Veiled Empire: Gender and Power in Stalinist Central Asia* (Ithaca, NY: Cornell University Press, 2004). See also Shoshanna Keller, *To Moscow, Not Mecca: The Soviet Campaign against Islam in Central Asia, 1917–1941* (Westport, CT: Praeger Publishers, 2001); and Adeeb Khalid, *Islam after Communism: Religion and Politics in Central Asia* (Berkeley: University of California Press, 2006).

5. The anthropologist Catherine Wanner has drawn a distinction between the Soviet state and the Communist Party with regard to religion. She argues that the Soviet state took an overall neutral position toward religious organization and practice (the state never formally outlawed religions, for example), while the Communist Party was staunchly hostile to it. See her introduction in Catherine Wanner, ed., *State Secularism and Lived Religion in Soviet Russia and Ukraine* (New York: Oxford University Press, 2012), 12. This paradox, in term, illuminates a crucial distinction between theory and practice in the case of early Soviet religious policy—if the communist project was fundamentally hostile to religion, the Soviet state could also be pragmatic.

6. See Michael David-Fox, *Showcasing the Great Experiment: Cultural Diplomacy and Western Visitors to the Soviet Union, 1921–1941* (Oxford: Oxford University Press, 2012); Sylvia R. Margulies, *The Pilgrimage to Russia: The Soviet Union and the Treatment of Foreigners, 1924–1937* (Madison: University of Wisconsin Press, 1968); Matthias Heeke, *Reisen zu den Sowjets: Der ausländiche Tourismus in Russland, 1921–1941* (Munster: LIT, 2003).

7. The expression is that of David-Fox, *Showcasing the Great Experiment*.

8. Peter Hopkirk, *Setting the East Ablaze: Lenin's Dream of an Empire in Asia* (London: John Murray Publishers, 2006).

9. Massell, *The Surrogate Proletariat*.

10. See, for instance, Andrew D. W. Forbes, *Warlords and Muslims in Chinese Central Asia: A Political History of Republican Sinkiang, 1911–1949* (Cambridge: Cambridge University Press, 1986), 66; Lars-Erik Nyman, *Great Britain and Chinese, Russian, and Japanese Interests in Sinkiang, 1918–1934* (Stockholm: Esselte Studium, 1977), 68–72; and Jon Jacobson, *When the Soviet Union Entered World Politics* (Berkeley: University of California Press, 1994).

11. Jacobson, *When the Soviet Union Entered World Politics*, 181.

12. On the USSR as a self-consciously anti-imperialist empire, see Francine R. Hirsch, *Empire of Nations: Ethnographic Knowledge and The Making of the Soviet Union* (Ithaca, NY: Cornell University Press, 2005).

13. John Baldry, "Soviet Relations with Saudi Arabia and the Yemen, 1917–1938," *Middle Eastern Studies* 20, no. 1 (Jan. 1984): 58. On Muslim anticolonial nationalist leaders in the 1920s who saw Mecca as a forum for spreading their ideas and overthrowing empire, see Ayesha Jalal, *Partisans of Allah: Jihad in South Asia* (Cambridge, MA: Harvard University Press, 2008), 221.

14. "K. Khakimov—pervyi sovetskii polpred v Saudovskii Aravii," *Ekho vekov*, May 1995.

15. Ibid.

16. Ibid.

17. DAOO, f. R-1965, op. 6, d. 66; f. R-1965, op.6, d. 65.

18. DAOO, f. R-1965, op. 6, d. 85, ll. 33–34.

19. *SSSR i arabskie strany 1917–1960: dokumenty i materialy* (Moscow: Gosudarstvennoe izdatel'stvo politicheskoi literatury, 1961), 60; *Dokumenty vneshnei politiki SSSR* (Moscow: Gosudarstvennoe izdatel'stvo politicheskoi literatury, 1963), 7, 215; John Baldry, "Soviet Relations with Saudi Arabia and Yemen," 58–60. Also serving alongside Khakimov was N. T. Tiuriakulov, a Kazakh from Kokand who also joined the Bolshevik Party in 1918. He served as Soviet consul general in Jeddah from 1928 to 1935. See *Nazir Tiuriakulov—polpred SSSR v Korolevstve Saudovskaia Araviia: pis'ma, dnevniki, otchety (1928–1935)* (Moscow: Russkii raritet, 2000); T.A. Mansurov, *Polpred Nazir Tiuriakulov* (Moscow: Molodaia gvardiia, 2004); and Baymirza Hayit, *Turkestan im XX Jahrhundert* (Darmstadt: C.W. Leske Verlag, 1956), 184, 227, 306, 314–315.

20. Bose, *A Hundred Horizons*, 204.

21. Jacobson, *When the Soviet Union Entered World Politics*, 181.

22. RGAE, f. 7795, op. 1, d. 262, ll. 2–6, cited in Norihiro Naganawa, "The Red Sea Becoming Red? The Bolsheviks' Commercial Enterprise in the Hijaz and Yemen, 1924–1938" (unpublished paper, 2013).

23. RGAE, f. 7795, op. 1, d. 260, ll. 6–6ob, cited in Naganawa, "The Red Sea Becoming Red?"

24. DAOO, f. R-1965, op. 6, d. 85, ll. 49–50.

25. Sunil S. Amrith, *Crossing the Bay of Bengal: The Furies of Nature and the Fortunes of Migrants* (Cambridge, MA: Harvard University Press, 2013), 3.

26. DAOO, f. R-1965, op. 6, d. 85, ll. 49–50.

27. Ibid.

28. Ibid.

29. David-Fox, *Showcasing the Great Experiment*, 5.

30. Ibid., 175–177.

31. Shawn Salmon, "Marketing Socialism: Inturist in the Late 1950s and Early 1960s," in *Turizm: The Russian and East European Tourist under Capitalism and Socialism*, ed. Anne E. Gorsuch and Diane P. Koenker (Ithaca, NY: Cornell University Press, 2006), 189. On Torgsin (the All-Union Association for Trade with Foreigners on the Territory of the USSR), see Elena Osokina, *Zoloto dlia industrializatsii: TORGSIN* (Moscow: ROSSPEN, 2009).

32. DAOO, f. R-1965, op. 6, d. 66, ll. 5–5ob.

33. DAOO, f. R-1965, op. 6, d. 136, ll. 5, 25.

34. Ibid., l. 25.

35. Michael B. Miller, "Pilgrims' Progress: The Business of the Hajj," *Past & Present* 191 (May 2006): 189–228.

36. DAOO, f. R-1965, op. 6, d. 86, ll. 2–4.

37. Forbes, *Warlords and Muslims in Chinese Central Asia*, 66; Nyman, *Great Britain and Chinese, Russian, and Japanese Interests*, 68–72.

38. DAOO, f. R-1965, op. 6, d. 85, ll. 25–28.

39. Ibid.

40. Ibid., ll. 43–46.

41. DAOO, f. R-1965, op. 6, d. 66, ll. 3–4.

42. DAOO, f. R-1965, op. 6, d. 85, ll. 23–24.

43. Ibid.

44. Ibid., ll. 6–7.

45. Ibid., ll. 11–12.

46. Ibid.

47. David Edwin Long, *The Hajj Today: A Survey of the Contemporary Pilgrimage to Makkah* (Albany: State University of New York Press, 1979), 109.

48. DAOO, f. R-1965, op. 6, d. 86, ll. 55–56; f. R-1965, op. 6, d. 85, l. 35.

49. DAOO, f. R-1965, op. 6, d. 85, ll. 35, 40.

50. DAOO, f. R-1965, op. 6, d. 86, l. 15.

51. Ibid., ll. 16–17.

52. Ibid.

53. DAOO, f. R-1965, op. 6, d. 85, ll. 25–30.

54. Ibid., ll. 25–28.

55. Ibid., ll. 14–15.

56. Ibid., ll. 21–22.

57. DAOO, f. R-1965, op. 6, d. 86, ll. 29–30.

58. Ibid.

59. Ibid., ll. 22–28.

60. DAOO, f. R-1965, op. 6, d. 85, ll. 14–15.

61. Ibid., ll. 18–19.

62. Ibid., ll. 12–13.

63. DAOO, f. R-1965, op. 6, d. 110, ll. 28–37.

64. DAOO, f. R-1965, op. 6, d. 85, ll. 14–15.

65. Ibid., ll. 18–19.

66. DAOO, f. R-1965, op. 6, d. 110, ll. 46–47.

67. See st. 248, "O perevozke morem palomnikov-musul'man iz portov Soiuza SSR v porty Gedzhasa i obratno," in *Sobranie zakonov i rasporiazhenii raboche-krest'ianskogo pravitel'stva Soiuza Sovetskikh Sotsialisticheskikh Respublik*, 537.

68. DAOO, f. R-1965, op. 6, d. 110, l. 3.

69. "Sovetskii diplomat N. T. Tiuriakulov," *Ekho vekov*, no. 3/4 (1997), cited in Naganawa, "The Red Sea Becoming Red?" 13. For a comparative look at Soviet and European medical missions set up in Arabia, see Martin Thomas, "Managing the Hajj: Indian Pilgrim Traffic, Public Health, and Transportation in Arabia, 1918–1930," in *Railways and International Politics: Paths of Empire, 1848–1945*, ed. T. G. Otte and Keith Neilson (London: Routledge, 2006), 173–191.

70. DAOO, f. R-1965, op. 6, d. 110, l. 42.

71. DAOO, f. R-1965, op. 6, d. 113, l. 7.

72. DAOO, f. R-1965, op. 6, d. 143, l. 3.

73. DAOO, f. R-1965, op. 6, d. 110, ll. 51–54.

74. Ibid., ll. 28–37.

75. DAOO, f. R-1965, op. 6, d. 113, ll. 8–10.

76. DAOO, f. R-1965, op. 6, d. 110, ll. 28–37.

77. Ibid.

78. DAOO, f. R-1965, op. 6, d. 113, ll. 9–10.

79. DAOO, f. R-1965, op. 6, d. 110, ll. 17–27.

80. Ibid., ll. 11–15.

81. DAOO, f. R-1965, op. 6, d. 143, l. 5; f. R-1965, op. 6, d. 136, l. 7.

82. DAOO, f. R-1965, op. 6, d. 110, l. 2.

83. DAOO, f. R-1965, op. 6, d. 136, l. 7.

84. DAOO, f. R-1965, op. 6, d. 110, ll. 4–5.

85. Ibid., ll. 51–54.

86. Ibid.

87. Ibid.

88. On the interwar colonial hajj, see, for example, Kris Alexanderson, "'A Dark State of Affairs': Hajj Networks, Pan-Islamism, and Dutch Colonial Surveillance during the Interwar Period," *Journal of Social History* 7, no. 4 (June 2014): 1021–1041.

89. See, for example, the website for an exciting just-launched interdisciplinary research project on "Socialism Goes Global." Framed conventionally as a post-WWII story (1945–1989), it seeks to illuminate linkages and exchanges that animated what might be called the global socialist world, and to integrate the history of this world into narratives of late twentieth-century globalization. http://socialismgoesglobal.exeter.ac.uk. See, also, *Mongolia in the Twentieth Century: Landlocked Cosmopolitanism*, ed. Stephen Kotkin and Bruce A. Elleman (New York and London: M. E. Sharpe), 1999. In this book, the authors challenge the idea of 1945 as a starting point for the global spread of socialism; they remind us that Mongolia was the first Soviet satellite state, created in 1921.

Conclusion

1. Michael Schwirtz, "Putin Opens Mecca Path for Muslims," *New York Times*, December 17, 2007.

2. The Saudi quota allows each country 1,000 hajj pilgrims per one million inhabitants. Robert R. Bianchi, *Guests of God: Pilgrimage and Politics in the Islamic World* (Oxford: Oxford University Press, 2004), 51–53.

3. Schwirtz, "Putin Opens Mecca Path for Muslims."

4. Abdürrechid Ibrahim, *Un Tatar au Japon: Voyage en Asie, 1908–1910* (Paris: Sindbad-Actes Sud, 2004).

BIBLIOGRAPHY

Archives

Arkhiv vneshnei politiki Rossiiskoi imperii (AVPRI), Moscow, Russia
Başbakanlık Osmanlı Arşivi (BOA), Istanbul, Turkey
Derzhavnyi arkhiv Odeskoi oblasti (DAOO), Odessa, Ukraine
Rossiiskii gosudarstvennyi arkhiv voenno-morskogo flota (RGAVMF), St. Petersburg, Russia
Rossiiskii gosudarstvennyi istoricheskii arkhiv (RGIA), St. Petersburg, Russia
Sakartvelos Sakhelmtsipo Saistorio Arkivi (SSSA), Tbilisi, Georgia

Unpublished Hajj Memoirs

Otdel Rukopisei, Institut Vostokovedeniia, Rossiiskaia Akademiia Nauk (IV RAN), St. Petersburg, Russia.
A1522, "Opisanie puteshestviia trekh tatarskikh palomnikov v Mekku i Medinu." Or "Awwali hajj al-haramayn. Al-hajj sighri sabil katib hajji al-haramayn Ayyub Bikan thalith al-hajji Ghubaydullah bin Arali katib thani Abu'l-Ghazi bin Baynaki."
Otdel Rukopisei, Ufinskii Nauchnyi Tsentr, Rossiiskaia Akademiia Nauk (UNT RAN), Ufa, Russia.
f. 7, "Makhammed Khasan Akchura tarzhemaikhale."

Published Accounts of the Hajj

Al'mushev, Khamidullah. *Khadzh-name: Kniga o khadzhe.* Nizhnii Novgorod: Izd. NIM "Makhinur," 2006.
Sayahatnama, Astarkhan ghubernasi Krasni Yar uyezi Sayyid qaryasining al-hajj al-haramayn Er ʿAli: Rahimberdiyef al-Qaraghachining hajj safarinda kurganlari. Astrakhan: Tipografiia Torgovogo Doma "Umerov i Ko." 1911.

Farmayan, Hafez, and Elton T. Daniel, eds. and trans. *A Shiʿite Pilgrimage to Mecca, 1885–1886: The Safarnameh of Mirza Mohammad Hosayn Farahani.* Austin: University of Texas Press, 1990.

Ismail sayahati. Ed. Rizaeddin Fahreddin. Kazan: Lito-tipografiia I.N. Kharitonova, 1903.

Ishaev, Sh. "Mekka—sviashchennyi gorod musul'man (rasskaz palomnik)." *Sredne-aziatskii vestnik,* November 1896, 60–81; December 1896, 45–83.

Nurimanov, I. A. *Khadzh Rossiiskikh musul'man: sbornik putevykh zametok o khadzhe.* Nizhnii Novgorod: Izd. "Medina," 2008.

"Rixlätel-Märcäni," in *Bolğar wä Qazan Töreklär,* ed. Rizaeddin Fakhreddinev, 130–150. Kazan: Tatarstan kitap näşriyati, 1997.

Sultanov, Khadzhi Salim-Girei. "Sviashchennaia oblast' musul'man v Aravii (iz vospominanii palomnika)." *Zemlevedenie* kniga 1–2 (1901): 85–144.

Published Document Collections

Akty, sobrannye Kavkazskoiu arkheograficheskoiu kommissieiu, ed. A. P. Berzhe. 12 Volumes. Tiflis: Arkhiv glavnago upravleniia namiestnika Kavkazskago, 1866–1904.

Dokumenty vneshnei politiki SSSR. Moscow: Gosudarstvennoe izdatel'stvo politicheskoi literatury, 1963.

Dvizhenie gortsev severo-vostochnogo Kavkaza v 20–50 gg. XIX veka: sbornik dokumentov. Makhachkala: Dagestanskoe knizhnoe izdatel'stvo, 1959.

La question des lieux saints de Jérusalem dans la correspondance diplomatique russe du XIX siècle. Ed. Alexandre Popoff. Vol. 1. St. Petersburg: Imprimerie Russo-Française, 1910.

Materialy dlia biografii Porfiriia Uspenskogo. Ed. P. V. Bezobrazov. Tom 1. St. Petersburg: Tipografiia V.Th. Kirshbauma, 1910.

Ocherki russkoi politiki na okrainakh. Ed. Arslan Krichinskii. Part 1. Baku: Soiuz musul'manskoi trudovoi intelligentsia, 1919.

Records of the Hajj: A Documentary History of the Pilgrimage to Mecca, ed. A. de L. Rush. 10 vols. Cambridge: Archive Editions, 1993.

Recueil d'actes internationaux de l'empire ottoman: traités, conventions, arrangements, déclarations, protocoles, procés-verbaux, firmans, bérats, lettres patentes et autres documents rélatifs au droit public extérieur de la Turquie, recueillis et publiés par Gabriel Effendi Noradounghian. vol. 1. Paris: Librairie Cotillon, 1897.

Russko-Indiiskie otnosheniia v XIX v.: sbornik arkhivnykh dokumentov i materialov. Moscow: Vostochnaia literatura RAN, 1997.

Russko-Indiiskie otnosheniia v 1900–1917 gg.: sbornik arkhivnykh dokumentov i materialov. Moscow: Vostochnaia literatura RAN, 1999.

SSSR i arabskie strany 1917–1960: dokumenty i materialy. Moscow: Gosudarstvennoe izdatel'stvo politicheskoi literatury, 1961.

Other Sources

Adamov, Aleksandr. *Irak arabskii: Bassorskoi vilaiet v ego proshlom i nastoiaschem.* St. Petersburg: Tip. Glav. Upr. Udielov, 1912.

Akhunov, Azat. "Gde nasha Mekka?" *Tatarstan* 11 (2005): 53–55.

Alder, G. J. *British India's Northern Frontier, 1865–95: A Study in Imperial Policy.* London: Longmans, 1963.

Alexanderson, Kris. "'A Dark State of Affairs': Hajj Networks, Pan-Islamism, and Dutch Colonial Surveillance during the Interwar Period." *Journal of Social History* 7, no. 4 (June 2014): 1021–1041.

Alroey, Gur. "Shtetl on the High Seas: The Jewish Emigration from Eastern Europe and the Cross-Oceanic Experience." In *Tales of Transit: Narrative Migrant Spaces in Atlantic Perspective, 1850–1950,* ed. Michael Boyden, Hans Krabbendam, and Liselotte Vandenbussche. Amsterdam: Amsterdam University Press, 2014, 81–99.

Amrith, Sunil S. *Crossing the Bay of Bengal: The Furies of Nature and the Fortunes of Migrants.* Cambridge, MA: Harvard University Press, 2013.

——. *Migration and Diaspora in Modern Asia.* Cambridge: Cambridge University Press, 2011.

Anderson, Barbara A. *Internal Migration during Modernization in Late Nineteenth-Century Russia.* Princeton, NJ: Princeton University Press, 1980.

Anderson, M. S. *The Eastern Question, 1774–1923: A Study in International Relations.* London: Macmillan, 1966.

ʿAnqawi, ʿAbd Allah ʿAqil. "The Pilgrimage to Mecca in Mamluk Times." *Arabian Studies* 1 (1974): 148–150.

Arapov, D. Iu., comp. *Imperatorskaia Rossiia i musul'manskii mir: sbornik statei.* Moscow: Natalis, 2006.

Arapov, D. Iu. *Sistema gosudarstvennago regulirovaniia Islama v Rossiskoi imperii.* Moscow: MPGU, 2004.

Ascher, Abraham. *P. A. Stolypin: The Search for Stability in Late Imperial Russia.* Stanford, CA: Stanford University Press, 2001.

Atalar, Münir. *Osmanlı Devletinde Surre-i Hümayûn ve Surre Alayları.* Ankara: Diyanet İşleri Başkanlığı, 1991.

Aust, Martin, Ricarda Vulpius, and A. I. Miller, eds. *Imperium inter pares: Rol' transferov v istorii Rossiiskoi imperii (1700–1917).* Moscow: Novoe literaturnoe obozrenie, 2010.

Avrutin, Eugene M. *Jews and the Imperial State: Identification Politics in Tsarist Russia.* Ithaca, NY: Cornell University Press, 2010.

Badone, Ellen, and Sharon R. Roseman. *Intersecting Journeys: The Anthropology of Pilgrimage and Tourism.* Urbana: University of Illinois Press, 2004.

Baldry, John. "Soviet Relations with Saudi Arabia and Yemen, 1917–1938." *Middle Eastern Studies* 1 (1984): 53–80.

Barbir, Karl. *Ottoman Rule in Damascus, 1708–1758.* Princeton, NJ: Princeton University Press, 1980.

Bardin, Pierre. *Algériens et tunisiens dans l'empire ottoman de 1848 à 1914.* Paris: Éditions du Centre National de la Recherche Scientifique, 1979.

Baron, Nick. "New Spatial Histories of Twentieth-Century Russia and the Soviet Union: Surveying the Landscape." *Jahrbücher für Geschichte Osteuropas* 55 (2007): 374–401.

Baron, Nick, and Peter Gatrell. "Population Displacement, State-Building, and Social Identity in the Lands of the Former Russian Empire, 1917–1923." *Kritika: Explorations in Russian and Eurasian History* 4, no. 1 (Winter 2003): 51–100.

Bayly, C. A. *The Birth of the Modern World, 1780–1914: Global Connections and Comparisons.* Oxford: Blackwell Publishing, 2004.

Bazili, Konstantin Mikhailovich. *Siriia i Palestina pod turetskim pravitel'stvom v istoricheskom i politicheskom otnoshenii.* Moscow: Mosty kul'tury; Gesharim, 2007.

Belov, E. A. "Tibetskaia politika Rossii (1900–1914 gg.) (po russkim arkhivnym dokumentam)." *Vostok* 3 (1994): 99–109.

Bennigsen, Alexandre. "Colonization and Decolonization in the Soviet Union." *Journal of Contemporary History* 4, no. 1 (1969): 141–152.

Bennigsen, Alexandre A., and S. Enders Wimbush. *Muslim National Communism in the Soviet Union: A Revolutionary Strategy for the Colonial World.* Chicago: University of Chicago Press, 1980.

Bennigsen, Alexandre, and Chantal Lemercier-Quelquejay. *La presse et le mouvement national chez les musulmans de Russie avant 1920.* Paris: Mouton, 1964.

Bhardwaj, S. M. *Hindu Places of Pilgrimage in India: A Study in Cultural Geography.* Berkeley: University of California Press, 1973.

Bianchi, Robert R. *Guests of God: Pilgrimage and Politics in the Islamic World.* Oxford: Oxford University Press, 2004.

Bose, Sugata. *A Hundred Horizons: The Indian Ocean in the Age of Global Empire.* Cambridge, MA: Harvard University Press, 2006.

Boyer, Pierre. "L'administration française et la reglementation du pèlerinage à la Mecque (1830–1894)." *Revue d'histoire maghrébine* 9 (July 1977): 278–279.

Breyfogle, Nicholas B. *Heretics and Colonizers: Forging Russia's Empire in the South Caucasus.* Ithaca, NY: Cornell University Press, 2005.

Breyfogle, Nicholas B., Abby Schrader, and Willard Sunderland, eds. *Peopling the Russian Periphery: Borderland Colonization in Eurasian History.* London: Routledge, 2007.

Brower, Daniel. "Russian Roads to Mecca: Religious Tolerance and Muslim Pilgrimage in the Russian Empire." *Slavic Review* 55, no. 3 (1996): 567–584.

——. *Turkestan and the Fate of the Russian Empire.* London: RoutledgeCurzon, 2003.

Brower, Daniel R., and Edward L. Lazzerini, eds. *Russia's Orient: Imperial Borderlands and Peoples, 1700–1917.* Bloomington: Indiana University Press, 1997.

Burbank, Jane, and Frederick Cooper. *Empires in World History: Power and the Politics of Difference.* Princeton, NJ: Princeton University Press, 2011.

Burbank, Jane, Mark von Hagen, and Anatolyi Remnev, eds. *Russian Empire: Space, People, Power, 1700–1930.* Bloomington: Indiana University Press, 2007.

Can, Lale. "Connecting People: A Central Asian Sufi Network in Turn-of-the-Century Istanbul." *Modern Asian Studies* 46, special issue no. 2 (March 2012): 373–401.

Carter, Paul. *The Road to Botany Bay: An Exploration of Landscape and History.* Minneapolis: University of Minnesota Press, 1987.

Chernukha, V. G. *Pasport v Rossii, 1719–1917.* St. Petersburg: Liki Rossii, 2007.

Chrissidis, Nikolaos. "The Athonization of Pious Travel: Shielded Shrines, Shady Deals, and Pilgrimage Logistics in Late Nineteenth-Century Odessa." *Modern Greek Studies Yearbook* 28/29 (2012/2013): 169–191.

Clancy-Smith, Julia. *Mediterraneans: North Africa and Europe in an Age of Migration, c. 1800–1900.* Berkeley: University of California Press, 2011.

Cohn, Bernard S. *Colonialism and Its Forms of Knowledge: The British in India.* Princeton, NJ: Princeton University Press, 1996.

Coleman, Simon, and John Eade, eds. *Reframing Pilgrimage: Cultures in Motion.* London: Routledge, 2004.

Crews, Robert D. "Muslim Networks, Imperial Power, and the Local Politics of Qajar Iran." In *Asiatic Russia: Imperial Power in Regional and International Contexts*, ed. Uyama Tomohiko, 174–188. New York: Routledge, 2012.

——. *For Prophet and Tsar: Islam and Empire in Russia and Central Asia*. Cambridge, MA: Harvard University Press, 2006.

——. "Russia Unbound: Historical Frameworks and the Challenge of Globalism." *Ab imperio* 1 (2010): 53–63.

——. "The Russian Worlds of Islam." In *Islam and the European* Empires, ed. David Motadel, 35–52. Oxford: Oxford University Press, 2014.

Crisp, Olga, and Linda Edmondson, eds. *Civil Rights in Imperial Russia*. Oxford: Clarendon Press, 1989.

David-Fox, Michael. *Showcasing the Great Experiment: Cultural Diplomacy and Western Visitors to the Soviet Union, 1921–1941*. Oxford: Oxford University Press, 2011.

Deringil, Selim. *The Well-Protected Domains: Ideology and the Legitimation of Power in the Ottoman Empire, 1876–1909*. London: I.B. Tauris, 1998.

Dirks, Nicholas B., ed. *Colonialism and Culture*. Ann Arbor: University of Michigan Press, 1992.

Dixon, Simon. "Nationalism versus Internationalism: Russian Orthodoxy in Nineteenth-Century Palestine." In *Religious Internationals in the Modern World: Globalization and Faith Communities since 1750*, ed. Abigail Greene and Vincent Viaene, 139–162. New York: Palgrave Macmillan, 2012.

Dobson, George. *Russia's Railway Advance into Central Asia*. London: W.H. Allen & Company, 1890.

Dördüncü, Mehmet Bahadır. *The Yıldız Albums of Sultan Abdülhamid II. Mecca-Medina*. Somerset, NJ: The Light, 2006.

Dukel'skii, V. "Dobrovol'nyi Narodnyi Flot, istoricheskii ekskurs." *Moskovskii zhurnal* 8 (2006): 2–7.

Edgar, Adrienne Lynn. *Tribal Nation: The Making of Soviet Turkmenistan*. Princeton, NJ: Princeton University Press, 2004.

Edney, Matthew H. *Mapping an Empire: The Geographical Construction of British India, 1765–1843*. Chicago: University of Chicago Press, 1990.

Eickelman, Dale F., and James Piscatori, eds. *Muslim Travellers: Pilgrimage, Migration, and the Religious Imagination*. Berkeley: University of California Press, 1990.

Eltis, David, ed. *Coerced and Free Migration: Global Perspectives*. Stanford, CA: Stanford University Press, 2002.

Engel, Barbara Alpern. *Between the Fields and the City: Women, Work, and Family in Russia, 1861–1914*. Cambridge: Cambridge University Press, 1996.

Escande, Laurent. "D'Alger à la Mecque: L'administration française et le contrôle du pèlerinage (1894–1962)." *Revue d'histoire maghrébine* 26 (1999): 277–292.

Etherington, Norman, ed. *Missions and Empire*. Oxford: Oxford University Press, 2005.

Fahrmeir, Andreas, Olivier Faron, and Patrick Weil, eds. *Migration Control in the North Atlantic World: The Evolution of State Practices in Europe and the United States from the French Revolution to the Inter-War Period*. New York: Berghahn Books, 2003.

Farah, Megan Dean. "Mobility, Commerce, and Conversion in the Caucasus." PhD diss., Stanford University, 2013.

Farooqi, Naim R. "Moguls, Ottomans, and Pilgrims: Protecting the Routes to Mecca in the Sixteenth and Seventeenth Centuries." *International History Review* 10, no. 2 (May 1988): 198–220.

Faroqhi, Suraiya. *Pilgrims and Sultans: The Hajj under the Ottomans*. London: I.B. Tauris, 1990.

Fawaz, Leila Tarazi, and C. A. Bayly, eds. *Modernity and Culture: From the Mediterranean to the Indian Ocean*. New York: Columbia University Press, 2002.

Forbes, Andrew D. W. *Warlords and Muslims in Chinese Central Asia: A Political History of Republican Sinkiang, 1911–1949.* Cambridge: Cambridge University Press, 1986.

Frank, Allen J. *Islamic Historiography and "Bulghar" Identity among the Tatars and Bashkirs of Russia.* Leiden: Brill, 1998.

——. *Muslim Religious Institutions in Imperial Russia: The Islamic World of Novouzensk District and the Kazakh Inner Horde, 1780–1910.* Leiden: Brill, 2001.

Frank, Allen J., and Mirkasyim A. Usmanov, eds. *Materials for the Islamic History of Semipalatinsk: Two Manuscripts by Ahmad-Wali al-Qazani and Qurban ali Khalidi.* Berlin: Das Arabische Buch, 2001.

Freitag, Ulrike, Malte Fuhrmann, Nora Lafi, and Florian Riedler, eds. *The City in the Ottoman Empire: Migration and the Making of Urban Modernity.* New York: Routledge, 2011.

Frieden, Nancy A. "The Russian Cholera Epidemic, 1892–93 and Medical Professionalization." *Journal of Social History* 10 (1977): 538–599.

Games, Alison. *The Web of Empire: English Cosmopolitanism in an Age of Expansion, 1560–1660.* Oxford: Oxford University Press, 2008.

Gatrell, Peter. *A Whole Empire Walking: Refugees in Russia during World War I.* Bloomington: Indiana University Press, 1999.

Gelvin, James L., and Nile Green, eds. *Global Muslims in the Age of Steam and Print.* Berkeley: University of California Press, 2014.

Gorsuch, Anne, and Diane Koenker, eds. *Turizm: The Russian and East European Tourist under Capitalism and Socialism.* Ithaca, NY: Cornell University Press, 2006.

Greene, Robert. "Bodies in Motion: Steam-Powered Pilgrimages in Late Imperial Russia." *Russian History* 39 (2012): 247–268.

Grigor'ev, S. E. "Rossiiskie palomniki v sviatykh gorodakh Aravii v kontse XIX-nachale XX v." In *Istoriografiia i istochnikovedenie istorii stran Azii i Afriki,* ed. N. N. D'iakov, 88–110. St. Petersburg: Izd. S.-Peterburgskogo universiteta, 1999.

Groot, A. H. de. "The Historical Development of the Capitulatory Regime in the Ottoman Middle East from the Fifteenth to the Nineteenth Centuries." *Oriente moderno* 83, no. 3 (2003): 575–604.

Hammoudi, Abdellah. *A Season in Mecca: Narrative of a Pilgrimage.* New York: Hill and Wang, 2006.

Harris, Ruth. *Lourdes: Body and Spirit in the Secular Age.* New York: Viking Penguin, 1999.

Harvey, David. "Space as a Keyword." In *David Harvey: A Critical Reader,* ed. Noel Castree and Derek Gregory, 270–293. Malden, MA: Wiley-Blackwell, 2006.

Hayit, Baymirza. *Turkestan im XX Jahrhundert.* Darmstadt: C.W. Leske Verlag, 1956.

Heeke, Matthias. *Reisen zu den Sowjets: Der ausländiche Tourismus in Russland, 1921–1941.* Munster: LIT, 2003.

Henze, Charlotte E. *Disease, Health Care, and Government in Late Imperial Russia: Life and Death on the Volga, 1823–1914.* London: Routledge, 2011.

Herlihy, Patricia. *Odessa, a History: 1794–1914.* Cambridge, MA: Harvard Series in Ukrainian Studies, 1986.

Hicaz Demiryolu: Istanbul'dan Medine'ye bir Tarih Belgeseli. Istanbul: Albaraka Türk Yayinları, 1999.

Hirsch, Francine. *Empire of Nations: Ethnographic Knowledge and The Making of the Soviet Union.* Ithaca, NY: Cornell University Press, 2005.

Ho, Engseng. *The Graves of Tarim: Genealogy and Mobility across the Indian Ocean.* Berkeley: University of California Press, 2006.

Hoerder, Dirk. *Cultures in Contact: World Migrations in the Second Millennium*. Durham, NC: Duke University Press, 2002.

——. *Migrations and Belongings: 1870–1945*. Cambridge, MA: Harvard Belknap Press, 2014.

Hopwood, Derek. *The Russian Presence in Syria and Palestine, 1843–1914: Church and Politics in the Near East*. Oxford: Clarendon Press, 1969.

Hurgronje, C. Snouck. *Mekka in the Latter Part of the 19th Century*. Leiden: Brill, 2007.

Husband, William B. *"Godless Communists": Atheism and Society in Soviet Russia, 1917–1932*. DeKalb, IL: Northern Illinois University Press, 2000.

Ibrahim, Abdürrechid. *Un Tatar au Japon: Voyage en Asie, 1908–1910*. Paris: Sindbad-Actes Sud, 2004.

Ilovaiskii, S. I. *Istoricheskii ocherk piatidesiatiletiia Russkogo obshchestva parokhodstva i torgovli*. Odessa: Iuzhno-Russkoe obshchestvo pechatnogo dela, 1907.

İnalcık, H. "Imtiyazat." In *Encyclopedia of Islam*, 3:1179a–1189b. New ed. Leiden: Brill, 1971.

Iskander, Fayiz Najib. *Misr fi kitabat al-hujjaj al-Rus fi al-qarnayn al-khamis ʿashar wa-al-sadis ʿashar al-Miladiyayn*. Alexandria: Dar al-Fikr, 1988.

Izmirlieva, Valentina. "Christian Hajjis—The Other Orthodox Pilgrims to Jerusalem." *Slavic Review 3*, no. 2 (Summer 2014): 322–346.

Jacobson, Jon. *When the Soviet Union Entered World Politics*. Berkeley: University of California Press, 1994.

Jalal, Ayesha. *Partisans of Allah: Jihad in South Asia*. Cambridge, MA: Harvard University Press, 2008.

Jelavich, Charles, and Barbara Jelavich, eds. *Russia in the East, 1876–1880: The Russo-Turkish War and the Kuldja Crisis as Seen through the Letters of A. G. Jomini to N. K. Giers*. Leiden: E. J. Brill, 1959.

Jersild, Austin. *Orientalism and Empire: North Caucasus Mountain People and the Georgian Frontier, 1845–1917*. Montreal: McGill-Queen's University Press, 2002.

Johnson, Robert. *Peasant and Proletarian: The Working Class of Moscow in the Late Nineteenth Century*. New Brunswick, NJ: Rutgers University Press, 1979.

Jones, Ryan Tucker. *Empire of Extinction: Russians and the North Pacific's Strange Beasts of the Sea*. New York: Oxford University Press, 2014.

Kappeler, Andreas. *The Russian Empire: A Multiethnic History*. London: Routledge, 2001.

Kappeler, Andreas, Gerhard Simon, Georg Brunner, and Edward Allworth, eds. *Muslim Communities Reemerge: Historical Perspectives on Nationality, Politics, and Opposition in the Former Soviet Union and Yugoslavia*. Durham, NC: Duke University Press, 1994.

Kaufman, Suzanne K. *Consuming Visions: Mass Culture and the Lourdes Shrine*. Ithaca, NY: Cornell University Press, 2005.

Keller, Shoshanna. *To Moscow, Not Mecca: The Soviet Campaign against Islam in Central Asia, 1917–1941*. Westport, CT: Praeger Publishers, 2001.

Kemper, Michael. "Khalidiyya Networks in Daghestan and the Question of Jihad." *Die Welt des Islams*, vol. 42, 1 (2002): 41–71.

——. "Von Orenburg nach Indien und Mekka: Ismails Reisebuch als Genremischung." In *Istochniki i issledovaniia po istorii tatarskogo naroda: Materialy k uchebnym kursam. V chest' iubileia akademika AN RT M.A. Usmanova*, ed. Diliara Usmanova and Iskander Giliazov, 318–330. Kazan: Kazanskii gosudarstvennyi universitet, 2006.

Kemper, Michael, Anke von Kügelgen, and Dmitry Yermakov, eds. *Muslim Culture in Russia and Central Asia from the 18th to the Early 20th Centuries*. 4 vols. Berlin: Schwarz, 1996.

Khalid, Adeeb. *Islam after Communism: Religion and Politics in Central Asia*. Berkeley: University of California Press, 2006.

——. *The Politics of Muslim Cultural Reform: Jadidism in Central Asia*. Berkeley: University of California Press, 1998.

——. "Russian History and the Debate over Orientalism." *Kritika: Explorations in Russian & Eurasian History* 1, no. 4 (2000): 691–699.

Khevrolina, V. M. *Nikolai Pavlovich Ignat'ev: Rossiiskii diplomat*. Moscow: Kvadriga, 2009.

Khodarkovsky, Michael. *Bitter Choices: Loyalty and Betrayal in the Russian Conquest of the North Caucasus*. Ithaca, NY: Cornell University Press, 2011.

——. *Russia's Steppe Frontier: The Making of a Colonial Empire, 1500–1800*. Bloomington: Indiana University Press, 2002.

King, Charles. *The Ghost of Freedom: A History of the Caucasus*. Oxford: Oxford University Press, 2008.

Klier, John Doyle, and Shlomo Lambroza, eds. *Pogroms: Anti-Jewish Violence in Modern Russian History*. Cambridge: Cambridge University Press, 2004.

Kobrin, Rebecca. *Jewish Bialystok and Its Diaspora*. Bloomington: Indiana University Press, 2010.

Komatsu, Hisao, Chika Obiya, and John S. Shoeberlein, eds. *Migration in Central Asia: Its History and Current Problems*. Osaka: Japan Center for Area Studies, National Museum of Ethnology, 2000.

Kratkii putevoditel' po Palestine dlia turistov evreev. Vil'na: Izd. Kadima, 1911.

Laffan, Michael Francis. *Islamic Nationhood and Colonial Indonesia: The Umma below the Winds*. London: Routledge, 2003.

Laue, Theodore H. von. *Sergei Witte and the Industrialization of Russia*. New York: Columbia University Press, 1963.

Lewis, Martin W., and Kären E. Wigen. *The Myth of Continents: A Critique of Metageography*. Berkeley: University of California Press, 1997.

Lieven, Dominic. *Empire: The Russian Empire and Its Rivals*. London: Yale University Press, 2000.

Litvinov, V. P. *Vneregional'noe palomnichestvo musul'man Turkestana (epokha novogo vremeni)*. Elets: EGU im. I.A. Bunina, 2006.

Lockman, Zachary. *Contending Visions of the Middle East: The History and Politics of Orientalism*. Cambridge: Cambridge University Press, 2004.

Long, David Edwin. *The Hajj Today: A Survey of the Contemporary Pilgrimage to Makkah*. Albany: State University of New York Press, 1979.

Ludden, David. "Presidential Address: Maps in the Mind and the Mobility of Asia." *Journal of Asian Studies* 62, no. 4 (Nov. 2003): 1057–1078.

——. "The Process of Empire: Frontiers and Borderlands." In *Tributary Empires in Global History*, ed. Peter Fibiger Bang and C. A. Bayly, 132–150. London: Palgrave Macmillan, 2011.

Mann, Gregory, and Baz Lecocq, "Between Empire, Umma, and the Muslim Third World: The French Union and African Pilgrims to Mecca, 1946–1958." *Comparative Studies of South Asia, Africa, and the Middle East* 27, no. 2 (2007): 365–381.

Mansurov, T. A. *Polpred Nazir Tiuriakulov*. Moscow: Molodaia gvardiia, 2004.

Ma'oz, Moshe. *Ottoman Reform in Syria and Palestine, 1840–1861: The Impact of the Tanzimat on Politics and Society*. Oxford: Clarendon Press, 1968.

Margulies, Sylvia. *The Pilgrimage to Russia: The Soviet Union and the Treatment of Foreigners, 1924–1937*. Madison: University of Wisconsin Press, 1968.

Masonov, E. A. "Sh.M. Ibragimov–drug Ch.Ch. Valikhanova." *Vestnik akademii nauk Kazakhskoi SSR* 9 (1964): 53–60.

Massell, Gregory J. *The Surrogate Proletariat: Moslem Women and Revolutionary Strategies in Soviet Central Asia, 1919–1929*. Princeton, NJ: Princeton University Press, 1974.

McChesney, R. D. "The Central Asian Hajj-Pilgrimage in the Time of the Early Modern Empires." In *Safavid Iran and Her Neighbors*, ed. Michel Mazzaoui, 129–156. Salt Lake City: University of Utah Press, 2003.

McKeown, Adam M. "Global Migration, 1846–1940." *Journal of World History* 15, no. 2 (June 2004): 155–189.

The Mecca Pilgrimage: Appointment by the Government of India of Thos. Cook and Son as Agents for the Control of the Movements of Mahomedan Pilgrims from All Parts of India to Jeddah for Mecca, Medina, etc., and Back. London: Printed for Private Circulation, 1886.

Metcalf, Thomas R. *Imperial Connections: India in the Indian Ocean Arena, 1860–1920*. Berkeley: University of California Press, 2007.

Meyer, James H. "Immigration, Return, and the Politics of Citizenship: Russian Muslims in the Ottoman Empire, 1860–1914." *International Journal of Middle East Studies* 39 (2007): 15–32.

——. *Turks across Empires: Marketing Muslim Identity in the Russian-Ottoman Borderlands, 1856–1914*. New York: Oxford University Press, 2014.

Mikoulski, Dimitri. "The Study of Islam in Russia and the former Soviet Union: An Overview." In *Mapping Islamic Studies: Genealogy, Continuity and Change*, ed. Azim Nanji. Berlin: Walter de Gruyter, 1997: 95–107.

Miliband, S. D. *Vostokovedy Rossii, XX–nachalo XXI veka: bibliograficheskii slovar' v dvukh knigakh*. Moscow: Vostochnaia literatura RAN, 2008.

Miller, Michael B. *Europe and the Maritime World: A Twentieth-Century History*. Cambridge: Cambridge University Press, 2012.

——. "Pilgrims' Progress: The Business of the Hajj." *Past & Present* 191 (May 2006): 189–228.

Mishra, Saurabh. *Pilgrimage, Politics, and Pestilence: The Haj from the Indian Subcontinent, 1860–1920*. New Delhi: Oxford University Press, 2011.

Morrison, Alexander. *Russian Rule in Samarkand, 1868-1910: A Comparison with British India*. Oxford: Oxford University Press, 2008.

Mosse, Werner E. "Russia and the Levant, 1856–1862: Grand Duke Constantine and the Russian Steam Navigation Company." *Journal of Modern History* 24 (1954): 39–48.

Mostashari, Firouzeh. *On the Religious Frontier: Tsarist Russia and Islam in the Caucasus*. London: I.B. Tauris, 2006.

Motadel, David, ed. *Islam and the European Empires*. Oxford: Oxford University Press, 2014.

Naganawa, Norihiro. "The Red Sea Becoming Red? The Bolsheviks' Commercial Enterprise in the Hijaz and Yemen, 1924–1938." Unpublished paper, 2013.

Nazir Tiuriakulov—polpred SSSR v Korolevstve Saudovskaia Araviia: pis'ma, dnevniki, otchety (1928–1935). Moscow: Russkii raritet, 2000.

Ne-Moriak, *Za chto russkoe obshchestvo parakhodtsva i torgovli zhelaet poluchit' 22 milliona rublei?* Odessa: Tip. Odesskiia Novosti, 1910.

Nicholson, James. *The Hejaz Railway*. London: Stacey International, 2005.

Nikol'skii, M. E. "Palomnichestvo v Mekku." *Istoricheskii vestnik* 124 (April 1911): 603–638.

Northrop, Douglas. *Veiled Empire: Gender and Power in Stalinist Central Asia*. Ithaca, NY: Cornell University Press, 2004.

Nyman, Lars-Erik. *Great Britain and Chinese, Russian, and Japanese Interests in Sinkiang, 1918–1934*. Stockholm: Esselte Studium, 1977.

Oishi, Takashi. "Friction and Rivalry over Pious Mobility: British Colonial Management of the Hajj and Reaction to It by Indian Muslims, 1870–1920." In *The Influence of Human Mobility in Muslim Societies*, ed. Hidemitsu Kuroki, 151–75. London: Kegan Paul International, 2003.

Osokina, Elena. *Zoloto dlia industrializatsii: TORGSIN*. Moscow: ROSSPEN, 2009.

Osterhammel, Jürgen. *The Transformation of the World: A Global History of the Nineteenth Century*. Princeton, NJ: Princeton University Press, 2014.

Ostroumov, N. P. *Sarty: Etnograficheskie materialy*. Tashkent: Tip. Sredneaziatskaia zhizn', 1908.

Otchet o komandirovke v Dzheddu vracha D. Zabolotnago. St. Petersburg: Tip. V. Kirshbauma, 1897.

Otchet shtabs-kapitana Davletshina o komandirovke v Khidzhaz. St. Petersburg: Voennaia tipografiia [v zdanii Glavnago Shtaba], 1899.

Otte, T. G., and Keith Nelson, eds. *Railways and International Politics: Paths of Empire, 1848–1945*. London: Routledge, 2006.

Owen, Thomas C. *Dilemmas of Russian Capitalism: Fedor Chizhov and Corporate Enterprise in the Railroad Age*. Cambridge, MA: Harvard University Press, 2005.

Özyüksel, Murat. *Hicaz Demiryolu*. Istanbul: Tarih Vakfı Yurt Yayınları, 2000.

Pack, Sasha D. "Revival of the Pilgrimage to Santiago de Compostela: The Politics of Religious, National, and European Patrimony, 1879–1988." *Journal of Modern History* 82, no. 2 (June 2010): 335–367.

Paine, Sarah C. M. *Imperial Rivals: China, Russia, and Their Disputed Frontier*. Armonk, NY: M.E. Sharpe, 1996.

Papas, Alexandre, Thomas Welsford, and Thierry Zarcone, eds. *Central Asian Pilgrims: Hajj Routes and Pious Visits between Central Asia and the Hijaz*. Berlin: Klaus Schwarz, 2012.

Pearson, Michael N. *Pilgrimage to Mecca: The Indian Experience, 1500–1800*. Princeton, NJ: Markus Wiener Publishers, 1996.

Peris, Daniel. *Storming the Heavens: The Soviet League of the Militant Godless*. Ithaca, NY: Cornell University Press, 1998.

Peters, F. E. *The Hajj: The Muslim Pilgrimage to Mecca and the Holy Places*. Princeton, NJ: Princeton University Press, 1994.

Petersen, Andrew. *The Medieval and Ottoman Hajj Route in Jordan: An Archaeological and Historical Study*. Oxford: Oxbow Books, 2012.

Poggenpol', M. *Ocherk vozniknoveniia i deiatel'nosti Dobrovol'nago flota za vremia XXV-ti letniago ego sushchestvovaniia*. St. Petersburg: Tip. A. Benke, 1903.

Porter, Venetia, and Liana Saif, eds. *The Hajj: Collected Essays*. London: The British Museum, 2013.

Pravila perevozki na sudakh palomnikov-musul'man iz chernomorskikh portov v Gedzhasa i obratno. St. Petersburg: Pervaia tsentral'naia vostochnaia elektropechatnia, 1908.

Pypin, A. "Palomnichestvo i puteshestviia v staroi pis'mennosti." *Vestnik Evropy*, August 1896: 718–771.

Rafeq, Abdul-Karim. "New Light on the Transportation of the Damascene Pilgrimage during the Ottoman Period." In *Islamic and Middle Eastern Societies: A Festschrift in Honor of Professor Wadie Jwaideh*, ed. Robert Olson, 127–136. Brattleboro, VT: Amana Books, 1987.

Randolph, John, and Eugene M. Avrutin. *Russia in Motion: Cultures of Human Mobility since 1850*. Urbana: University of Illinois Press, 2012.

Randolph, John W. "The Singing Coachman Or, The Road and Russia's Ethnographic Invention in Early Modern Time," *Journal of Early Modern History* 11, nos. 1–2 (2007): 32–61.

Reynolds, Michael A. *Shattering Empires: The Clash and Collapse of the Ottoman and Russian Empires, 1908–1918*. Cambridge: Cambridge University Press, 2011.

Rezvan, Efim. *Al-hajj qabla mi'a sana: ar-rihla as-sirriyya lid-dabit ar-rus ʿAbdalʿaziz Dawlatshin ila Makka al-mukarrama, 1898–1899*. Beirut: Dar al-Takrib, 1993.

——. *Russian Ships in the Gulf, 1899–1903*. London: Garnet Publishing & Ithaca Press, 1993.

Rhinelander, Anthony L. H. *Prince Michael Vorontsov: Viceroy to the Tsar*. Montreal: McGill-Queen's University Press, 1990.

Robinson, David. "France as a Muslim Power in West Africa." *Africa Today* 46, nos. 3/4 (1999): 105–127.

——. *Paths of Accommodation: Muslim Societies and French Colonial Authorities in Senegal and Mauritania, 1880–1920*. Athens, OH: Ohio University Press, 2000.

Roff, William R. "Sanitation and Security: The Imperial Powers and the Nineteenth-Century Hajj." *Arabian Studies* 6 (1982): 143–160.

Rogger, Hans. *Jewish Policies and Right-Wing Politics in Russia*. Berkeley: University of California Press, 1986.

Rogger, Hans. *Russia in the Age of Modernisation and Revolution, 1881–1917*. New York: Longman, 1983.

Sarıyıldız, Gülden. "II. Abdülhamid'in Fakir Hacılar için Mekke'de İnşa Ettirdiği Misafirhane." *Tarih Enstitüsü Dergisi* 14 (1994): 134–141.

Sarıyıldız, Gülden, and Ayşe Kavak, eds. *Halife II Abdülhamid'in Hac Siyaseti: Dr. M. Şakir Bey'in Hicaz Hatıraları*. Istanbul: Timaş, 2009.

Schenk, Frithjof Benjamin. "Imperial Inter-Rail: Vliianie mezhnatsional'nogo i mezhimperskogo vospriiatiia i sopernichestva na politiku zheleznodorozhnogo stroitel'stva v tsarskoi Rossii." In *Imperium inter pares: Rol' transferov v istorii Rossiiskoi imperii (1700–1917)*, ed. Martin Aust, Ricarda Vulpius, and A. I. Miller. Moscow: Novoe literaturnoe obozrenie, 2010.

Schuyler, Eugene. *Turkistan: Notes of a Journey in Russian Turkistan, Khokand, Bukhara, and Kuldja*. Vol. 1. New York: Scribner, Armstrong and Co., 1876.

Sibgatullina, A. T. "'Delo' Saidazimbaeva—Rukovoditelia musul'manskogo palomnicheskogo dvizheniia iz Rossii." *Nauchnyi Tatarstan* 1 (2009): 76–89.

Sibgatullina, Al'fina. *Kontakty tiurok-musul'man Rossiiskoi i Osmanskoi imperii na rubezhe XIX–XX vv*. Moscow: Istok, 2010.

Skrine, C. P., and Pamela Nightingale. *Macartney at Kashgar: New Light on British, Chinese, and Russian Activities in Sinkiang, 1890–1918*. London: Methuen, 1973.

Smilianskaia, I. M. "K.M. Bazili—Rossiiskii diplomat i istorik Sirii." In *Ocherki po istorii russkogo vostokovedeniia*, sb. IV, 52–78. Moscow: Izdatel'stvo vostochnoi literatury Akademii nauk SSSR, 1959.

Smith, Grace Martin. "The Özbek Tekkes of Istanbul." *Der Islam* 57, no. 1 (1980): 130–139.

Smolkin-Rothrock, Victoria. "'The Confession of an Atheist Who Became a Scholar of Religion': Nikolai Semenovich Gordienko's Last Interview." *Kritika: Explorations in Russian and Eurasian History* 15, no. 3 (Summer 2014): 597–620.

Sokolov, D. F. *O palomnichestve musul'man v Dzheddu*. St. Petersburg: Tip. Stasiulevich, 1901.

——. "Poezdka v gorod Dzheddu." *Istoricheskii viestnik*. 5 (1902): 616–649.

Sorenson, Thomas C. "The End of the Volunteer Fleet: Some Evidence on the Scope of Pobedonostsev's Power in Russia." *Slavic Review* 34, no. 1 (March 1975): 131–137.

Spring, Derek W. "Railways and Economic Development in Turkestan before 1917." In *Russian Transport: An Historical and Geographical Survey*, ed. Leslie Symons and Colin White, 46–74. London: Collins Educational, 1975.

Stavrou, Theofanis George. *Russian Interests in Palestine, 1882–1914: A Study of Religious and Educational Enterprise.* Thessaloniki: Institute for Balkan Studies, 1963.

Sunderland, Willard. *The Baron's Cloak: A History of the Russian Empire in War and Revolution.* Ithaca, NY: Cornell University Press, 2014.

——. *Taming the Wild Field: Colonization and Empire on the Russian Steppe.* Ithaca, NY: Cornell University Press, 2004.

Sychev, Viktor. *Indoneziia i musul'masnkii mir v XX v.: Problema-religiozno-politicheskogo vzaimodeistviia i uchastiia v organizovannom islamskom dvizhenii stran Azii i Afriki.* Moscow: Rusaki, 2003.

Sylvester, Roshanna P. *Tales of Old Odessa: Crime and Civility in a City of Thieves.* DeKalb, IL: Northern Illinois University Press, 2005.

Tagliacozzo, Eric. *The Longest Journey: Southeast Asians and the Pilgrimage to Mecca.* Oxford: Oxford University Press, 2013.

——, ed. *Southeast Asia and the Middle East: Islam, Movement, and the* Longue Durée. Stanford, CA: Stanford University Press, 2009.

Tchalenko, John. *Images from the Endgame: Persia through a Russian Lens 1901–1914.* London: SAQI, 2006.

Thompstone, Stuart. "Tsarist Russia's Investment in Transport." *Journal of Transport History* 3, no. 19/1 (March 1998): 50–67.

Togan, A. Zeki Veilidi. *Bugünkü Türkili Türkistan ve Yakın Tarihi.* Istanbul: Enderun Kitabevi, 1981.

——. *Umumi Türk Tarihi'ne Giriş.* Istanbul: Enderun Kitabevi, 1983.

Torpey, John. *The Invention of the Passport: Surveillance, Citizenship, and the State.* Cambridge: Cambridge University Press, 2000.

Treadgold, Donald W. *The Great Siberian Migration: Government and Peasant in Resettlement from Emancipation to the First World War.* Princeton, NJ: Princeton University Press, 1957.

Tuna, Mustafa. *Imperial Russia's Muslims: Islam, Empire, and European Modernity, 1788–1914.* Cambridge: Cambridge University Press, 2015.

Turner, Victor, and Edith Turner. "Pilgrimage as a Liminoid Phenomenon." In *Image and Pilgrimage in Christian Culture,* 1–39. New York: Columbia University Press, 1978.

Usmanov, M. A. "Zapiski Isma'ila Bekmukhamedova or ego puteshestvii v Indiiu." In *Blizhnii i srednii vostok: Istoriia, ekonomika,* ed. L. M. Kulagina, 88–103. Moscow: Nauka, 1967.

Usmanova, Diliara. *Musul'manskie predstaviteli v Rossiskom parlamente: 1906-1916.* Kazan: Fan Akademiia nauk RT, 2005.

Uyama, Tomohiko, ed. *Asiatic Russia: Imperial Power in Regional and International Contexts.* New York: Routledge, 2012.

Vasil'ev, Aleksandr Dmitrievich. "Palomniki iz Rossii u Shiitskikh sviatyn' Iraka. Konets XIX veka." *Vostochnyi arkhiv* 1, no. 27 (2013): 9–17.

Vredenbregt, Jacob. "The Haddj: Some of Its Features and Functions in Indonesia." *Bildragan voor Taal-, Land-, en Volkenkunde* 118, no. 1 (1962): 92–153.

Weinberg, Robert. *The Revolution of 1905 in Odessa: Blood on the Steps.* Bloomington: Indiana University Press, 1993.

Werth, Paul W. *The Tsar's Foreign Faiths: Toleration and the Fate of Religious Freedom in Imperial Russia.* Oxford: Oxford University Press, 2014.

Wheeler, W. E. "The Control of Land Routes: Railways in Central Asia." *Journal of the Royal Central Asian Society* 21 (1934): 585–608.

White, Owen, and J. P. Daughton, eds. *In God's Empire: French Missionaries and the Modern World*. Oxford: Oxford University Press, 2012.

Wolfe, Michael, ed. *One Thousand Roads to Mecca: Ten Centuries of Travelers Writing about the Muslim Pilgrimage*. New York: Grove Press, 1997.

Worobec, Christine. "The Unintended Consequences of a Surge in Orthodox Pilgrimages in Late Imperial Russia." *Russian History* 36 (2009): 62–76.

Zipperstein, Stephen. *The Jews of Odessa: A Cultural History*. Stanford, CA: Stanford University Press, 1987.

INDEX

Page numbers in *italics* refer to figures.

borders, 12–13; of Russian Empire, *vi*, 12–13, 49, 84–85, 91, 215n2

Britain: campaign to prevent Soviet hajj transport, 172–73; colonies, 6, 10, 173, 211n26; competition with Russia, 91, 101, 149, 156, 160–61, 167; fear of Soviet involvement in Arabia, 161; hajj services, 14, 169; interests in Syria, 24–25; trade networks, 104

Brower, Daniel, 9

Bukhara: émigré community in Arabia, 76; pilgrims, 22, 62, 154; rulers, 2

Bushehr, 91

Cairo, religious study in, 49

Cairo hajj caravan, 27, 33

Capitulations, 25, 34

caravans. *See* Cairo hajj caravan; Damascus hajj caravan

caravanserais, 15, 66–67, 74, 79, 170

Caspian Sea ports, 44, 97, 109, 178

Catherine the Great, 5, 22

Caucasus, 2, 18, 83, 203n43; hajj pilgrims, 31–40, 65, 83; hajj routes through, 21, 88; Muslim anticolonial resistance, 20–23, 34, 37, 38, 44, 60; Russia's conquest of, 20–21, 35, 45–46

cavus (pilgrim-guides), 92

Central Asia, 2, 18, 21, 194n9; hajj pilgrims, 5, 58, *100*, 114, *168*; holy sites in, 174; Russia's colonization of, 73–74; Russo-British rivalries, 167; Soviet ambitions in, 159–61; Soviet assault on Islam in, 158–59; women's status in, 160

Central Odessa Office for Shipping Muslim Pilgrims to Jeddah by Steamship, 116

Charykov, N. V., 1

Chernyshev, A. I., 37

Chicherin, Georgii, 160–63

Chinese Muslims, 161–62, 167, 172–75, 178, 182

cholera outbreaks: in Arabia, 42, 70, 75, 100, 199n67; and discrimination against Muslims, 142, 144; fear of, 48, 77, 101, 171; global epidemics, 55–56, 74–75, 83; hajj bans during, 92, 154; in Jeddah, 13, 64–65; prevention of, 9, 92, 117, 132–33, 140

Christians: in Syria, 25. *See also* Eastern Orthodoxy; Russian Orthodox Church

civil rights, 142–43, 148

Committee of the Volunteer Fleet, 104, 128

Communist Party, 180, 215n5

Constantinople, 31, 57–59, 152; as center of Pan-Islamic activities, 86; holy sites, 49–51, 53, *58*; *misafirhane* (lodging house), 62; Russian ambassador to, 33, 61, 67; Russian consulate, 48; Soviet recruitment of hajj pilgrims, 163, 167–68; *tekkes* (lodging house), 62, 67; visits by hajj pilgrims, 113–14, 162. *See also* Istanbul

consulates. *See* Russian consulates; Soviet consulates

Cook, Thomas, 126

Council of Ministers, 120, 134

Crews, Robert, 5, 194n9

crime, 83, 124, 152; Bedouin attacks, 29–35, 39; pirate attacks, 53; robbery, 31, 40, 58–59, 68, 141

Crimea, 2, 18, 56, 65

Crimean Tatars, 53, 56, 57, 202n30

Crimean War, 3, 56

currency, Soviet policy on, 165–66, 168–69, 173, 175–78

Dagestan region, pilgrims from, 31–36, 39, 42, 60–61, 203n43

dalil system, 79–80

Damascus, 10, 44–45, *50*; Algerian émigré community, 205n90; economy, 127; European consulates, 24; holy sites, 49–51, 53

Damascus hajj caravan, 17, 27–35, 39, 42; commander with *mahmal*, 27; procession through Damascus, 29

David-Fox, Michael, 165, 215n7

Davletshin, Abdul Aziz, 82

diplomatic protection: for foreign Muslims, 162; for Russian subjects, 17, 33–35, 63, 67–68, 76

disinfection, 98–99, 114, 126, 140, 150

Dobson, George, 97–98

Duma, 120; Muslim representatives in, 121–22, 127–28, 143, 144, 211n5

Dutch colonies, 6, 78, 161, 197n19; financial requirements for pilgrims, 60; hajj services, 14

Eastern Orthodoxy, 1, 25–26, 184. *See also* Russian Orthodox Church

"Eastern Question," 24

Egypt, 24; occupation of Syria, 29–30

elites, Muslim: complaints about hajj ban, 22–23; as hajj brokers, 181; hajj memoirs, 58–59; hajj pilgrimages, 7, 13–14, 20, 31, 36–37, 65, 80, 153, 197n19; recruited into Russian administration, 38

El-Tor, 14, 103, 112

émigré communities: Algerians in Damascus, 205n90; Bukharans in Arabia, 76; Turkestanis in Jeddah, Mecca, and Medina, 79–81

Ermolov, A. P., 21–23

estate cases, 17–18, 36, 40–41, 62–63, 73, 75–77, 80

Europe: collapse of land empires, 164; Muslim communities in, 183, 185. *See also* Britain; France; Russian Empire

European imperialism: colonization of Muslim states, 6; competition in Ottoman and Persian territories, 2, 24–26, 42, 45–46, 91, 156, 160–62; co-opting Muslim hajj networks, 167; and hajj sponsorship, 7–9, 18, 53, 60, 69, 75–78, 87, 162; mapping and knowledge-producing projects, 54–55; in Muslim states, 6–7. *See also* Dutch colonies

extraterritorial privileges: of French subjects, 198n41; of Russian subjects, 17, 20, 34, 40, 76

facilities for hajj pilgrims. *See* caravanserais; lodging houses; Odessa hajj complex; quarantine facilities; railroads; steamships

Farahani, Hosayn, 95, *96*

Faroqhi, Suraiya, 27, 202n33

Feast of the Sacrifice, 90, 131–32

Feodosiia, 109, 112, 119, 150

Five-Year Plan, 165, 175

foreign hajj pilgrims, 21–22; mistreatment by Soviets, 178–80; petitions for access to Black Sea routes, 161–62; Soviet support for, 158–59, 163, 166, 171–74

France: colonies, 6, 10, 197n19; French subjecthood, 205n90; interests in Syria, 25, 30; Islamic studies, 193n6; Ministry of Foreign Affairs, 60; rivalries with Russia in Ottoman Arab lands, 42

Frank, Allen, 210n79

Georgian Orthodox Church, 26

global hajj networks, 2, 18–19, 84, 183–86; traffic within, 157–59, 162, 182

globalization, 15, 182, 185

Golovin, I. G., 31, 35

Great Depression, 159, 182

Gurzhi, Petr, 116–17, 132–34, 144, 150–51

hajj, 1, 8; costs of, 43–44; economic activity generated by, 127, 141; growth in, 57, 60, 67, 107–8; and illegal economic activity, 182; impact of modern transport on, 53–54; as mass event, 47, 54, 68, 84; in twenty-first century, 49, 183–86. *See also* itineraries; mapping the hajj; routes to Mecca

hajj director. *See* Saidazimbaev, Said Gani

hajj infrastructure: Soviet reconstruction of, 164, 166; tsarist-era, 1, 3–6, 15, 20, 46, 147, 151, 156, 158, 184. *See also* caravans; lodging houses; Ottoman Empire; railroads; steamships

hajj memoirs, 51–53, *52*, 57–59, 78–79, 154, 201n13

hajj pilgrims, *5*, *7*, *58*, *100*, *118*, *148*, *168*; exploitation of, 13, 68, 79–80, 124, 141, 144, 146; identity as Russian subjects, 39, 59–60, 68; numbers of, 28, 36; perceptions of tsarist Russia, 67–68, 151–53; responses to Russian involvement in hajj, 13–14, 123, 142–45, 147; treatment of, 94–99, 144–45, 147, 151, 154; as unsupervised and out of control, 63. *See also* elites; foreign hajj pilgrims; poor hajj pilgrims

hajj sponsorship, Russian, 1–6, 185–86; 1907–8 hajj season, 114–18, 121, 125; as decentralized and semisecret, 19, 88, 101, 151; development of services in Syria, 35–46; economic incentives for, 87, 89; force and coercion of pilgrims, 140–46, 151; goals of, 9–10, 72–73, 86–87, 147–49, 156; laws and regulations, 108–14, 117–19, 129–30; as mechanism of imperial integration and expansion, 3, 10–13, 19–20, 36, 84–85, 156, 184–85; newspaper articles promoting services, 72; officials' attitudes toward hajj sponsorship, 64–66, 151–53; officials' coordination of hajj services, 107, 154; origins of, 20, 23–24, 30–35; restrictions and efforts to discourage the hajj, 37–38, 43, 55–57, 60–61, 64–66, 149. *See also* hajj infrastructure; passports hajj sponsorship, Soviet, 14–15, 157–59; backlash against, 180; coordination among authorities, 170; end of, 182; goals of, 160–62; housing in Odessa, 166–67; ideological implications, 180–81; laws on, 176–77; logistical problems, 178–80; plan for, 162–66; political potential of, 173–74, 176, 178; recruitment of pilgrims, 167, 171–73; transit conditions, 169, 174–75, 178–80

hard currency, 165–66, 173, 175–78

Harvey, David, 12, 202n24

Hejaz railway, 5; connecting Damascus and Medina, 10; special cars, 111

Hejaz region, 28; Ottoman control over, 60, 69–70, 90; report on, 82

"Hejaz steamships," 1, 111, 111–16, 113, 115, 150–51, 154. See also steamships

holy sites and shrines, 27, 49–52, 174, 201n9; Shiʿi Muslims, 43–44, 48, 83, 201n7. See also Constantinople; Jerusalem; Mecca; Medina

Hurgronje, Snouck, 78

Husayn-Ibn Saud war, 161

Ibragimov, Shahimardan Miriasovich, 69–70, 204n74

Ibrahim, Abdürreşid, 14, 144–45, 186

Ignatʹev, N. P., 61–67, 209n55

Imperial Orthodox Palestine Society (IOPS), 26, 87–88, 102, 106

India, 83, 169, 172; hajj centralization, 126. See also routes to Mecca

Indonesia, 78, 197n19

infectious diseases, 48, 55–56, 67, 92, 125, 140, 152, 170. See also cholera outbreaks; sanitary threats

intelligence gathering, 37–38, 40, 43, 77–82. See also mapping the hajj

Intourist, 165

IOPS. See Imperial Orthodox Palestine Society

Irkeshtam, 178

Ishaev, Shakirdzhan, 78–81

Islamic law, 122; courts, 40

Islamic studies, 4–5, 11–13, 193nn6–7

Israel, 26

Istanbul, 28, 168. See also Constantinople

itineraries, 49–51, 93; influence of modern transport on, 54; pilgrims' choice of, 164, 171; Russian control over, 86, 113–14; Russian information-gathering on, 48, 55, 106; Soviet control over, 174; and steamship service, 99; through Constantinople, 57–59. See also routes to Mecca

Ivanov, I. A., 74–76, 81

Jaffa, 114

Jeddah: cholera outbreaks, 13, 64–65; European consulates, 24; European services, 14; Russian consulate, 46, 48, 68–79, 88, 93, 102, 116; Soviet consulate, 158, 163; Soviet recruitment of hajj pilgrims, 167; steamship service, 83, 104, 111, 114, 116, 122, 149–50, 154

Jerusalem: European consulates, 24; holy sites, 10, 49–51, 50, 53; Russian Compound, 87. See also Russian Orthodox pilgrimage to Jerusalem

Jewish population, Russian, 2, 11, 66. See also anti-Semitism

Jubilee Indian Pilgrims Relief Fund, 60

Kandahar, 172

Karbala: Russian consulate, 48; Shiʿi holy sites, 43, 83, 201n7

Kashgar pilgrims, 113–14, 161–62, 172–73, 175

Kaufman, K. P. von, 64, 66

Kazakh steppe, 2

Kazikumukh, 31–35, 32, 39

khadzhikhane. See Odessa hajj complex

Khakimov, Karim Abdraufovich, 161–62, 182

Khalid, Adeeb, 70, 194n9

Kharkov, 147

Kishinev Pogrom, 105

KOMOCHUM (Commission on Measures for Prevention and Struggle against the Plague, Cholera, and Yellow Fever), 89, 107

Kotsebu, P. E., 65–66

Kuropatkin, A. N., 82

Kushka, 170, 173–74, 182

Lamsdorf, V. N., 107–8

Lenin, Vladimir, 157, 159

Levitskii, A.D., 13, 70, 74–78, 89–90, 92

lodging houses (tekkes), 57, 62, 67, 74, 75–76. See also Odessa hajj complex

Lord Jim (Joseph Conrad), 7
Loris-Melikov, M. T., 60–61
Ludden, David, 73

mahmal (ceremonial palanquin), 27, 28
Mamluks, 27
mapping the hajj, 48, 54–55, 70–85; use of
  passports for, 23, 36, 38–39, 70, 72–73, 83
Marjani, Shihabetdin, 54
Mashhad: Russian consulate, 48; Shiʿi holy
  sites, 43–44, 201n7
Massell, Gregory, 160
McChesney, Robert, 202n33
Mecca, 10, 18, 44, 50, 82; holy sites, 27, 49–52,
  62; Muslim Russian officials in, 70; sharif
  of, 47–48, 80; as site of anticolonial political
  agitation, 8, 160–61, 186. See also routes to
  Mecca
medical examinations, 98–99
Medina, 10, 18, 48, 50, 82; holy sites, 27, 49–52,
  62; religious study in, 49
Menshikov, M. O., 148–49
Metcalf, Barbara, 51
migrations, 11–12, 185; influence on imperial
  policies, 45, 49, 84–85
Ministry of Finance, 132
Ministry of Foreign Affairs, 22, 25, 35–37, 57,
  64, 66, 67–69, 84, 100–101, 204n74; reports
  on hajj traffic, 77–82, 87
Ministry of Internal Affairs, 55, 66–67, 83, 84,
  86–87, 92, 108, 134, 142; removal of Saidazimbaev, 146; "Report on the Hajj, Its Meaning, and Measures for Organizing It," 88; on
  request to close Odessa to pilgrims, 140; and
  steamship service, 100–102, 110, 119, 147;
  support for hajj director's plan, 131
Ministry of Trade, 92, 110, 116, 119, 133–34,
  142, 147
Ministry of Transport, 92, 110–11, 125, 151
Ministry of War, 82
mobility revolution: global, 6–7; in nineteenth-century Russia, 11, 90–92
Moscow, 153
Mt. Arafat, 8
Muslim Bolsheviks, 161
Muslim clergy, 38, 106, 181
Muslim customs and cultural norms, 95,
  97–98, 112–13, 125, 175

Muslim "fanaticism," 21, 44, 48, 64, 108, 148
Muslim press, 123, 142–45, 150
Muslims, in Russia, 2–3, 18, 43, 47, 184–86;
  discontent with unequal treatment, 142–45,
  147; as Duma representatives, 121–22,
  127–28, 143, 144, 211n5; integration into
  empire, 3, 5–6, 21–24, 44, 48–49, 61, 67, 74,
  84–85; migrations, 11–12; political activity,
  143, 145; recruited as officials and special
  agents, 37, 106–7, 131, 204n74; scholarship
  on, 4–5, 11–13. See also elites
Muslim Tatars, 50, 78, 161

Najaf, 48; Shiʿi holy sites, 43, 83, 201n7
Naval Ministry, 101, 104
Neidgardt, A. I., 37
Nelidov, A. I., 67–69, 83
Nesselrode, Karl, 22, 37, 42, 44
New Russia, 65
Nicholas II, 86, 89, 118
Niedermiller, A. G., 133
NKID (Commissariat of Foreign Affairs),
  160–63, 166, 177–81; Near East
  Division, 173

October Manifesto, 120, 130–31, 143
Odessa: as central port for hajj traffic, 47–48,
  54, 65–66, 88; Jewish population, 66, 134,
  140–41; khadzhikhane on Primorskii
  Boulevard, 166–67; Port Pilgrimage Commission, 119; quarantine port, 98; Russian
  conquest of, 46; sanitary facilities, 98–99; as
  state-sanctioned port for hajj traffic, 124–27,
  145; steamship service, 91, 93, 102, 114–16,
  122, 149–50
Odessa hajj complex (khadzhikhane), 131–45,
  136–39, 148, 150, 167; Muslim press on, 123,
  142–45; pilgrims forced into, 140–46
Odesskii listok, 135–40
OGPU (Soviet state security service), 163,
  170–71, 179–82
"On the Sea Transport of Hajj Pilgrims from
  the Soviet Union to the Hejaz and Back"
  (Soviet law), 176
Orenburg, 51. See also Tashkent-Orenburg-Odessa railroad
Orenburg Muhammadan Ecclesiastical Assembly, 5, 13

Ottoman Empire: Arab provinces, 10, 14, 24, 42, 69; collapse of, 24, 161, 164; control over Hejaz region, 60, 69–70, 90; estate cases, 40, 62–63, 75–77; and European imperialism, 2, 6, 24–26, 42, 45–46, 91, 156, 160–62; hajj sponsorship, 28, 75–77, 102, 116; imperial caravans, 9, 15, 17, 27, 52 (*see also* Cairo hajj caravan; Damascus hajj caravan); investiture ceremonies, 18, 28, 57; political revolutions, 121; resistance to European consuls in Arabia, 76–77; resistance to European hajj sponsorship, 75–77; Russo-Ottoman treaties, 21, 196n2; steamship tickets for poor pilgrims, 68, 126; sultan's role as "protector" of the hajj and Holy Cities, 27

Ottoman Syria, 10, 20, 24–27, 35, 45–46

Pan-Islamism, 3, 9, 48, 86, 121, 143, 152, 186
Pan-Turkism, 121, 143
Paris Sanitary Convention (1894), 75
passports: 1857 passport law, 61; applications by Soviet Muslims, 181; applications by the poor, 56–57; cost of, 37–38, 61, 65, 105–6; Dutch policy, 197n19; for foreign hajj pilgrims, 163; illegal travel without, 83, 92, 153; obtained in Black Sea ports, 106, 149; Persian government policy, 171; "pilgrim passports," 108, *109*; restrictions on, 55–57, 64–65; use in mapping and regulating hajj traffic, 23, 36, 38–39, 70, 72–73, 83
Penza, 132; railway station, 124
Persia, 2, 6, 21, 163, 181; passport policy, 171; political revolutions, 121; Russian treaties with, 21; Soviet hajj campaign in, 170–72
Persian Muslims, 22, 30, 95, 162, 167, 170–72, 179
"Pilgrimage-Sanitary Khadzhikhane (Lodging House)," 117
pilgrim-guides, 48, 79–80, 168, 173, 182; *cavus*, 92
pilgrims. *See* hajj pilgrims; Russian Orthodox pilgrimage to Jerusalem
Pleve, V. K., 105–10
political threats, 9, 44, 48, 67–68, 89, 121
poor hajj pilgrims, 7, 36, 81; access to transportation, 54; exploitation of, 124; financial assistance for, 59–61, 63–65, 203n43; free tickets for, 116, 125–26; passport

applications by, 56–57; stranded, 60, 64, 73; use of state-sponsored Black Sea routes, 153–54. *See also* hajj pilgrims
Port Pilgrim Commission, 146
ports. *See* Black Sea ports; Caspian Sea ports
public health, 83, 87, 130. *See also* sanitary rules and procedures; sanitary threats
Putin, Vladimir, 183–84

quarantine facilities, 14, 56, 59, 72, 75, 153–54; border stations, 170; in Feodosiia, 109, 119; observation posts, 89; in Odessa, *98*, 133, 141, 145, 164

racism, 144, 147
railroads, modern, 3, 7–8, 53–54
railroads, Russian state-owned, 9, 11, 47, 83, 124, 204n62; conditions on, 92–98, 103, 125, 129–30; cost of long-distance travel, 207n18; "hajj cars," 125, 146, 151; modernization and expansion of, 90–92; revenue from hajj traffic, 87, 89–90; subsidies for hajj transport, 110. *See also* Hejaz railway; Tashkent-Orenburg-Odessa railroad; trans-Caspian railroad; trans-Caucasian railroad; trans-Siberian railroad
railroads, Soviet, conditions on, 174–75
Randolph, John W., 200n5
Red Crescent, 180
religious equality, 120–22, 130–31, 143
religious scholars, 49, 54, 57
religious toleration, 1, 9, 22, 43, 61, 64–65, 131, 148
Roff, William, 9
ROPiT (Russian Steamship Company), 89, 117, 128, 149–50, 165, 177; advertisements, 93, *111*, 111–13, *113*, *150*, 154, 208n25; combination tickets, 93–94, 99, 110; competition with Volunteer Fleet, 102–3, 141–42, 144, 147; founding of, 207n13; "Persian Line," 91; Sevastopol service, 142, 150; ticket sales and prices, 99–100; travel conditions, 116
routes to Mecca, 4, 18, 35, 48, 55, 70–85, 106; Central Asian, *71*, *152*; from Damascus, 28; dangerous conditions, 29–37, 45; influence of modern transport on, 54; informal Muslim networks on, 83, 93–94, 153, 167; informal Turkic networks on, 53; from Kazikumukh, *31*; old land routes, 94, 100,

129–30, 147; pilgrims' choice of, 4, 38, 49–51, 88, 164; restrictions on, 108–9; sea routes, 38; secret routes through Afghanistan and India (old land routes), 72, 81, 83, 86, 88, 92, 100–101, 130, 153; through Central Europe, 153–54, *155*; through India, 169, 172; through Ottoman lands, 22–23, 47; through Syria, 29–41, 45–46; through the Caucasus, 21, 88. *See also* Black Sea routes; itineraries

"Rules on the Transport by Ship of Muslim Pilgrims from Black Sea Ports to the Hejaz and Back," 119, 130

Russian consulates, 13, 20, 48, 90; in Aleppo, 35, 41; along Orthodox pilgrim routes, 207n6; in areas of strategic interest, 42–43, 46; in Beirut, 24–25; in Bombay, 48, 100–101; in Damascus, 35–41; financial assistance to poor hajj pilgrims, 59–61, 63–65, 203n43; in Jeddah, 46, 48, 68–79, 88, 93, 102, 116; in Mecca (proposed), 42–44, 46; services to hajj pilgrims in Syria, 31–41. *See also* mapping the hajj

Russian Empire, 1–2; archives, 15; borders, *vi*, 12–13, 49, 84–85, 91, 215n2; collapse of, 164; emigration, 56; imperial conquests, 18; industrialization, 90–92; institutionalization of Islam, 5, 194n9; interests in Syria, 25, 30; migration patterns, 11–12, 49; moderniza- tion, 3, 47, 90–92; political instability, 101; religious toleration policy, 1, 9, 22, 43, 61, 64–65, 131, 148; scholarship on, 4–5, 11–13; security measures, 23; travel restrictions, 55. *See also* hajj infrastructure; hajj sponsorship

Russian Orthodox Church: and the Capitula- tions, 34; in Jerusalem, 26; privileged status of, 1, 19, 88, 92, 108, 121–22, 131, 185; and Putin, 184

Russian Orthodox pilgrimage to Jerusalem, 19, 25–26, 48, 68; privileged treatment, 99, 144–45, 147; Russian state sponsorship, 87–88, 91, 106, 110; steamship service, 93

Russian Political Agency, 193n1

Russian Steamship Company. *See* ROPiT

Russian subjects, extraterritorial privileges of, 17, 20, 34, 40, 76

Russo-British rivalries, 91, 101, 149, 156, 160–61, 167

Russo-Japanese War, 128

Russo-Ottoman trade agreement (1783), 77

Russo-Ottoman War (1877–78), 61

Safarov, Sabirzhan, 13, 93–94, 102, 116, 141

Saidazimbaev, Said Gani, *123*; appointment and removal as hajj director, 120–21, 146; family background, 123–24; hajj plan and Odessa complex, 124–36, 140–48, 167; legacy, 147–48; reputation, 150–51; Tashkent "Muslim station" (musul'manskii vokzal), 126, 132, 146; Volunteer Fleet contract, 122, 128–29, 133, 141–42, 144, 146–47, 150

Samara, 132; railway station, 124

Samarkand railway station, *118*

Sanitary Conference on the Mecca Pilgrimage, 75

sanitary rules and procedures, 114, 117, 119, 126, 132–33; inspection of, 180; medical examinations, 98–99. *See also* disinfection; KOMOCHUM; quarantine facilities

sanitary threats, 9, 48, 55–56, 67, 74–75, 121, 130. *See also* cholera outbreaks; infectious diseases

Saudi Arabia, 162, 171; annual hajj quotas, 183–84, 218n2; control of hajj, 49, 173

Schuyler, Eugene, 124

security threats, 38–39, 63, 67

Seniavin, L. G., 44

services for hajj pilgrims, 14–15, 59–79, 72–73. *See also* Russian consulates

Sevastopol, 54, 88, 93, 99, 102; lodging house (*khadzhilar-sarai*), 111; steamship service, 111–12, 114, 145, 149–50

shamail prints, 8, 10, 50, 50–51, *62*

Shamil, Imam, 38

Shi'i Muslims, 2, 171; holy sites, 43–44, 48, 83, 201n7

Sinkiang, 161–62; Chinese pilgrims from, 175–76; hajj brokers, 167–68; Soviet consul- ate, 163

Sipiagin, D. S., 100, 105

socialist revolution, 105; spread of, 158–60, 178, 182, 218n89

Society for the Transport of Muslim Pilgrims, 150

Sokolov, D. M., 82

Soviet-British rivalries, 167

Volunteer Fleet (steamship line), 89, 110, 151, 177, 207n13; advertisements, 114–16, *115*, *150*, 154; Committee of the Volunteer Fleet, 104, 128; competition with ROPiT, 102–3, 141–42, 144, 147; contract with Saidaz-imbaev, 122, 128–29, 133, 141–42, 144, 146–47, 150; hajj services, 101–5, 114–17, 149–50, 164–65; ticket prices, 144
Vorontsov, M. S., 38, 40–41, 43
Vrevskii, A. B., 81

Wanner, Catherine, 215n5
Warsaw, 153–54

Witte, Sergei, 90–92, 105, 121
World War I, 157, 164

xenophobia, 182

Yanbu, 88, 114
Yemen, 180
Young Turks, 121

Zabolotnyi, D., 82
Zimmerman, V. V., 102–3
Zlatoust station, *152*
Zuev, N. P., 141–42

9 781501 748509